Sean Oliver-Dee is Associate Researcher of Inter-Religious Affairs at the Office of the Archbishop of Canterbury's Representative to the EU and Associate Research Fellow at the London School of Theology. He is also a consultant on religio-political issues for a number of think-tanks, NGOs and government departments in the UK and overseas. His PhD was published as *The Caliphate Question: British Government and Islamic Governance* in 2009.

MUSLIM MINORITIES AND CITIZENSHIP

Authority, Communities and Islamic Law

SEAN OLIVER-DEE

Published in 2012 by I.B.Tauris & Co Ltd
6 Salem Road, London W2 4BU
175 Fifth Avenue, New York NY 10010
www.ibtauris.com

Distributed in the United States and Canada
Exclusively by Palgrave Macmillan
175 Fifth Avenue, New York NY 10010

Library of Modern Religion 23

ISBN 978 1 84885 388 1

A full CIP record for this book is available from the British Library
A full CIP record for this book is available from the Library of Congress

Library of Congress catalog card: available

Typeset by Newgen Publishers, Chennai
Printed and bound by CPI Group (UK) Ltd, Croydon, CR0 4YY

To

Philippa, my children, wider family and the many friends who walk their journeys with mine: grace and peace go with us all.

CONTENTS

A NOTE ON STYLE AND TRANSLITERATION

This book makes extensive use of a number of Arabic words and includes some French quotations. I have decided to keep the Arabic words in plain text and have done the same for the French quotations. This has left book titles and names of organisations in italics. The Arabic terms do not include the accents and do not differentiate letters that appear the same in English script; for example, 'sa' and 'siin' are not differentiated in the English transliterations.

INTRODUCTION

This book examines the historical issues and questions raised by the interaction of Western imperialism with the Muslim societies they encountered as a way of informing the current debates on Muslim-Western integration issues. Central to this discussion are the issues of 'citizenship' and 'belonging' that underlie the debates in the public domain concerning Muslim loyalty to non-Muslim authority, the place of Islamic law within a Western legal system and the nature of the ummah.

Such an approach is not without its potential problems: policymakers are rightly wary of setting too much emphasis on historical anecdote and analogy when thinking through current public policy issues. The vastly differing geo-political settings and the social attitudes that were preva-lent in former periods would make any direct transfer of policy from history to the present, deleterious. However, if one is aware of such pitfalls and is prepared to factor them into developing current policy, history provides a rich seam of wisdom to be tapped in the modern day. Above all, his-torical situations that to a large degree mirror our own can be an essential pool of knowledge from which to draw out the framework of 'dos' and 'don'ts' that will form the struc-ture of a well-informed policy solution in the present day.

It is precisely this technique that this book will seek to employ: not to propose policy, but to develop a framework of analysis, questions and anecdote that can form the basis of effective solutions.

Key to the construction of an effective framework are the choosing of relevant historical 'mirror moments', an understanding of what we mean by 'citizenship' and a choice of voices that will articulate all sides of this debate.

Turning to the terminology, one definition of the term 'citizenship' is given in the *Encyclopaedia Britannica* as:

> ... relationship between an individual and a state in which an individual owes allegiance to that state and in turn is entitled to its protection. Citizenship implies the status of freedom with accompanying responsibilities. Citizens have certain rights, duties, and responsibilities that are denied or only partially extended to aliens and other noncitizens residing in a country. In general, full political rights, including the right to vote and to hold public office, are predicated upon citizenship. The usual responsibilities of citizenship are allegiance, taxation, and military service.[1]

As the nature of the freedoms and responsibilities this term encapsulates are broadly understood in its Western context, this book will not be examining the nature of 'citizenship' in the West. Instead, Chapter One contains an examination of the concept from a Muslim perspective, and a brief exposition of the transition the concept has undergone from the classical to the modern periods. This will be linked with a discussion of the nature and the broader concept of 'loyalty' in theology and the role of shari'a. Chapter One therefore acts as a foundation for the discussions concerning the place of shari'a and perceptions of citizenship in a Muslim context, which are conducted over Chapters Three and Four of the book.

Of course, when the term 'Muslim' is used, there is a real possibility that the erroneous picture of a single, homogeneous group of people can be imagined. Clearly, this is far from the truth: even within the UK, 'Muslim' covers a multitude of ethnic and sectarian divisions. For example, the Bangladeshis are not particularly close to the Pakistanis and the Pakistanis themselves are divided into biraderis that may despise each other. Furthermore the Arabs and Iranians consider themselves classes apart and there are the Muslims from the Horn of Africa who are divided between Salafi-Wahhabi creeds and Sufi, or Folk Islam.[2] The same phenomenon is seen in France where North African Muslims, who make up the majority of French Muslims, will be separate again from the Turkish and Arab Muslims who also inhabit the country.[3]

However, although Muslim communities in the UK and France are both ethnically and culturally diverse, there is a sizable majority within each country that come from a particular area: in the UK, the Mirpuris who are believed to make up two-thirds of the total Muslim population, and the Saharan peoples in France, who constitute approximately three-fifths of the total French Muslim population. For that reason, it is possible to explore the writings of Muslim reformers from relevant cultural backgrounds for these majorities when trying to engage with the perceptions of Muslims on the issues of citizenship and identity. Therefore, this book will be exploring the writings of Muslim reformers, politicians and thinkers from both the Indian subcontinent and North Africa from the colonial period as well as the present, as they impinge most directly on the citizenship discussions in the UK and France. Unfortunately, this will necessitate omitting discussion of several influential theologians and thinkers such as Farid Esack, Farish A. Noor, Khaled Abou El Fadl, Ebrahim Moosa, Aziz Esmail, Amyn Sajoo, Ali Shari'ati and Abdol Karim Soroush. Their important contributions to the Muslim discourse in the area of theology, citizenship and authority are certainly acknowledged and it is regrettable that their cultural backgrounds place them outside of the rubric of this book. However, in encompassing the writings of North Africa and the subcontinent, the majority of the key reformist ideologues are able to be covered in a way that speaks most relevantly to the vast majority of European Muslims, not just in the UK and France, but also in Germany, Spain, Belgium and Italy, who also have large minority Muslim populations that come from either Turkey and Morocco and whose shari'a background also reflects those of the groups already mentioned in France and the UK.

One of the most difficult decisions concerning the scope of this book has been whether to include the writings of Jamal ad-Din al-Afghani, given that he was originally from Iran. However, since he spent so much time in both India and North Africa over the course of his life and in the light of his seminal influence, it seemed appropriate to include him in the analysis.

From a structural point of view, in order to do this complex and delicate subject some justice, it is important to view the issue from the perspectives of both of the ruler and the ruled. So, following on from the coverage of Islamic theology and political theory in Chapter One. Chapter Two provides a brief historical background on the geo-political reality that these reformers were writing in, as well as outlining the aims and objectives of the British and French.[4]

This historical survey is by no means comprehensive, but it is designed to highlight those events and themes that will inform the reader's understanding of the analysis and debates that follow it.

Having explored the context of the debates historically and strategically, Section Two examines the perspective of the ruled on questions of citizenship through their answers to two questions, each of which forms one chapter: should Muslims always obey those in authority over them, even if they are not Muslims? and on what level should the notion of the Muslim community function?. Chapters Five and Six will then switch focus to the perspective of the rulers, examining case studies from India and briefly, Algeria before Chapter Seven brings the discussion out of the historical and into the present. All this will provide the foundation for the observations and conclusions arrived at in the final chapter.

This book therefore explores the complex interaction between Muslim minorities and their rulers during the European colonial period in order to understand this very delicate and important issue in the present day. The debates raging in the government and media of European nations such as France, Belgium and the Netherlands fueled recently by the actions of Mohammad Merah in Toulouse, along with flirtations with shari'a in both the UK and Canada lend urgency and focus to the issues this book deliberates upon.[5]

One book already exists that covers almost the same territory that is covered in this one: Adrian Favell's *Philosophies of Integration: Immigration and the Idea of Citizenship in France and Britain*. However, Favell's book focuses on studying government policy specifically, whilst this book seeks to explore all aspects of the question of citizenship for Muslims in a non-Muslim state taking into account both government and minority perspectives.[6]

Recently there have been several books that have attempted to engage with aspects of shari'a and more broadly Islamic interaction with the West. Notable amongst these are Kathleen Moore's *The Unfamiliar Abode: Islamic Law in the United States and Britain,* and Wael Hallaq's *Shari'a: Theory, Practice and Transformations,* both of which critically examine the struggles that Islamic law has experienced as Muslim communities have begun to adapt to Western cultural norms.[7] However, whereas these works principally examined the issue of integration from the perspective of Muslims alone, this book seeks to consider the perspectives of both Muslims and government in developing its conclusions.

Many past studies have approached the rise and development of Islamic revivalism as a political force through historical analysis, providing a survey of the ideas and the history of their development. These writers frequently use case studies, either from one part of the world, or selected from varying areas, to reveal patterns: the studies of Hiro, Choudhury and Burgat are examples of this.[8] This book does not tell the history of Islamic revivalism, although many of the foremost names in its history are included here: rather, it is an analysis of citizenship that takes place in a historical context, but without tracing that story as those named above have already done so expertly.

Other revivalist studies published thus far broadly fall into three categories: firstly, those that tended to use historical or geographical parameters, or a combination of both on a local, national or regional level to frame their research. Examples of this would be those undertaken by Ishtiaq Ahmed[9], Moin Zaidi[10], Barbara Metcalf[11], Syed Nadvi[12], or the essays edited by Rafiuddin Ahmad[13], looking at the Bengali Muslims. Secondly are those linking Islam with a political ideology, or movement, within the same kinds of historical and geographical parameters.[14] Furthermore, others, such as McDonough and Rizvi, have taken a more author-based approach, where the analysis has taken an overview of the opinions of the author in many different areas.[15] Finally, previous approaches to analyzing revivalist ideology and movements in India such as Baljon's[16] have been content to analyse the doctrines and debates in terms of explaining the author's philosophy, either through elucidating the author's standpoint or in relation to how it influenced their contemporaries and later generations. This book moves away from all these approaches by looking at one particular issue, and setting it, not just in a historical and geographical framework, but also in a theological perspective. By so doing, this book seeks to give the theological facet of this integration, and citizenship debate the space that it requires but is so often denied when policymakers and opinion-formers engage with this issue. As such, the book makes an implicit plea for theology and faith perspectives to be given due consideration when the issue demands it.[17]

In a survey such as this, it would be entirely possible to get buried under the weight of available material, allowing for only a cursory glance in each direction. Therefore, in order to avoid this, those figures included within the study in Chapters Three and Four have been selected by virtue of their contribution, not simply to general Muslim philosophical or theological ideas, but to the Muslim debate upon the specific issues discussed in this book. The great strength of this approach is that the views expressed on the subject of non-Muslim authority and the role of the ummah are not those of outsider non-Muslims. So the opinions of the writers considered carry the weight of personal conviction behind them and they express their views from a genuine desire to see Islam resurgent.

It should also be clearly stated from the outset that, whilst its importance cannot be overestimated, this book does not seek to engage with the present internal Muslim sectarian conflicts. This is done principally to control the volume of material being engaged with given that it already proposes to deal with the issue of citizenship from two differing perspectives, each of which in turn has two differing perspectives within them. Should the further element of inter-sectarian struggle be added, this already complex discussion might become unmanageable. In terms of the book's aims and context however, it is right to acknowledge the importance and relevance of this internal struggle, therefore, comment will be made on the possible policy impact of the Sunni-Shi'a engagement in relation to Western policymaking in the Conclusions.

For those wishing to delve further into the issues and consequences of the Sunni-Shi'a struggle, Nathan Gonzalez's book, which looks at the sectarian conflict in the Middle East, provides some useful insights into the issues, background and course of the disputes.[18] Furthermore, Vali Nasr offers invaluable insights in his 2007 book, which examines the phenomenon of the 'Shi'a Crescent', an important facet of the future shape of global Islam.[19] Both of the books cited above were published before the current upheavals that have changed the picture of the Middle East so radically began. However, both titles serve as useful commentaries on the current unrest seen in recent months in Egypt, Syria, Pakistan and Bahrain.[20] Struggles for the very narrative of Islam in the twenty-first century and beyond.

Finally, it is important to say that this book is written from a desire to see confident and properly integrated societies emerge from the identity debates that have been taking place for more than a decade and from the belief that Muslims can play an active part in those societies.

SECTION ONE

HISTORICAL AND
THEOLOGICAL
BACKGROUND

CHAPTER ONE

STATE, CITIZENSHIP AND THE LAW: ISLAMIC THEOLOGY AND HISTORY

State and Citizenship in Islam

The nature of the Islamic state in theology and developing political theory in the first centuries of Islam were examined in detail in *The Caliphate Question: British Government and Islamic Governance*.[1] It seems therefore unnecessary to repeat the same material once again here. However, it is worthwhile highlighting one or two of the pertinent points and examining the more modern concept of 'citizenship' that emerged in the later years of the Muslim Empire as it will have a direct bearing upon the discussions in this book.

The nature of what constitutes 'the Islamic state' is currently the subject of legitimate, intensive debate both inside and outside the heartlands of Islam where the vast majority of geopolitical states which characterise themselves as 'Islamic' exist. Such debates are continuations of arguments that have been ongoing from the early-modern period when the loss of the Islamic Empires have forced the re-evaluation of terms such as ummah, watan and quwah: terms that had been largely understood in the preceding centuries. These debates have been given a fresh impetus following the rise of Arab nationalism, the creation of independent post-colonial states and the advent of global jihadism.

These debates have drawn in contributions that run the spectrum from the intensely pragmatic to the heavily theological. Two brief examples will illustrate this.

Recently, Abdullahi Ahmed an-Na'im, the Charles Howard Candler Professor of Law at Emory University, proposed that the state should be kept separate from discussions on the development of shari'a. Indeed, state law, even in 'Islamic states', should be separate from shari'a so that all communities within that state can participate in it.[2] This reasoning of course begs the question whether the state may still be called 'Islamic' in that situation, but it seems likely that an-Na'im has in mind the concept of Islam as the official religion of the state, rather than having an integral part in its Constitutional definition. An-Na'im is advocating an inovative approach to defining the place of shari'a within modern constitutional arrangements, but the key weakness of his argument lies in the fact that he struggles to give his perspective the kind of theological foundation that would make his argument persuasive to pious Muslims. At present he concentrates on historical narrative and legal principle rather than scriptural quotation for the positions he outlines.[3]

At the other end of the scale, there is the more scripturally focussed Sunni-Shi'a debate between protagonists who both espouse all-encompassing definitions of what constitutes the 'Islamic state', such as Ayatullah Khomeini on the Shi'a side and Hizb-ut Tahrir for the Sunni's.[4] One might argue that their vision of a global Islamic state is very similar, and what differs is how Islamic authority is legitimized. Both perspectives are being heavily pushed by the Iranian and Saudi governments, each of whom are using their money to resource their perspectives throughout the world. The Canadian broadcaster and activist, Tarek Fatah, skilfully analyses and dissects the issues and manoeuvrings of both governments in his 2008 book.[5] For the purposes of this book though, it is judicious to side-step this fundamental debate to focus upon how statehood in Islam relates to citizenship itself.

Whatever definition is now given to the term 'Islamic state', it is beyond doubt that the years of Muhammad's rule in Madina, then Mecca and into the rule of the Caliphs, following his death, instituted a religio-political entity in which the developing apparatus of state also functioned as a religious guide.[6] It is broadly true to say that the 'ummah' this 'salvation community' was identified by its beliefs, rather than through its ethnic grouping.[7]

Thus, although the original definition of 'the ummah' also included non-Muslims who accepted Muhammad's political headship, the more generally accepted understanding of the term quickly shifted to become 'believers' alone.[8] As such, the developing laws and systems that were instituted to administer the rapidly growing Empire reflected that definition. Citizenship of the state therefore focussed around adherence to the beliefs, and those that chose to remain outside of that faith whilst continuing to live within its territorial boundaries had to be defined differently.[9]

As that system began to break down over the course of the Middle Ages and European Reformation periods, new understandings of what it meant to be both 'citizens' in the Islamic Empire, and 'Muslims' under non-Muslim headship were explored.[10] The theoretical expediency of the task was given particular impetus when the Mongols smashed through considerable portions of the Islamic Empire, although they themselves eventually converted.[11] Thus, this period saw such luminaries as Ibn Taymiyya himself engaging with how Muslims living under non-Muslim rule should live in relation to their new masters. Perhaps surprisingly, given his label as the 'Father of Revolutions', he concluded that Muslims could live peaceably under non-Muslim rule. However, this same Ibn Taymiyya declared the Mongols 'takfir' following their conversion to Islam and their continued rule under Mongol customary law, rather than shari'a. It is therefore important to point out that, whilst Muslims were being instructed to obey their non-Muslim overlords, once conversion had happened and those same overlords had been declared 'takfir', it became the duty of Muslims to overthrow them.[12]

For those Muslims in the modern world searching for answers on the issue of 'citizenship' in non-Muslim contexts and reading Taymiyya's opinions in isolation, Taymiyya's actions would logically suggest that, for those governments who cannot be characterised as 'Islamic', ruling without the shari'a is perfectly acceptable for Muslim citizens. That said, events and theoretical positions developed during the colonial period and since have somewhat muddied the Ibn Taymiyya ruling.

It was through the changing geopolitical realities of the rise of Europe during Ottoman hegemony that questions of statehood and citizenship moved significantly away from classical theology and theory. The institution of the Mughal Caliphate in India, the Wahhabi revolts in Arabia, the self-determination of Greece and Egypt and the European inroads into Algeria, India and Southeast Asia forced the Ottoman Caliphs to rethink the concepts of state and citizenry for a new era.[13]

This new constitutionalism for the Ottoman Empire was complicated by the revivalist Pan-Islamic ideology that they nursed and encouraged over the course of the late nineteenth century.[14] Certainly in theory, the universalist rule of the Caliph over the whole of the Islamic Empire had never ended, however, the situation was complicated by the nature of governance in places such as Egypt where the Caliph retained theoretical headship, including the power to appoint the Judges, whilst the French and British administered the state that was, from the 1820s onwards, declared independent under the rule of Muhammad Ali.[15] Egypt was an extreme example of an issue that became prevalent all over the former Islamic Empire; the central question of which, for both Caliphs and the European rulers, was what powers constituted part of the Caliph's religious authority and what constituted temporal or administrative authority?[16] For the British at least, the issue was found to be irresolvable. On the Ottoman side, the construction of an authoritative religious identity, which encouraged the patronage and money they so desperately needed, had to be reconciled with reforming and modernist elements both within and without.[17] The Ottomans therefore found themselves in the somewhat contradictory position of both defending the validity of non-Muslim governance, whilst at the same time encouraging Pan-Islamic sentiment. Neither the Europeans nor the Ottomans were able to reconcile the theoretical tensions that threatened to undermine the situation, and the result was that the issue was simply allowed to drift until such time as events demanded engagement with it. That time came with the Ottoman declaration of war against France, Britain and Russia in the form of a proclamation of jihad in 1914 and the subsequent treaty of Lausanne. Even so, the situation was only resolved by Kemal Atatürk's abolition of the Caliphate in 1923. Thus, even though the British opposed him, Atatürk did the British government of the time a favour, opening a route for resolution in a situation which had the potential to escalate cataclysmically for them.[18]

In light of this changing reality, the traditional Muslim definition of citizenship as 'believer' was becoming increasingly anachronistic; new definitions which also fitted within Muslim beliefs therefore had to be found.[19]

The traditional Ottoman term for a citizen was 'ra'wiyya' and it denoted anyone, regardless of religion or race, who lived within the borders of Ottoman jurisdiction. That status was codified in 1869 with the *Ottoman Citizenship Law*, which departed from the previous norm insofar as it put all non-Muslims on an equal footing with Muslims.[20] This innovation was enshrined in the 1876 Constitutional document.[21]

From then on, three differing terms denoting 'citizenship' began to be used and are still used in Middle Eastern countries today: Taba'iyya, Jinsiyya and Muwatana.

'Taba'iyya', literally 'subordination', is ascribed to minority groups living within a Muslim state. The Kurds in Iraq are given that term and indeed take the term for themselves, as it is the title of one of their political parties.[22] The same epithet is also given to the Shi'as in Saudi Arabia.[23] Therefore it can be, for the modern Islamic state, a description of both an ethnic minority and a religious one. It is important to note, however, that it does not appear to be a replacement for the classical 'dhimmi' status insofar as no inferiority of status is implied in the term. That said, whilst the term itself is free of overtones of inferiority, this does not necessarily mean that those on the ground do not experience it.

As for 'jinsiyya', Wehr offers 'sexuality' as the initial translation, before adding 'nationality' and 'citizenship'.[24] Davis characterises this as 'inferior citizenship' or 'passport citizenship' where the citizen does not have the full participatory rights of the 'muwatana' or 'democratic citizenship'.[25]

Thus far, we have traced the broad conceptual and historical understandings of what it means to be a 'citizen' in the Islamic context and how those constructs developed over time in relation to changing circumstances. The next section seeks to develop the fluid definitions presented here by examining the place and nature of shari'a within conceptions of Islamic statehood, both theologically and historically.

The Development of shari'a

In one sense, it is impossible to do justice to any historical or theological discussion of shari'a without examining the broader nature of political philosophy in Islam, perhaps even an examination of the whole faith as a system. This is due the theoretical centrality of shari'a to Islam which American scholar Joseph Schacht, in his seminal work on shari'a, described as the very 'kernel of Islam itself'.[26] Schacht's observation is confirmed by the British orientalist scholar D.B. MacDonald who argued that

> Muslim law, in the most absolute sense, is the science of all things human and divine ... .Whilst Muslim theology defines everything that a man shall believe about all things in Heaven and on Earth ..., Muslim law prescribes everything that a man shall do to God, his neighbour and to himself.[27]

The essence of the place of shari'a within the Islamic religion is captured perfectly by MacDonald's summary here. Islam without shari'a would be like Christianity without the writings of St. Paul, the Apostle, for in the same way as the Pauline writings are critical to a complete theological understanding of the place of Christ and the doctrinal implications of his life and teachings, shari'a captures the very essence of Muhammad's message as described in the Qur'an and Sunnah.

Furthermore the suggestion that shari'a itself captures the essence of Islam as a religion is borne out by an examination of the etymological and theological roots of the term.

Etymology of shari'a

According to the American Islamicist Bernard Lewis, the word 'shari'a' was designated to the Law of Islam and he gives its primary meaning as 'the way to the watering hole'.[28] Lewis' illuminating cultural insight is given substantiation by Orientalist Edward Lane's monumental *Arabic- English Lexicon,* in which he highlights the oasis imagery for the 'sha-ra-ayn' root in his definitions, citing the *al-Misbah* by al-Fayyumi, the *Taj al-Arus* by Mutada al-Zabidi and the *Mohkam* by Ibn Sidah for authority.[29] However, the connection to law is made via al-Zabidi and al-Fayyumi, both of whom also give shari'a as 'a road', which al-Zabidi specifically connects to God 'showing the way': the way to God, the goal of religion.[30]

These translations offer a potent image for a religion that grew out from the desert. If one followed the cultural logic from which Islam springs, the finding of the watering would have been is a matter of life and death. The watering hole must therefore represent life and safety, a natural image of Paradise. Further still, the directions to find such a place must be the most valuable map for a Muslim. Thus, shari'a itself has become the most important facet of a Muslim's day-to-day life, for it explains precisely what will and what will not enable the adherer to pass the terrible judgement that awaits all.

The truth of this perspective on the nature of shari'a can be found within the Qur'an itself.

In terms of doctrine, the absolute sovereignty of Allah over the earth, indeed the whole universe is beyond contestation.[31] Further, there is no doubt that, according to the Qur'an, this same sovereign God will one day judge all people: the very opening of the Qur'an specifies this.

In the name of Allah, The Most Gracious, the Most
Merciful. Praise be to Allah The Cherisher and
Sustainer of the Worlds; The Most Gracious, The Most
Merciful; Master of the Day of Judgement. (1;1–4)[32]

This doctrine is seen explicitly and consistently elsewhere
in the Qur'an, such as Q76: 30–31.

He [Allah] will admit to His Mercy whom He will;
but the wrongdoers – for them He has prepared a
grievous penalty.[33]

For the Muslim who fears judgement therefore, the most
important question in their life becomes: what actions will
enable a pathway into Paradise and what will go against
that? Furthermore, are there actions that are more serious
than others and if so, can the effects of those be counter-
balanced?

The Qur'an provides some direction on the answers to
these questions: Q5:95 tells the reader that killing a wild
creature whilst on pilgrimage is an offence that can be for-
given once, but not again. Other specific details of what
constitutes sin and what will be counted as credit are given
variously at Q2:274–275, Q4:31–35, Q17:31–33 and Q9:34,
amongst many others. However, in the light of the fact that
Allah is 'ever watchful,' the Muslim wanting an assurance
of Paradise will want a breakdown every action's consequences so that the moment of judgement, whenever it may
be (Q7:187) can be faced with confidence.

It is here that the shari'a guides those who follow it
towards the pathway to Paradise, for it draws from scriptural and other sources precisely to specify all that needs to
specified in order to achieve Paradise.

This discussion therefore highlights the shari'a's unique-
ness with the corpus of legal literature, for it stands as both
state law code and salvation pathway. No other legal system
in the modern world purports to offer the hope of Paradise
through any state code and it highlights for the non-Muslim
and Muslim alike, the conjoined nature of faith and state that
Muhammad instituted. This perspective is validated further
by the acknowledgement of the Caliph's role as the 'implementer of shari'a' in early Islamic political theory[34] and serves
to underline the validity of Calder's observations in his article on shari'a in the *Encyclopaedia of Islam*. Where the author
observes that the word is 'usually applied to a system of law
or the totality of the message of a particular prophet.'[35]

Thus, the term 'shaari'' (law-giver) is frequently applied
to Muhammad himself, although it is occasionally applied
to jurists as well.[36]

There can therefore be little doubt from this brief etymological discussion that Schacht's statement on the place of
shari'a given at the opening of this chapter appears to be verified in relation to early and dogmatic Islam. Yet Schacht's
association of shari'a as Islam forgets, or factors out, the
considerable swaths of the Muslim diaspora who practice
more mystic or 'folk' manifestations of the religion.

Amending Schacht's observation therefore, one might
say that "shari'a is the root and kernal of doctrinal Islam",
rather than Islam as a whole. As most of the world's Muslim
adherents practice forms of folk Islam, seeking to character-
ize 'Islam' as a belief within one definition which does not
express the perspectives even of the majority of Muslims
only adds weight to those Muslims within the Wahhabi/
Salafi/Deobandi tradition who seek a 'one size fits all' definition of 'true Islam' that tries to subjugate and eradicate all
other definitions of the faith.

The Term 'shari'a' in the Qur'an and Hadith

In the Qur'an itself, the word shari'a is used once in Q45:18:

> Then We put you, [O Muhammad], on an *ordained way* concerning the matter [of religion]; so follow it and do not follow the inclinations of those who do not know.
>
> (Sahih Translation)

> Then we put thee on the [right] *way of religion*: so follow thou that (way) and follow not the desires of those who know not.
>
> (Yusuf Ali Translation)

The Arabic translated in the italicized portions of the ayah above is *'shari'atin'*, which, according to Penrice, is defined as 'a law or institution prescribed by God: the right way or mode of action.'[37] Even though the word carries a 'tan-win', indicating what is usually cited as an indefinite article, *'shary'atin'* remains definite and consequently has become the name for the developing body of guidance rulings.[38] Kamali helpfully points out that the ayah is set up as a contrast: the guidance or ordained way offered by Allah: strong and directive, versus 'desire', which can change and fluctuate.[39]

Several cognates are found elsewhere: Q5:48: 'to each we have appointed a shir'a ('path' or 'way') and 'minhadj.' As well as Q42:13 and Q7:163, in which 'shara'a' is used, meaning 'laid down'.

In the Hadith, the term 'shari'a' occurs just once, in the writings of the jurist Ibn Hanbal, although the plural form occurs eleven times.[40] Given the extent of the Hadith, this limited reference to shari'a might suggest that the word was not in common use in relation to the developing body of Islamic law in this formative period. However, Calder suggests instead that the very lack of usage of the term would be an indicator of a pre-Islamic, commonly held understanding of the term.[41] Indeed, Schacht and Viktor, who hints at the pre-Islamic origins, not just of Islamic law, but also of many Islamic rituals and practice, share his opinion.[42] This space does not offer the luxury to investigate these differing opinions. The excellence of the scholarship combined in the opinions of Calder, Schacht and Victor render their viewpoint worthy of weighty investigation, yet on the surface, the logic of their conclusion is not immediately apparent.

Whatever the truth of the extent of 'shari'a's' pre-Islamic origins, the importance of shari'a as presenting the right-path for the believer cannot be doubted, although its presence is frequently implied rather than explicit in developing dogma.

Having established shari'a's centrality in doctrinal Islam, it is important to move onto exploring how this developing body of guidance dealt specifically with issues of citizenship, particularly 'loyalty' in order to understand the theological background against which the Muslim subjects and non-Muslim rulers were developing their positions. This will provide the foundation for the critique and analysis that comes later in the book.

The Concept of 'Loyalty' in shari'a[43]

The first written codes were set down in about 767 CE, and by the ninth century CE each code had a 'school' that had developed around it made distinctive by the cultural norms around it. To this day, each school has become the key shari'a text in differing geographical locations. Thus, when thinking about emigration to the West, it is important to understand that, when a Muslim migrates from a particular area, he/she brings the shari'a interpretation of that geography with them.

The geographic origins of the majority of Muslim immigrants into the UK suggests that they are likely to be principally of the Hanafi madhahib,[44] whereas for the French, the overwhelming majority of their Muslim immigrants being from North Africa, it will be the Maliki madhahib that will dominate. It is therefore worthwhile exploring what the two schools have to say about citizenship and loyalty to authority in their legal streams before moving on to examining the Qur'anic teaching.

Hanafi Approach

Abu Hanifa himself left no law books although he is credited with a number of seminal works including the *fiqh al-akbar* that contained the creedal doctrines of Sunni Islam.[45] Its heavy reliance on the Hadith and its underlying principles of reason and expediency give the school broad flexibility when engaging with issues of loyalty to non-Muslim rulers. For Hanafis, the central question when thinking through this issue concerns whether the governing body could be classed as dar al-Harb or dar al-Islam. It is for this reason that both the proclamation of the British Empire as dar al-Islam by the Ottoman Caliph and the later fatwa proclaiming the same thing by the North Indian 'ulama was of such import in undermining any attempts by Muslim groups to encourage rebellion against British rule.[46]

However the concept of dar al-Harb and dar al-Islam in relation to Muslim relations to non-Muslims in the Hanafi tradition was articulated by al-Shaybani in his *Law of the Nations*.[47] The central premise of this developing body of legal theory was expediency and the adoption of ra'y as an instrument of the science.[48] However, even amongst such pious pragmatism, Abu Hanafi himself held to the principle that a Muslim should rather emigrate than live permanently under the authority of a non-Muslim. Al-Shaybani countered the teaching of his master and decreed that the necessity for emigration had ended in the lifetime of Muhammad himself and that there was therefore no need for Muslims who found themselves under non-Muslim authority to consciously seek to live under Muslim authority instead.[49]

Thus, in this pragmatic system, the initial principle of emigration rather than living under non-Muslim rule was abrogated by the pupil and, in so doing, opened the way for any Muslim living under non-Muslim rule to do so freely without imperilling their walk along the 'straight path'.

Maliki Approach

In her book tracing the origins of Islamic law, Yasin Dutton tackles the question citizenship and loyalty to non-Muslim rule by referring to a tradition which records that Imam Malik was flogged by the then governor of Madina for using a Hadith related by Thabit Ibn al-Ahnaf concerning the invalidity of a forced divorce with the implication that any forced oath of allegiance was also invalid.[50] In the *Muwatta*, Malik quotes two Hadith for guidance, each of which confirms the other:

> Malik related to me from Abdullah ibn Dinar that Abdullah ibn Umar said, "When we took an oath of

allegiance with him to hear and obey, the Messenger of Allah, may Allah bless him and grant him peace, said to us, 'In what you are able.' " Hadith 55.1.1

Malik related to me from Abdullah ibn Dinar that Abdullah ibn Umar wrote to Abd al-Malik ibn Marwan, making an oath of allegiance. He wrote, "In the name of Allah, the Merciful, the Compassionate. To the slave of Allah, Abd al-Malik, the amir al-muminin, Peace be upon you. I praise Allah to you. There is no god but Him. I acknowledge your right to my hearing and my obedience according to the sunna of Allah and the sunna of His Prophet, in what I am able." Hadith 55.1.3[51]

For Malik therefore, the principle of allegiance was a straight-forward one: that the Hadith call upon the Muslim to obey their leaders as far as one is able to. A teaching that echos the sentiment of the first Caliph Abu Bakr when he called on Muslims to obey him so long as he obeyed the law of God. This is a consistent principle in line with the scholarship per-taining to Q4:59, which is discussed shortly. The issue there-fore concerns the extent to which any government which is not Islamic can claim the allegiance owed to the Caliph, or leadership of the ummah in any form. Meir Litvak observes that Qaradawi and Huwaydi draw a

distinction between sovereignty and the source of leg-islation – the Quran and Shariah. Accordingly popular sovereignty means that no one can rule over Muslims against their will and without their allegiance, but excludes its most common form of manifestation – legislation.[52]

In the framework of such an argument, democratic consent through voting permits anyone, whether Muslim or not, to rule over a Muslim. However, it still does not empower that government to enact legislation that remains within the purview of the religious scholars and jurists unless they can be classified as 'those that loosen and bind'. Caliphs, commanders and clerics have, over the course of Islamic history, generally been defined in those terms.[53] However, should the term be reinterpreted in the modern era to include the role of any government, then the way would be open to allegiance in this form.

It is in this context that the Qur'an itself should be turned to in relation to defining who has that appropriate authority.

Obedience to Authority in the Qur'an

Given the nature of Islam as a religion that began as both faith and state, it is perhaps somewhat surprising that there is so little upon the subject of 'obedience to authority' within it, outside of injunctions to obey Muhammad himself.[54] Indeed, there is a clear doctrine of obedience to Muhammad being equated to obedience to Allah. It is a natural and indivisible link.

Other than the injunctions to obey Muhammad, the Qur'an does contain the story of Joseph in Surah 12 that has been used as an allegorical device to understanding how to behave in a non-Muslim state. However, one further ayah speaks more directly into the question of obedience to authority; Q4:59, an ayah described by Maulana Al'a Maududi as

... the very cornerstone of the entire religious, social and political structure of Islam and the very first clause of the constitution of an Islamic state.[55]

The first part of the ayah translates 'Oh you who believe: Obey Allah, Obey the Messenger and those in authority among you ...', and it is the phrase 'those in authority among you' that is the focus of all the exegetical arguments.[56] As the meaning of this phrase has been discussed extensively in the *Caliphate Question,* there is little point going over the same ground again here. However, some points in relation to differing interpretations do need to be drawn out for the purposes of this book.

Before discussing the interpretations of the key phrase itself, it is important to bear in mind the Qur'anic context of the ayah. In the case of Q4:59, it is the preceding ayah which many exegetes have especially considered, in order to enhance their understanding of Q4:59 itself. Particular attention falls on the word translated 'entrusted', 'amanah' and the consequential doctrine of the direct sovereignty of God himself over the Earth and the role of human authority within that framework.

God is over all, but he has delegated his authority to human authorities, entrusting them with the task of governance in His stead. This interpretation is advocated by Azad.

Political power is held in trust (amanah) from God; and His will, as manifested in the ordinances comprising the Law of Islam, is the real source of all sovereignty.[57]

Who are those human authorities? According to Q3:26, all human authorities are raised or brought down by Allah himself. Therefore, the logical conclusion would be that all human authorities are to be obeyed. However, as has been seen in the words of Abu Bakr, obedience to authority is conditional upon them acting in the way of righteousness. Thus, although all human authorities are raised and brought down by the will of Allah, obedience to them is not specified unless they rule in the way of Allah. What therefore can be considered 'the way of Allah?' This is the core of the issue, for it is here that the interpretation of Q4:59 become all important.

It is clear that Muslim headship was initially assumed, but in the course of history, as that changed and could no longer be assumed, the broadening of the concept to include any authority that ruled in the 'way of Allah' became permitted. Thus, should a non-Muslim power that permitted a role for shari'a also have authority, then obedience to it became not only possible, but obligatory. This was the core of Sayyid Ahmed Khan's interpretation of the ayah. The all-important ruling therefore was whether any non-Muslim headship constituted dar al-Islam or not.

In recent times, the original Arabic of the phrase '. . . those in authority among you' from Q4:59 has been translated in such a way as to preclude obedience to anything other than Muslim authority. This has been done through the inclusion of the word 'from' in the phrase '(from) among you', for the inclusion or absence of this word in the translation makes a significant difference to the Muslim's relationship with their own rulers and the way that their faith is lived out. The earlier English translations produced by Bell, Rodwell, Dawood, Sale and Arberry left the 'from' out from their translation, permitting the range of interpretations of the ayah's meaning that become impossible with that word inserted. These translations remain closer to the translated Ibn Kathir version than any of the others. The most plausible reason that can be advanced for their contentment to leave the text ambiguous is that, in each of these cases, the motivation of the scholars was simply to discover the text and understand it more.[58] Their more open approach to Muslim scriptural translation and exegesis opened up a new phase in Western engagement with the Qur'an that had long been hostile.[59] As such, it would seem reasonable to assume that their interpretations of the text, more ambiguous though they are, more truly convey the original meaning of the text.

Sale himself only comments upon this passage with a brief footnote directing the interpretation of the phrase '... refer it unto God', as talking about the authority of the Qur'an.[60]

In his brief notes on the verse, Bell makes no comment upon who those in command might be, and is inclined towards a literal interpretation of the text insofar as he interprets the second half of the verse as

> Disputes are to be referred to Allah and the messenger, i.e. to Muhammad as the representative of Allah.[61]

Of course, this leaves no clue as to what to do once Muhammad has died, though it would be reasonable to argue as Ibn Kathir did, that the Sunnah is the natural point of reference for resolving disputes in his absence. This view, perhaps implicit rather than explicit, very much brings Bell into line with Ibn Kathir and the other Classical exegetes, although he leaves no room for the inclusion of the Qur'an itself as they argue should be the case. What is more fascinating about Bell's interpretation though is his assertion that this ayah and its predecessor were placed in this position much later than the ayah's around it. This opinion is based on the fact that ayah fifty-eight makes reference to 'judges in the community', which must have come later on, though not as late as Baydawi places it in his *Commentary*.[62]

The question therefore is 'why has it been inserted at this point?' Such a question can only lead to endless conjecture, but it does come in the middle of a passage on warnings to believers to stay close to God and not to follow other false teachings. In this context, its inclusion at this point would seem sensible; however, it does remove the ayah from whatever its original context might have been and in so doing, possibly changed its meaning.

It is in the writings of Maududi and Qutb that a strong shift away from the open approach of Sale, Bell and the medieval scholars is seen.

Maududi includes the word 'from' in the phrase 'and those (from) among you who are invested with authority' – a move that closes the door to any who could argue that Muslims must obey anyone in authority over them, no matter who they are and it means that, by implication, a Muslim is therefore obliged to ensure that it is a Muslim in authority.[63] He draws out that theme by articulating four principles: loyalty first to God, loyalty to Muhammad, loyalty to fellow Muslims in authority and the primacy in law of 'the injunctions of God and the way of the Prophet . . .'[64]

He ties his argument together by allowing the principle laid down in the ayah to be carried through after the death of Muhammad through the concentration on the authority of the Sunnah and Qur'an as his foundation for all Islamic state legislation. Indeed, he is at pains to point out that even a (the) Prophet cannot expect obedience in his own right; it must be under the authority of the Sunnah and Qur'an, as it must be for any Muslim ruler. Interestingly enough, he quotes a tradition that he attributes to both Bukhari and Muslim, but without the references he commonly gives for his other quotations. This is unfortunate, for it has massive implications:

The Prophet (peace be upon him) also made us pledge not to rise against our rulers unless we see them in open disbelief, so that we have definite evidence to lay before God.[65]

In tone and style, it is in keeping with Abu Bakr's pronouncement mentioned earlier, however, it is more specific in its language and for that reason it would have been useful to have been able to have referenced more accurately.

What is fascinating about Qutb's exegesis is that it is surprisingly free of political discussion. Given Qutb's position amongst the founding fathers of the modern Islamist movement, one would naturally expect the exegesis upon such a vital passage to be much more in line with Maududi's. However, its tone is actually moderate and spiritual, concentrating upon the importance of the believer's relationship with God and the power of that witness, rather than calling all Muslims to strive for Islamic worldwide rule. That being said, the idea of Allah's headship can be seen as bubbling below the surface, implicit in all the statements that he makes concerning the interpretation and implication of the ayah for, like Maududi, Qutb is at pains to point out that, in terms of earthly authority,

> ... the whole issue rests on believing in God's absolute oneness, and that, as such, all sovereignty belongs to Him alone.[66]

He too inserts the 'from' with its commensurate assumption that it is only believers that should be in command.

Qutb's free-flowing commentary also points at the crux of the difficulty when trying to interpret this ayah in a worldwide context, or even Muslim minority context, for,

like Maududi, he is happy to go along with the wider
Baydawi/Tabari non-military interpretation of 'those in
authority'. However, Qutb also talks in terms of the 'community', never in terms of the state.[67]

The purpose of Shi'a translators of this passage is to
challenge the Sunni interpretation, before explaining their
own point of view. Thus, the translations and commentaries of Ali and Imain both cite the Hadith of ul-Burhan
to lend weight, both to their criticisms of Sunni theology
and the interpretations they offer, as well as identifying the
'immaculate Imams' as those identified by the phrase 'ulil-
'amr'.[68] They diverge slightly in their handling of the ayah
insofar as Ayatullah Imain draws points from subtleties in
the phrasing of the ayah, principal amongst them being
that:

> The name of those charged with authority' is men-
> tioned nesct [sic] to the names of Allah and the Apostle,
> accompanied with an absolute obedience. This is a sign
> to show that the one in charge of Islamic government
> should be qualified with high saintliness.[69]

The exegete is focussing on the leadership of the community here, whereas, Maududi and Qutb continuously highlight the importance of 'community'.[70]

Ali, however, focuses on the historical errors of the Sunni
Caliphs (such as Yazid) to enforce the point that their interpretation of the idea of succession was incorrect. He further
cites Q33:33 to lend weight to the notion that, in the same
way that the ayah makes a link between Allah – Apostle –
'those charged with authority', so Q33:33, added to that
link, identifies Muhammad's view that succession is inher-
ited through the familial seed rather than election.

This argument is therefore based around legitimacy through inheritance, rather than obedience in line with righteous behaviour.

Summary

Shari'a has a central place in the Muslim doctrinal system of belief, for it specifies the path to be taken in order to pass the terrible judgement that awaits all and enter into Paradise. Its centrality is confirmed when the cultural translation of the term is done, for being shown the 'way to the watering-hole' for a desert people would literally mean salvation for them.

As a consequence, the large and complex body of literature – that extrapolates from the foundational sources the rulings and precedents that make up the corpus of shari'a literature – underlines the importance placed upon the directives that guide the believer towards Paradise.

The ancient Islamic state was therefore geared towards the 'forbidding of wrong and enjoining of good' as the Caliph (as the implementer of the Law of God) became both state and religious head of the community. As a consequence, loyalty to the head was conditional upon his leading the people along the pathway towards Paradise. Should he fail to do so, then loyalty was no longer required. Thus, loyalty to Islamic rule was always conditional. However, when Islamic rule began to decay and fade, fresh examinations of the scriptures had to be found. It is in this light that a valid interpretation of Q4:59 became of paramount importance to the now developed shari'a doctrines.

The discussion of Q4:59 showed that several interpretations of this vital ayah are possible, taking into account text positioning, historical context and accurate translation. This

gave space for the Muslim reformers, theologians, scholars and commentators of the Raj to address the necessity
for shariʿa compliance in the context of non-Muslim rulers.
The ummah of Muhammad's years was indeed the original
'community' of believers that Qutb still spoke in terms of.
Muhammad was reciting and preaching to a relatively small
group, bound together by a shared belief or idea, rather than
a geographically defined nation-state and he addressed his
followers at that level.[71] This is why Bell's theory of this ayah
and its predecessor being 'dropped in' at a later date becomes
more persuasive, for their placement at this point, within a
discussion of authority in many differing social contexts, provides a natural protectable conclave which rejects wide interpretation. On the other hand, if these two ayahs are removed
from their context, as Bell suggests they should be, then this
ayah can sound very different indeed. For, removed from the
context of engagement with earthly rulers, 'those in authority
over you' could be interpreted as being on a purely spiritual
level, talking about the need to adhere to God in the practice
of one's belief and to respect the direction of those Imams and
people of spiritual authority as they lead the community of
Muslim believers. This interpretation frees the Muslim completely from deciding whether to obey a non-Muslim leader,
for the teaching itself becomes mute and the endless discussion and pulling apart of the ayah in terms of who governs
whom becomes irrelevant.

If indeed the ayah was addressing his small early 'community' (his address is simply to 'those who believe': the
ummah) then his teaching makes sense for it is teaching
a reliance upon himself as God's Apostle and any others that might come from within the group. Indeed, the
'Constitution of Madina' shows that one did not have to
be a Muslim to be considered part of the ummah, only

accepting of Muhammad's political leadership. In this light, therefore, the ayah can be seen not as spiritual advice, but as a legal directive to those who are living within the 'community'. He is directing it towards a means of arbitration in the case of dispute so that they may remain unified, an essential requirement if it was to survive outside pressure. Possible alternative placement aside, the ayah is where it is and therefore, whatever other interpretations might be feasible, this book needs to engage with what exists, rather than what might exist. Therefore, leaving such speculation behind, Sections Two and Three seek to engage with the issues of citizenship and loyalty in the light of what is currently accepted as true.

Before getting to that material however, further groundwork in the shape of some analysis of the historical developments, and imperial strategies of the European colonial period is needed. This is vital in order to understand the goals perspectives of the rulers with respect to their Muslim minorities.

CHAPTER TWO

ANGLO-FRENCH IMPERIAL INTERACTION WITH ISLAM: HISTORICAL CONTEXTUALISATION

Introduction

Following the Crusades in the Middle East between the eleventh and sixteenth centuries, formal contacts at government level between the Europeans and the Ottoman rulers of Turkey had been few and far in between, although regular contact through trade and commerce had continued throughout the whole period.[1] In that period, both the Europeans and the rulers in the Muslim Empire had been involved in events that had torn apart, or broken up the social and political structures that had existed over much of the medieval period. For the Europeans, it had been the new nationalism that emerged from the Reformation; for the Muslims, it was the sharp decline in centralised authority that had been, notionally at least, directing the affairs of the entire Islamic Empire. Europe broke into states under their own sovereign authority, whilst Muslim administrators ruled with ever-increasing autonomy, some of whom took the title of Caliph for themselves.[2]

As each of these denominations began to emerge from its internal restructuring, a cautious interest in each other's affairs began to take hold and, whilst each was disparaging of the other's civilisation, diplomatic links were nevertheless tentatively forged.[3]

Of particular significance for the purposes of this book were the agreements made between the Ottoman Caliph Suleiman the Magnificent and Francis I of France in 1535 as well as that between the same Caliph and Queen Elizabeth I of England in 1580.[4] For they were the first time that a Muslim Caliph had moved away from the classical theory of jihad in which only temporary treaties were signed with non-Muslims. The wording of both agreements also treated each ruler, Muslim and non-Muslim, with equality – a concept that was once again an innovation from classical shari'a.[5] Indeed, such was the relationship created by the treaty between Suleiman and Elizabeth that Elizabeth felt able to appeal to Suleiman for aid against the Spanish Armada.[6]

In more modern times, the Ottomans had also been invited to become co-signatories with the other European Great Powers to the 'Concert of Europe' in 1856. Fascinatingly, one of the articles of the Concert contained the offer for the Ottomans 'to participate in the public law and concert of Europe.' According to Hugh Wood's article on the treaty, this clause above all others was the cause of much confusion for the lawmakers and officials in the rest of Europe with regard to what role this gave the Ottomans in European affairs.[7] Indeed, no clarification seems to have been attempted and the implications of the phrase appear to have remained unexplored. Thus, the rather ambiguous relationship between

Turkey and the rest of continental Europe seen in the late twentieth and early twenty-first centuries appears to be somewhat mirrored in the nineteenth century.

On the colonial front, the beginning and early part of the nineteenth century saw the British East India Company advance its influence throughout the subcontinent through a system of military alliances with regional Mughal rulers at war with each other. This advance was to a great extent, at the expense of the French, who had lost ground following the defeat of Napoleon at Waterloo in 1815. Under the terms of the Vienna Settlement signed nine days before the battle, the British were given control of a substantial number of French Asian colonies, including the island of Martinique and several mainland French settlements in India.[8] This gave the British a platform to expand, unhindered into the rest of India, leaving the French to focus instead upon North Africa. So it was that in a relatively short period of time, the Mughal Empire that had been established by Babur in India and that founded by Ottomans in Algeria were subsumed into new European power.[9] It is therefore not surprising that the Muslim elites, who bore the brunt of the shift of power, began to question what had gone wrong even as early as the middle of the eighteenth century.

This questioning coincided with the rising tide of frustration with a new foreign rule that finally exploded with the 'First War of Independence', or 'Indian Mutiny', of 1857–58. The fact that it was crushed only with great difficulty and was widely believed to have been instigated by the Muslims left an indelible mark on the psyche of both the rulers and the ruled.[10]

That said, it appears that both the British and the French colonial administrations spent time and effort in developing good relations with Islam. This diplomatic effort produced varied results. Patricia Lorcin, Paul Sanders and John Bowen argue that the French had a reputation for special relations with Islam, even given their somewhat interventionist approach to citizenship (which shall be discussed later).[11] The British also desired good relations with Islam, which it attempted to establish through an express policy of freedom of religion. The policy achieved some success insofar as it won a declaration from both the Ottoman Caliphs and the North Indian 'ulama, declaring the British Empire dar al-Islam, thereby ensuring that any rebellion by Muslims against British rule could not be religiously justified. However, it was not without its problems, chief of which was the development of the Shari'at Act 1937, which will be discussed in Chapter Five.[12]

What then was the nature of British and French interaction with Islam as a religion in their imperial contexts?

Britain in India

Islamic Resurgence and Imperial Expansion

Since the time of the Delhi Sultanate, the Muslim sultans had styled themselves as rulers in the name of the Caliph.[13] Ideologically, they had therefore held their positions as implementers of the will of the Caliph, who was himself the implementer of the shari'a. Theoretically therefore the Sultans ruled India in the name of Islam; however, in practice, many of the Sultans were lax about the imposition of Islamic law in a systematic way owing to the pragmatic problem of bringing the vast Hindu majority under dar al-Islam. For that reason, amongst the rulers of both the Delhi Sultanate and the later Mughal Empire, only the Mughal

Emperor Aurangzeb seems to have made a concerted effort to bring a shari'a state to Muslim rule on the subcontinent. It was he who implemented the Hanafi shari'a in India that remained in situ into the British period of imperial rule. Indeed, aspects of it remained until the 1870s before it was subsumed into the developing Anglo-Mohammadan law.[14]

As this administrative takeover and shift towards British law was taking place over the course of a century, a realisation and reaction to these developments amongst the Muslim elites, as well as a more grass-roots level, began to crystallize. As Ann Marie Schimmel observes:

> The various responses to British rule that emerged among the Indian Muslims of various denominations during the last quarter of the nineteenth century resulted in a growing self-consciousness of the Muslim community.[15]

This growing self-consciousness had developed as the direct rule by the British government, that had been going on since 1858, began to be felt at all levels of society. The British imposition of Western law and government on a fragmented and culturally disparate area was being felt increasingly since the Macaulite reforms going back to the 1830s had begun. However, even before the British East India Company had begun to take a significant grip on the country in the mid-eighteenth century, Shah Wali Ullah, the Mughal scholar, looked at what was happening within the Indian Muslim Empire, and saw the encroaching power of the Europeans. He had the foresight to see which way the wind was blowing and, as a consequence, began to call for Islamic revivalism in the form of a re-focussing on the sources of the faith within the Muslims of the subcontinent.[16] However, other than the revolt in the North-West Frontier Province and Punjab led by Sayyid Ahmad Barelwi,[17] his appeals appeared to fall on deaf ears, until British administrative rule of the country had grown more and more intrusive. At the same time, the Hindu majority, who had held only limited power under the Mughals, began to take advantage of the Western education on offer to advance into the administrative system. The Muslims tended to reject British education, a consequence of which was the virtual exclusion of Muslims from power in the Indian administration and government. At the same time, however, Sayyid Ahmad Khan, along with the Nizam of Hyderabad, founded the Aligarh school, which became a centre for progressive Muslim education, thought and debate.

Sayyid Ahmad Khan himself was both a staunch citizen of the British Empire and a Muslim. Many, such as al-Afghani, Muhammad Ali and Maududi were appalled at the way Khan appeared to submit to their foreign masters,[18] but his stance was not simply a frightened reaction to their power, or a grovelling ploy to allay the suspicions of his colonial masters after the events of 1857–58. His opinions were born from extensive personal study of the Qur'an, and he wrote his own commentary (tafsir) as well augmented this scriptural foundation through the Persian philosophical education that formed a natural part of his upbringing.[19] He saw no dichotomy between being both a Muslim and an imperial citizen, and his pamphlets, speeches and books are a reflection of this stance. The documents this book is analysing – 'Review on Dr. Hunter's Indian Musalmans: Are they bound in conscience to rebel against the Queen?'[20] and 'The Truth about the Khalifat'[21] – illustrate this very clearly. What it also shows is that Khan's primary aim was not the recreation of Islamic power on the subcontinent, but rather Islamic resurgence as an important, valued and active voice in the new India that was slowly being formed. For, though Muslims were intellectually active within India, their separation from the rest of society meant that they did not have an effective voice with which to make their desires and thoughts known. Consequently they were badly placed when the British began to move, with surprising swiftness, towards Indian Self-Government at the turn of the century. The story of this move to self-government sharpened the developing thinking of Muslim theologians and intellectuals on the subcontinent regarding 'citizenship' and 'loyalty' and the fruits of their thinking are an important element of Chapters Three and Four. Furthermore, it provides a fascinating backdrop to the British government's engagement with Muslim politicians in this period and, as this includes the passage of 1937 shari'a law Bill which is discussed in Chapter Five, it is important to explore the key elements of the narrative as it relates to the perspectives of both Muslims and the British government.

The Drive for Independence

India was the 'Jewel in the Imperial Crown', but had not been profitable for Britain since the administrative costs were taken on by the government following the turmoil of 1857–58. Allowing Indians a measure of self-rule appeared to be the obvious answer: it had already worked in Canada and Australia and, with cautious steps, they felt it could also work in India.[22] It also had the advantage of satisfying increasingly vocal Indian nationalist sentiments at the same time. However, the reforms of 1861 and 1909 (which included separate voting rights for Muslims) did not go far enough to satisfy the nationalists and, though they supported the British in the First World War, they expected to get something in return for their support.[23] In an increasingly political atmosphere, the *All-India Muslim League*, founded in 1906, first began discussions with the *Indian National Congress* and the British Government on greater self-rule, as a response to the Partition of Bengal in 1905.

That said, no discernible desire for a separate Muslim nation can be found at that early stage. The Muslims and Hindus were as keen to break away from direct British rule as the British themselves appeared to be and so the concern of the *Muslim League* was not the separation of the two religious communities, but the representation of Muslims within any future self-governing Indian state.[24] This remained the case right through the First World War and into the 1920s, by which time the British had clearly stated their intent in the 1918 *Montague/Chelmsford Report*, which had been written in response to the Indian support of Britain in the war:

> The policy of his Majesty's government and the government of India are in complete accord,[sic] is that of increasing association of Indians in every branch of the administration and the gradual development of self-governing institutions with a view to the progressive realisation of responsible self-government in India as an integral part of the British Empire.[25]

This document focused attention on the political goals of parties in a way that had not been experienced before. The number of people voting increased and the country seemed to take on a new energy, invigorated by the knowledge that self-government would become a reality in the future.[26] The only question was when? Even in these years, there was tension between the Muslims and Hindus, but this was temporarily hidden beneath the Khilafat Movement of the early 1920.[27] By 1935, however, this had changed and this can be traced to three main sources: the abolition of the Caliphate in 1924, the publication of the *Nehru Report* in 1928 and the calls of the poet and mystic, Muhammad Iqbal.

The abolition of the Caliphate was important because it came at a time when the entire Indian population, including the Muslims, were suddenly awakening to the very real possibility of political power within their lifetime. Thus, although Gandhi and other *Congress* leaders were very supportive of Indian Muslims in their Khilafat Movement, the abolition became a distinctive rallying cry for a minority who felt that their very faith was under attack. For, though the Khilafat Movement had been a cause of unification between the Hindus and Muslims up to its abolition in 1924, after 1924, that unity broke down, as communal violence began. This violence was exacerbated by the call of the 'tabligh', whose preachers called Muslims back to 'pure Islam' through religious education. Implicit in that 'call', was rejection of any perceived, or actual, non-Muslim influence. The abolition of the Caliphate, therefore, not only increased Islamic awareness amongst Muslims in a heightened political atmosphere, but it also served to exacerbate divisions between the two main religious communities that had managed a measure of unity in the preceding twenty years through their joint opposition to British rule. This breakdown in relations was cemented by the publication of the *Nehru Report* in 1928: a document that had been designed to try and bring the communities back together, but whose lack of commitment to Muslim political representation alienated the very people it was trying to calm.[28] It was in response to this document that Jinnah left the *Congress Party* to concentrate on the *Muslim League*, and it was two years after this that the poet and politician Muhammad Iqbal stood up to address the *All India Muslim League* over which he had been asked to preside, and made a speech which contained the first public call for a separate homeland for Indian Muslims:

> I would like to see the Punjab, North West Frontier Province, Sind and Balochistan amalgamated into a single state … .the formation of a consolidated North West Indian State appears to me to be the final destiny of Muslims …[29]

Although the idea of a Muslim state on the subcontinent was not very new, the fact that it was being articulated in an atmosphere of heightened political stakes and against a background of deepening communal tensions made the message more potent. Once Rahmet Ali had given a name to the country, the Muslims of India now had a vision to aim for and the support for the *Muslim League* increased rapidly from this point on. Iqbal's influence at this pivotal moment was immense. Gibb described it as:

> Perhaps the right way to look at Iqbal is to see him as one who reflected and put into vivid words the diverse currents of ideas that were agitating the minds of the Indian Muslims.[30]

Iqbal seemed to be able to bring together all the currents of debate and the frustration within the Muslim community, and re-direct it with a goal to aim for. Unfortunately, it also led to a time when the practicalities of power politics pushed theological and philosophical debates within the Muslim community in India to one side. Many theories have been advanced for this; amongst the plethora of material, historians such as Ikram, Chaudhuri Muhammad Ali, Jalal, Sayeed and Robinson have all analysed the social, political, religious and economic factors that drove the move towards Pakistan.[31] Undoubtedly important as all these elements were, there was a missed opportunity to discuss the question of the theological validity of the call for Pakistan within the Muslim intellectual community as well as the wider Indian Muslim community. Consequently, communalism and fear triumphed, shutting down meaningful discussion at this vital moment.

However, it must also be said that although this separatist urge was fuelled from within Indian Islam by Jinnah, Iqbal and others in the *Muslim League* hierarchy, it was certainly not helped by Gandhi's extraordinary insensitivity in insisting on going to the Third Round Table discussions in 1932, as the sole Indian representative at the conference. The idea on his part was to diffuse Muslim-Hindu tensions by going as an impartial non-religious leader to represent everybody. Unfortunately though, his plan backfired and the communal violence continued in India as nothing was achieved in London.

The struggle for independence was a time marked by ongoing strife and political stubbornness on all sides as the *Government of India Act 1935* pulled all power back to the centre in the wake of increasing non-cooperation.[32]

The elections of 1937 saw the *Muslim League* take the Muslim vote decisively and use it as a platform to push for a separate state when the *Congress* leadership was imprisoned. It was in this context that the passage of the *Shariat Act* took place.

This is not to say that Muslims were all united behind Jinnah and the *Muslim League*, indeed, this period saw the formation of the *Jama'at-i Islami* party under the leadership of Maududi, who was concerned that Jinnah and the *Muslim League* hierarchy were not Muslim enough. He was also concerned with the very notion that a separate Muslim state was a final goal to be aimed for: for Maududi, the Muslim community worldwide should be a single entity. However, objections to the aims of the *Muslim League* did not come from the Maududists alone: Ghulam Murtaza Shah Sayed inaugurated his *Progressive Muslim League* in 1943, breaking away from the *All-India Muslim League* that he had been a significant member of, in order to strive for Sindhi Muslim autonomy during the same period. The organisation he left behind continued to struggle for Sindh independence as the *Sindh United Front* even after the creation of Pakistan.[33] It has been this struggle between the nation-state, Pan-Islamism and provincial politics that has dogged Pakistan ever since its independence, and its roots can be seen in the pre-independence developments.

In the struggle to find the shape of the two independent states during the 1930 and 1940, there can be no doubt that the British pushed the *Muslim League*'s desires to the forefront of the agenda on post-colonial India in order to cause problems amongst the leadership of the Independence Movement. However, the British manoeuvres were one part of a wider communal problem, for, Mushirul Hasan has shown through an examination of the election results during the 1940, that the *Muslim League* was capturing a large percentage of the Muslim vote through its portrayal as the defender of Islam.[34] The desire to maintain identity and a voice within a newly independent state appears to have been a significant issue within the consciousness of many Indian Muslims. However, as Chapter Five will show, there was perhaps not the universal Indian Islamic consciousness that the work of Hasan suggests.

With the end of the Second World War and the release from incarceration of the core *Congress* leadership due to their lack of support of the British, the negotiators engaged a new Viceroy who, under pressure from the British government, was appointed so that Britain could free herself from India as quickly as possible. It was in these conditions that Jinnah was able to stall and harry the *Congress* leadership at the Stafford-Cripps negotiations to the extent that the *Congress* leadership realised that they would have to agree to the creation of the new Muslim state if they ever wanted to be able to concentrate on developing the institutions of the newly independent nation.[35] As it was, there was such a rush after Mountbatten had announced the date for independence without consultation, that the reactionary British legislation of 1935 became the bedrock of the new Constitution in both India and Pakistan, as there was no time to develop a new one before independence. Although both eventually created their own (India 1950 and Pakistan 1956), the *Government of India Act* remained an integral part of the new Constitutions, although it can be argued that this was less so in Pakistan given the theocratic foundational principle. Indeed, the *Shariat Act* also passed into the post-colonial statute book.

There can be little doubt that, once the idea of a separate state had taken root, the achievement of the goal justified the means in the minds of the protagonists. As Sir Percival Spear said in his *History of India*:

> The ideology of Iqbal, the visions of Rahmat Ali, and the fears of the Muslims were ... united by the practical genius of Jinnah to bind Muslims together as never before during the British period and led to an act of political creation.[36]

The cost, in human tragedy, had been enormous and the creation of the state with the disputed boundary in

Kashmir had caused great suffering. As was summed up by a peasant's angry words to the British civil servant Malcolm Darling,

> The English have flung away their Raj like a bundle of old straw and we have been chopped in pieces like butcher's meat.[37]

Even so, the general euphoria in the Muslim world that greeted the creation of the first fully Muslim state of the modern era could not be dampened. It would be fair to say that the establishment of Pakistan as a geographical entity was a politico-religious act rather than a linking together of culturally common peoples. Islam was the glue that bound together a large number of disparate groups and drove the push for the creation of the nation-state.[38] The glue began to lose its grip shortly after independence and the issue of ethnicity within the state has remained a thorn in the side of all successive Pakistani governments.

India and Pakistan Post-Independence

With the enormous administrative problems that they encountered in the first year, through the flood of refugees and the first war with India over Kashmir, very little was done on the Constitutional side apart from the adoption of the 'Objectives Resolution' in 1949, which remains the preamble to the Pakistan Constitution even now. It was followed in 1952 by the *Basic Principles Committee Report* and the first *Constitution of the Islamic Republic of Pakistan 1956*. Its essential principles were that temporal sovereignty in Pakistan had been delegated to its people by 'Almighty

God' as a sacred trust within the limits of God's law and that the founding Islamic principles of democracy, freedom and social justice should be implemented. It further described that Muslims would be 'enabled' to live their lives in accordance with Islamic principals and that facilities would be provided to allow them to do this.[39] Thus, from its very beginnings, Pakistan characterised itself as an Islamic state, this was its reason for existence and the institutions and legislative framework of the Constitution reflected that raison d'être. However, the country over the first ten years of its life appeared paralysed by indecision along with ongoing economic and ethnic struggles. Not only that, but the government also rapidly lost support from the clerics and intellectuals who had driven its creation on the basis that it was not Islamic enough. This frustration is clearly captured by Maududi, in the introduction to *Islamic Law and Constitution*:

> It [the government] had fed the people on slogans, but when the hour of implementation came, it could not deliver the goods. It was from this situation that the ideological conflict arose. People waited for some time. But gradually they began to become restless. Protests and demands began to pour in. Dissatisfaction began to mount ... [40]

The author's annoyance is self-evident, though it appears to have had less to do with the fact that many people did not have basic necessities and more to do with the government's failing to live up to its status as the ideal Islamic nation.

Given this groundswell of anti-government feeling from so many differing quarters, it is therefore not surprising that the Constitution and the democracy it enshrined, lasted only two more years, before the coup led by General Khan swept it all away. Thus, when Maududi was writing and compiling his *Islamic Law and Constitution*, it was against the background of martial law and dictatorship in Pakistan. It seemed that vision and desire of Jinnah, Iqbal and others back in the 1930 and 1940 had buckled under the weight of the enormous administrative, political, economic and sectarian issues that prevented the fledgling Islamic nation from achieving its full potential. Not only that, but the Muslim nation was having difficulty in defining what that label meant in the governmental and social life of the country. Thus, when Maududi's book was published in 1960, he wrote the situation that he saw around him at the time and as such, his book drives at what he felt to be the essential weakness of the state: its failure to be true to its inherent Islamic identity. His book is a plea to see the relevance and necessity of an Islamic state expressing itself as that in every aspect of its life. This is the Muslim philosopher appealing to the administration to govern in line with the teachings, as he saw them, of Muhammad, the Companions and the imperial ummah, and using them to qualify what a truly Islamic nation was and should be.

For the Muslims left in India, their issues revolved around two main areas: firstly, the ongoing debate over loyalty to a non-Muslim leadership, especially when that leadership was at war with Muslim neighbours. Secondly, the essential difficulty of a minority culture fighting for its identity within the state, which brought with it increasing concerns over the influence of 'secularism' and then the tide of Hindu nationalism. In the face of these pressures and issues, the works of Abid Husain, amongst others, have been instrumental in attempting to reconcile Indian Muslims to the culture around them and bringing them back into mainstream Indian culture.[41] For that reason, their work is of particular value in the context of the European Muslim minorities engaging with the secular society around them.

French North Africa

Islamic Resistance to French Conquest

The French had had a long relationship with Islam in North and West Africa that stretched back to the Napoleonic invasion of Egypt in the late 1790s, and the struggle for control of the Mediterranean with the Barbary Pirates. Indeed, several historians have suggested that Napoleon himself converted to Islam.[42] Whether this is true or not, there can be little doubt that the French had a fascination with the religion they described as 'Islam noir', which they encountered all over the region.[43]

Despite the relative ease with which the French initially embedded themselves within North and West Africa, resistance to them steadily grew and in order to motivate the resistance, the French were characterised as 'takfir', enabling the invocation of jihad to expel them.[44] The leadership of the jihad fell upon Shaykh Muhyi al-Din, an aging Sufi scholar from Algeria who, with the help of his son Amir Abd al-Qadir was able to defeat the French at two battles near Oran in 1832. This achievement was all the more remarkable in the light of the lack of support, though requested, from the Moroccans and their neighbours, the Tijani.[45] The victories brought many flocking to their banners as Muhyi al-Din handed complete control of the campaign to his son who had won acclaim on the battlefield.[46]

Abd al-Qadir quickly realised that support could be improved by a conscious shift away from the mystic symbolism of the mahdi, to the use of the classical Sunni term 'Amir al-Muminun' (Commander of the Faithful) that had been used for the Caliphs.[47] The switch proved astute as the Algerian 'ulama threw their support behind al-Qadir who were pleased by the image of a Muslim standing up to the invaders, in sharp contrast to the Beys who had negotiated away their power in a series of compromises.[48] In what has become a theme of the modern revivalist movements, al-Qadir looked to the example of Muhammad himself for his strategic inspiration, from whom he drew the principle of tactical withdrawal in the face of opposition that was too strong.[49]

Once his capital at Mascara in modern-day Algeria had been captured and razed by General Clauzel in 1835, Abd al-Qadir withdrew once more into the hills and continued to wage a successful guerrilla war right up to 1847, when he was forced to surrender to General Bugeaud.[50] Al-Qadir's chief difficulty during his long campaign against the French had come from internal opposition and from his inability to unite a broader support base amongst other North African leaders.[51] Even so, al-Qadir's resistance had shown both the colonialists and the indigenous population that European military might could be opposed and that Islam could be victorious. For the French therefore, there was a resultant desire not to provoke further reaction of this kind and so, even though their policy of assimilation was far more culturally imperial than that of the British, they were at pains to accommodate Islam within their structures as far as their desire for assimilation would allow.[52]

It is not possible to cite al-Qadir's campaign as the inspiration for subsequent rebellions, however al-Qadir's use of early Islamic symbolism and employment of the Sunnah were certainly mirrored in the Kabylia rebellions of 1852–64 and 1871 as well as in the Saharan Revolt of the 1860s. Thus, there is good evidence to suggest that al-Qadir's methodology became something of a blueprint for North African Islamic Resistance. That said, whilst there can be little doubt that Islam was the motivating factor in the al-Qadir campaign, the other revolts are harder to classify as jihads rather than nationalist uprisings given that elements of both can be found.[53] For, as Pessah Shinar argues in his chapter in *Studies in Islamic History and Civilization: In Honour of Professor David Ayalon*, the Kabyle people had valued their independence from all invaders and therefore countered the influence of Algerian rulers even before the arrival of the French.[54] So whilst there can be little doubt, that Kabyle independence was asserted against all-comers whether Muslim or not, Islamic identity was a significant factor in motivating resistance to non-Muslim leadership. Given the fact that Shinar characterises their Islam as infused with the animism they retained following their conquest in the ninth century, one might assume that this mystical folk, or Sufi Islam, would not lend itself to religious violence.[55] In the modern day, Sufism has been contrasted with jihadism in relation to the possibility of integration within Western systems, and so this example of armed resistance lead by Sufis in both the nineteenth century and in the run-up to independence (and beyond) in the twentieth century would seem to sit uncomfortably with that perception. For that reason, it serves as a stark reminder that jihadism itself is simply a methodology with an ideological foundation that can be employed by any Muslim sect that wishes to do so, whether they be Wahhabi or Sufi.

Consolidation and Law-Making

It would be fair to say that the French control of Algeria was completed by 1870 although periodic revolts continued throughout the duration of their imperial stay, rising to a crescendo in the late 1950s, early 1960s as a move to independence gained momentum.[56] However, by the middle of the nineteenth century, much of Algeria was under French rule and, accordingly, they began to set up their administration.

During both the periods of the French Second Republic (1848–52) and the Second Empire (1852–1870), Algeria was organised into three departments with a prefect over the French colonialists living in each department. The southern part of Algeria was administered by the military and came under the purview of the Governor General as the head of the 'Arab Bureaus'. Local chiefs administered the indigenous Algerian population, answering directly to the Governor General. As the Republic ended and the Empire began, a conscious policy of increased European colonisation was adopted whilst the Algerian economy was moved towards foodstuff export.[57] Here, the cultural differences in land ownership caused tensions as the colonialists, who were used to private ownership of land, met an ancient system of tenantship under complex customary and shari'a law. The apparent deprivation of land by the new masters became one of the chief causes of the sporadic rebellions discussed above. It was not the only one however, and Hiskett has helpfully highlighted the religious division between the colonialists, who were generally poor, Catholic peasants and the indigenous population, who were overwhelmingly Sunni Muslims.[58] Thus, religious rivalry existed even at grassroots level in French colonial Algeria for, no matter how bad the pre-French Turkish masters had been, they were at least Muslims. These new masters, whether good or bad, were not and it was a fact that Algerians were faced with in their interaction with their colonial masters at all levels. For that reason, religious division and motivation was bound into Algerian nationalism against French rule in a way that it could not have been against Turkish rule.[59]

This delineation between Islam and non-Islamic was exemplified in the mind of both ruler and ruled by the legal actions of Emperor Napoleon III in the 1850s and 1860s under the pressure of an economic crisis. For he allowed indigenous Algerians to adopt French nationality under the *Senatus Consulté* of 1865 having already protected tribal lands under a previous *Senatus Consulté* of 1863, with a view to binding them to French civil law, rather than to the shari'a. The Chancellor of State, Fladin, revealed the thrust of the decree:

> We do not even ask him [a Muslim] to renounce, by an explicit statement, his Muslim personal status; the Sénatus-Consulté deduces implicitly this renunciation from his demand, since Muslim status is incompatible with French Law.[60]

The decree was simply one in a series that had begun back in the 1840s when Algerian shari'a penal law was replaced by French criminal law.[61] However, it is interesting to note that declaration of 1865 differentiated between any Algerian wishing to take French nationality, who was free to remain under shari'a, and any Algerian who wished to take French citizenship, who had to renounce the shari'a and put themselves under French Civil Code.[62] For the French imperial government, therefore, being a Muslim was incompatible with being French.

Had the French been afforded the time to fully implement their policy of extreme *laïcité*, the resultant struggle would have had fundamental repercussions beyond the borders of Algeria, however, the opportunity was never given to them as the Second Empire fell to the march of the Prussian advance. The French colonialists in Algeria seized the opportunity of the chaos in France to eject the imperial administrators and to set up their own civil 'Commune of Algiers'. The Cantonments and Arab Bureaus that had been the model were gradually shifted to an integrated pattern where colonialists and indigenous Algerians lived side by side. Paris was unable to reassert centralised control and complete autonomy was achieved in 1900, enabling Algeria to pursue her own economic policies.[63] The result was an increase in colonial immigration on the back of the employment opportunities stimulated by the extensive road, ship and factory building that developed to service the rapidly developing agricultural and mining economy. It was during this period, in the new spirit of pragmatic accommodation, that the eminent jurist and expert on Maliki shari'a, Marcel Morand, was asked by Paris to work upon a legal corpus which would fuse French civil code with shari'a. His efforts and the issues associated with it will be the subject of Chapter Six.

In his article in the *EI2* on Algeria, Emerit summarises the period thus:

> The economic achievement was very considerable, but the social policy continued to be very paternal in spirit.[64]

The accuracy of this statement is born out by the fact that real social reform, including universal, equal suffrage for colonialists and Algerians, along with comprehensive education for all, was only brought in following the Second World War, in recognition of the service rendered by the Algerian people in the North African campaign.

Independence and Beyond

Perhaps the most long-lasting effect of French rule in Algeria was the new social class of professionals it produced as traditional tribal loyalties were eroded. It was these teachers, civil servants and lawyers that became the backbone of the growing nationalistic feeling that were nurtured in the newly developing trade unions and cultural associations.[65] It was a nationalism that could, unlike India, be bound up completely in a single religious identity; for the Algerian population were Muslim to a far higher degree than on the subcontinent.

The road to independence might be said to have begun with the call by Messali Hajj to create an independent Algeria that was grounded in Islam in 1937. The newly formed *Parti du Peuple Algérien* that he led called for the creation of an Algerian government, universal suffrage, total political independence and compulsory Arabic classes.[66] Above all, it called upon all Algerians to adhere to the principles of Islam.[67] In practical terms, this centrality of Islam within the milieu of nationalism was seen in the absorbing of the PPA and Islamic movements within the *Algerian Muslim Congress* in late 1936.[68]

Thus, the calls for Algerian independence could be backed wholeheartedly by the leaders of the Algerian Islamist movements, even though they came from very different political origins than their PPA colleagues. Most notable among the religious revivalists or *Islah Movement* was Abd al-Hamid b. Badis who had been influenced by the writings of the prominent Egyptian reformers Muhammad Abduh and Rashid Rida.[69] According to Lapidus, Badis also stressed belief in the unity of God and emphasized the Qur'an and Hadith whilst roundly denouncing the Sufi beliefs and practices that had actually been at the heart of the sustained resistance to French rule in the first place.[70] Central to Badis' outlook was the example of Muhammad himself, so his institution of a new Algerian 'ulama in 1931 aimed to encourage Muslims to the example of Muhammad and away from the influence of the Sufis through a new emphasis on preaching and religious publication.[71]

The outworking of this revivalism was the creation of a social movement alongside the religious one in the hope that the principles of the movement would be passed onto the young. Thus, a strong scout movement was encouraged, as was the teaching of Arabic, and the Qur'an and Algerian history were put alongside arithmetic and geography. Few went on to higher education, but, by 1954 it was said that the schools were also training militants that were fed into the independence campaign.[72]

Unsurprisingly, the French government reacted against the growing and coordinated resistance to their rule by passing the *Statut d'Algérie* of 1947 in response to the development of the new *Mouvement pour le Triomphe des Libertés Démocratiques* (MTLD) under the headship of Messali the year before.[73] It offered some compromise in the shape of recognition of the Arabic language and Islamic religious culture of Algerian people, but continued to define Algeria as an entity in terms of a group of departments within the French state.[74] It also consciously excluded Muslim reformist parties from participation in the elections that took place that year. Thus, for many Algerians, the concept of a peaceful transition of power from one regime to another through political pressure seemed to become less possible with every passing year. Indeed, massacres of either French or Algerian citizens by each side became an alarming new feature of the post-war independence struggle and the violence itself persuaded a section of the young Algerian population from poorer, more Arabic, Islamic backgrounds that the only recourse was to armed insurrection. Thus, from 1949 on, the MTLD began to organise militant cells within it under the command of Badis, which became the *Front de Libération Nationale* (FLN) and who, in 1954, launched their coordinated campaign against French colonial rule.[75] It announced that Algeria could only be freed with violence and that they desired to create an independent, democratic and socialist state, which was based on Islamic principles.

The aims of the organisation were therefore clear-cut in terms of independence, yet the precise role of Islam in any future government was less easy to discern. As was discussed above, Islam was intertwined in national identity in Algeria in a way that could not be so in India, however the calls for universal suffrage and national identity sat less well with the principles that appeared to motivate Badis personally.[76] This was brought into sharp focus in 1956 when the MTLD-FLN conference in Summam announced that the war had been inaugurated with the express intention of destroying colonialism, but that it was not a religious war, in spite of the very pietist orthodox views of the fighters themselves.[77] This was a dichotomy that continued to haunt the post-independence Algerian government.[78]

The end to the war was facilitated by a change in French government as the incoming President and hero of the Second World War, Charles de Gaulle, announced the prospect of a 'self-determined' Algeria. At a stroke, he reversed the policy of his predecessors who had managed some notable military victories, including the capture of Badis himself over the previous two years. However, the urban fighting and economic woes that accompanied it had brought the mass demonstrations of a tired people that proved the catalyst for the change of government.[79]

Independence quickly followed in 1962 through the signing of the *Accord* at Evian, which recognised Algerian independence on the basis that the French were allowed to maintain some airfields in the country.[80] The government was formed under the presidency of Badis from elements in FLN, as well as a broad spectrum of opinions and parties from across the political elite and bourgeoisie. The central issue for the post-independence government therefore, aside from economic issues, was the composite nature of the decision-making body. The long history of Islamic reformist resistance and social engagement, coupled with a century of French assimilation and a heavy socialist nationalist influence, produced a consistent struggle for domination from each of these perspectives in the independence era.[81]

It is somewhat ironic that Badis himself became the de-facto spokesman for modernising, progressive socialist Constitution that evolved in the early years given his personal piety and that he was ousted in a military coup by Houari Boumedienne, who was seen to represent Arabic-orientated Muslim viewpoints. Indeed, this tussle between socialism and religious identity has been the unresolved fault line running through Algerian politics ever since. This has been seen most clearly in the state attempts to control the agendas of religious schools in the country and the banning of the *Association of the 'Ulama* as far back as 1962. In spite of the ban however, and in the wake of constant fiscal and economic inefficiency, religiously focused opposition to the state has grown and developed in Algeria, in common with many of the North African countries that have experienced the so called "Arab Spring" over the course of 2011.[82]

Islam in Algeria therefore has been both the heart of national identity and the element of post-independence that has yet to have found its appropriate place within the new structures. At the same time, expressions of Islam itself within the new state have struggled to speak with a unified voice. No group attests to this more than the *Islamic Salvation Front* (FIS), formed in 1989 when the formation of alternative political expressions was finally permitted, for they include radical, conservative and modernist movements. Their leaders also express this dichotomy: 'Abassi Madani was the modernist politician apparently committed to pluralism and 'Ali Belhadj was a pious salafi. These splits have produced further violence and this central dichotomy has continued to haunt the post-independence Algerian state.[83]

Summary

From the point of view of the ruled, the loss of power for Muslims in both Algeria and India would have been felt within a generation. The shock of sudden disempowerment would have been profound, especially for those amongst the ruling elites in both countries whose fathers would have brought them up to understand one thing about their place in the world, only for their children to have to deal with a completely new situation. The self-reflection that Islam went through over this period is therefore an entirely understandable response and it is interesting, as shall be seen in the following two chapters, that this internal reflection produced such varied responses from the same material. What is also clear however is that whatever the nature of the responses, the underlying desire to raise the status of Islam once again was consistent.

For the Muslims under non-Muslim rule in Algeria, the freedom from colonial rule was associated with the past glories of Islamic culture in the region, whereas in India, independence from British rule could not mean a rejuvenation of Muslim rule. Consequently, Indian Muslim calls were not inextricably linked with national freedom in the same way as it was in Algeria. The issue for Algerians therefore concerned the nature of the state within the umbrella of the ummah. In India, the issue was one of identity within a non-Muslim culture.

For the rulers, the British approach to Islam in India was one of cautious diplomacy. They were concerned about possible rebellion in the light of the 1857–58 rebellion as well as the calls of the Ottoman Caliph. At the same time, the Muslims became a useful pawn in the political games surrounding independence and so had to be courted. In proclaiming religious liberty, there is the suggestion that it would enable India to be peaceable so that the maximum economic advantage could be gained from it. Yet, in making that pledge, they had not understood how some of their Muslim subjects would hear that.

The French were in Algeria both to spike the threat of the Barbary pirates initially, but later, to spread the message of enlightened government to this apparently backward region. As with so many since who have hoped to show others the advantages of Western democratic concepts, they were surprised at the lack of enthusiasm for their new ways. 'Enlightened mission' therefore gave way into angry imposition in the mid-nineteenth century and then to pragmatic accommodation in the late nineteenth early twentieth centuries. In this learning process, they attempted to fuse some elements of shari'a with their civil code, as the British also did in India. The course and results of these attempts are the subject of Chapters Five and Six as they form an important element of the discussion on citizenship from a government point of view.

Both France and Britain had learnt that the call of renewed faith had the potential to explode into violence and could be used as a weapon by those who were savvy enough to manipulate it. Consequently, for the colonial rulers, the search for a peaceful, even passive interpretation of Muslim theology and political theory was the key to successful community living. For their Muslims subjects, thoughts focussed around whether their colonial masters could, even should be obeyed, and whether Islam as a political entity should be consigned to the past, or worked for once more.

For both ruler and ruled, the answers to these questions would provide the basis for their ongoing relationship and would determine the nature of the 'citizenship' that was either demanded or given.

* * *

Section Two will now go on to explore that relationship from a Muslim perspective before Section Three turns to look at them from the ruler's viewpoint.

SECTION TWO

ISLAM IN MINORITY: CITIZENSHIP AND THE UMMAH

Introduction

The aim of this section is to outline and analyse the broad spectrum of opinion within the Muslim world in order to examine two pertinent questions that reside at the heart of the issue of citizenship from the perspective of the Muslims themselves. Firstly, should Muslims always obey those who are in authority over them, even if they are not Muslims? The second question has two sub-questions within it: on what level should the notion of the Muslim community function – local, national or global – and does the ummah require a single leader (and if so, what would his remit be)?

As has been seen in the 'Theological Section', it would be reasonable to say that many interpretations of Q4:59 and the broader theory of Islamic governance were written with the assumption of Muslim rule. However, most modern-day Muslims do not live under Muslim rule[1], and, for the sake of those majority Muslims, it is important to examine the writings of those Muslims who have already been in that situation and how they worked out their duties as Muslims and citizens. The Muslims of North Africa and the sub-continent provide excellent source material on this subject in relation to their relevance for current Muslim communities in Europe. Egypt is home to the premier Sunni Islamic University in the world, Al-Azhar, and has given rise to the *Muslim Brotherhood* as well as producing revivalist luminaries such as Muhammad 'Abduh and Sayyid Qutb. India is home to the influential Dar ul-Ulum school in Deoband, Aligarh University and revivalists such as Maulana 'Ala Maududi, Sayyid Ahmad Khan, Muhammad Ali and Muhammad Iqbal. Between them therefore, they have produced some of the most influential thinkers, writers and activists of the revivalist movement. Many of those named above owed a debt to the Persian Shi'a revivalist, Jamal-ad-Din al-Afghani, who rose above sectarianism to spend a lifetime advocating support for the Ottoman Caliphs as a way into reinstituting a Pan-Islamic concept of the ummah.

The responses to each of the questions posed in this section will be grouped into two clearly defined positions: on one side are those that have been labelled 'visionary separatists', whose theological and political standpoint is exemplified by Maududi's books, *Islamic Law and Constitution* and *Let Us Be Muslims*. Those writings will be examined and critiqued along with the writings of other Muslim reformers whose answers to the questions put them in the same or similar camp as Maududi, no matter what their sectarian beliefs may be. The other group has been labelled the 'pragmatic philosophers' and their standpoint is exemplified in the political speeches and writings of Sayyid Ahmad Khan as well as a number of others. As with the 'visionary separatists', this label takes no account of sectarian background and includes those reformers whose viewpoints on the questions alone place them in this category. Both categories are homogeneous and there is considerable difference of opinion on the details of the positions being espoused within both camps.

The material has been grouped in this way in order to focus the reader on the positions being articulated, rather than the personalities or backgrounds of those articulating them. Furthermore, although this discussion has been set within the colonial and post-colonial eras as a parallel to the current situation facing Muslim minorities in the West, this section does not present a linear historical progression of ideas: commonality and difference of position between writers are observed, grouped and analysed irrespective of whether they were contemporaries or were generations apart. This has been done to place the positions they are taking at the centre of the critique, rather than any other external factor.

Maududi has been chosen as one of the two main writers on the basis of his standing and influence among Indian Muslim reformers, for he is called the 'South Asian architect of Islamic fundamentalism.'[2] The reason that the final three chapters of Maududi's book *Let Us Be Muslims* have been selected from his writings to discuss his ideas on question one is that they represent the culmination of all that he had been saying in the rest of the book, which calls Muslims back to 'purity of faith', and it is in these final chapters that he expounds the political implications of all that he has said before.

Maududi's chapter in *Law and Constitution* has been chosen as the basis for the discussion of his ideas on question two on the basis that it expands on his ideas contained within *Let Us Be Muslims*, and develops his philosophy of universal Muslim separatism. The chapter was originally a paper delivered to a meeting of the *Inter-Collegiate Muslim Brotherhood*, Lahore in October 1939 and the writing has the tone and feel of a political speech: a mix of scholarship, and emotional appeal designed to engender a sense of vision and possibility.

Acknowledging this potentially leaves me open to the criticism that the orator would be 'playing to the crowd'. However, the speech is clearly the result of great reflection and sets out what Maududi believed to be the fundamental ideals and basic tenets required of an Islamic state, in the context of a drive towards that very goal. Thus, Maududi is speaking into a situation where Islamic authority is not just discussed as an abstract, but as a fast approaching reality in which it was imperative to get the fundamentals right. This was no time for purely academic discussion; Maududi was talking to people who would hold the reigns of power for themselves within eight years and his desire was to see a state set-up, which would be a shining beacon of Islamic power, showing the world what an Islamic state could be. His message therefore had to be both idealistic and pragmatic, directing his listeners towards the theological principles of Islamic state authority and moving on to show how these principles should be translated into executive and legislative government organs. This was the visionary, attempting to cross into the pragmatic.

The rationalist Persian noble Sayyid Ahmad Khan has been chosen as a foil to Maududi for the principal reason that his views are diametrically opposed to Maududi in almost every sense. Despite this fact, he is still recognised as a great Muslim thinker[3] and reformer throughout the subcontinent. He was a man who was steeped in scriptural knowledge and stood up for Muslims in India under assault and suspicion from their colonial masters following the events of 1857–58.[4] Consequently, his opposing viewpoint cannot be lightly dismissed by those on the Maududi side of the Indian Muslim debate who may wish to attack many of his views as too synergetic and doctrinally not rooted in Muslim scripture.

When assessing the political philosophy of the Sayyid Ahmad Khan, the hardest part of the task is to choose the material to analyse, for he never wrote a piece of work that enshrined his political ideas in the same way that Maududi did. Much of his political thought was expressed through the general principles he applied to the situations he was discussing in the various letters and speeches he made in the period between the First Indian War of Independence/ Indian Mutiny and his death in 1898. Many of his speeches and correspondence were rebuttals of various other positions.[5] Therefore by proxy rather than by intention, as he expressed his opinions on the issues of the day such as the inclusion of Muslims in the Viceroy's government [6] the arguments he advances build a consistent position on how Muslims should live under non-Muslim authority. Two pieces in particular stand out: the first was his *Review on Dr. Hunter's Indian Musalmans: Are They Bound in Conscience to Rebel Against the Queen?* in which he deploys historical, cultural and limited theological arguments to strongly refute the accusations of disloyalty made against the Indian Muslims by Dr. Hunter. It therefore becomes an invaluable counter-argument to place against the stringent theology of Maududi's position on obedience to authority, and provides insight into Khan's understanding of the answer to both the first and second questions. The second main piece comes from a pamphlet he wrote titled: *'The Truth About the Khalifat'*, which sets out his beliefs concerning Muslim leadership and what form it should take, thus providing a suitable additional basis for discerning his ideas on question two.

Chapter Three sees the discussion of the broad question of citizenship in relation to non-Muslim leadership. The chapter following it takes that broadstroke argument and digs deeper into the issue by looking at the nature of the ummah following the end of the Islamic Empire.

Finally, before stepping into the debates, it is worthwhile highlighting one of the points made in the 'Introduction': that the Muslim thinkers included in the next two chapters come from very different religious and philosophical backgrounds, many of whom share little in common. Putting them in the groups they are could be seen as a gross injustice, perhaps even giving a false impression of proximity of belief when none actually exists. However, it has been done to make the question sovereign, not the ideas of the individual writers. This approach enables a wide variety of viewpoints on these questions to be gathered together and grouped to provide clarification of the central tensions that exist between the differing viewpoints. Those wishing to find a nuanced discussion of the views of any of these thinkers outside of these questions will need to explore other writings.

CHAPTER THREE

SHOULD MUSLIMS ALWAYS OBEY THOSE IN AUTHORITY OVER THEM, EVEN WHEN THEY ARE NOT MUSLIMS?

Maududi and the Visionary Separatists

Maududi

It is in section five of *Let Us Be Muslims* that Maududi's answer to the question given in the chapter title can be found. Much of what he says in this section is the outworking of the principles that he lays down throughout the rest of the book, but it is in this section that the political principles that are implicit in the rest of the book are made explicit. This is particularly seen in the chapters entitled 'Renewal of Society', 'Meaning of Jihad' and 'Central Importance of Jihad'[1] where he explains why he believes that Muslims in a non-Muslim nation should fight for a Muslim state that he defines as a shari'a state.

Maududi explains the terms he is to base his argument on at the beginning of his section on the 'Central Importance of Jihad':

> Acknowledging that someone is your ruler to whom you must submit means that you have accepted his Din. He now becomes your sovereign and you have become his subjects. The commandments and the codes he gives you constitute the law or Shari'ah which you must follow. Once you live in accordance to the law laid down by him, you are serving and worshipping him: this is 'Ibadah. You then give him whatever he demands, obey whatever he orders, abstain from whatever he forbids, observe whatever limits he sets for your conduct, and follow whatever he instructs or decides in all your affairs.[2]

For Maududi therefore, whatever political system becomes your ruler, the subject or citizen is seemingly reduced almost to the level of slavery. This central pillar of his whole argument concerning obedience to rulers, whether Muslim or non-Muslim, rests upon the huge assumption that he is making in these definitions. For Maududi clearly saw no delineation between personal faith and temporal rule in his perception of Western democracy in spite of the fact that he had seen that principle operating at close hand in the British rule of India.[3] Thus, Maududi's words here appear to bear out Mujeeb's critical summary of Maududi's philosophy:

> Maulana Maududi categorically rejects the Western view of life, and the moral, social and political views it claims to represent. His reasoning is apparently sound, and would convince anyone who knew the west

only from hearsay and did not feel the need to understand Muslim and Indian history or face the facts of contemporary life.[4]

Fascinatingly Maududi defines 'the law' as being the same as shari'a, even though, within the historical setting in which he was writing, he could have had no basis for doing so unless he applied the idea that all law is, in one sense religious, insofar as it transfers the moral principles of a society into a set of regulations. In making this statement, he displays the deep-rooted influence of his cultural heritage, rather than objectively observing the alternative systems on display around him.

However, if one chooses to accept the premise of his opening statement for the purpose of following his line of argument, the validity of what he goes on to say appears logical: for he specifies that either one is under Allah's sovereignty (and therefore shari'a) or under the diin of a nation or people. His choice of word in this context is interesting as Maududi is using it in a specifically political context and it is useful to spend a few moments unpacking the etymology of diin in order to understand fully the concept he is attempting to articulate.

Gardet's extensive entry on diin in the *Encyclopaedia of Islam* suggests three possible meanings: judgement or retribution, custom and religion.[5] These differing meanings are derived from the choice of root language the scholar is developing their translation from, for the notion of 'judgement' is derived from the Aramaic-Hebrew root, 'custom' from the Arabic for 'debt' and 'religion' from the Pelhevi word for 'revelation' or 'religion'.[6] Gardet dismisses the Pelhevi root meaning on the grounds that the concept of 'religion' in Islam is not similar to that of Mazdaism.

He concludes that the combination of the Aramaic-Hebrew meaning with the Arabic meaning gives an accurate understanding of how the word should be understood.[7] Thus, for Gardet, the true sense of the word is 'obligation, submission, judgement'.

In the most general sense, this could be understood as 'religion'; however, a more accurate understanding is a 'life of faith', which goes beyond the dogmatic practice of ritual to what Gardet describes as 'the radiance or essence of faith'.[8] This sense is captured by both Watt and Penrice where Watt translates the word as 'way of life'[9] and Penrice's entry includes 'custom, institution, the true faith, obedience and judgement'.[10]

On the evidence of these Arabists, it seems that Maududi's use of the term could be accepted and contested on different grounds insofar as he appears to have been articulating an accurate cultural perception of the term from the Muslim perspective, but a concept that would be entirely alien in a Western culture that separated Church and state.[11] Thus, one might say that validity of Maududi's argument rests upon a very Muslim understanding of Western concepts.

Whether this assessment can be validated or not, it is clear that Maududi's perception of the inextricable intertwining of religion and state sovereignty sees no possibility of duality in citizenship:

> ... you can see that it is impossible for you to follow more than one Din at a time. Of various rulers only one can rule your lives: of various systems of law, only one can be the law of your lives.[12]

This sentiment was almost precisely mirrored by Perwez in his book, where he argues that fiqh Islam is a parody of

'Western democracy', and that true Islam can only be found in the total immersion of every aspect of social, religious and legal life in its scriptures as well as its law.[13]

Thus, Maududi's description of 'shirk' that follows elucidates the point he has already made. The argument is essentially based on the idea that whatever law is being described, whether shari'a, secular or an alternative religious code, it must be 'all encompassing' and therefore leave no room for the co-existence of any other set of principles.

Such a black-and-white stance is almost impossible to understand from non-Muslim Western perspectives, where one is brought up on the notion of separation between personal faith and secular state and law.[14] Yet, given the apparently overarching nature of the shari'a as a social and legal instrument, the notion makes far more sense. This idea is mirrored in Asad's later work on state government and Islam, written in the post-colonial era,

> ... an individual, however well intentioned he may be, cannot possibly mold [sic] his private existence in accordance with the demands of Islam unless and until the society around him agrees to subject its practical affairs to the pattern visualised by Islam.[15]

Kalim Siddiqui cites this principle as the reason that Maududi founded the *Jama'at-i Islami* in 1941, opposing the *Muslim League* and their apparent desire to create an Islamic state using 'Western democracy' as its political system.[16] Siddiqui's observation helps us to understand that when Maududi later calls for jihad in order to create the perfect state, it flows naturally from the philosophical position he has already expounded:

> The Din of Allah, like any other Din, does not allow that you merely believe its truth and perform certain worship rites. If you are a true follower of Islam, you can neither submit to any other Din, nor can you make Islam a partner of it. If you believe Islam to be true, you have no alternative but to exert your utmost strength to make it prevail on this earth: you either establish it or give your lives in the struggle.[17]

His use of Qur'anic ayah in the course of the discussion are designed to lend apparently unimpeachable authority to his arguments, and in this section within the final chapter alone he deploys Q8:39, Q12:40, Q18:111, Q4:60–64, Q29:2–3, 10–11, Q3:179, Q9:16 and 58:14–21 to lend weight to what he is saying. The context of each verse cannot be examined here, but it clearly shows the author's ongoing desire to draw on the Qur'an itself, rather than classical exegesis, in order to form his opinions.

This same universalist principle in approaching the question of Muslim rule by non-Muslims is seen in al-Afghani's *Refutation of the Materialists*.[18]

Al-Afghani

Al-Afghani will feature more in the second question in the following chapter, but given his status amongst the leading ideologues of Islamic reform, it is worthwhile spending a few moments briefly articulating his ideas on the question of obedience to non-Muslims. His ideas are entirely in line with Maududi's and so there is little point revisiting arguments that have already been reported and analysed.

However, it is important to look at what al-Afghani's call for Muslims to rule Muslims is based upon as it differs slightly from Maududi's.

Although he does not specifically name it, al-Afghani's reasons for wanting Muslim leadership of Muslims is based upon his understanding of the rashidun period. This comes out most clearly in his quotation of Q49:13, where he suggests that, in the original ummah, leadership was based on piety, rather than ancestry.[19] It was therefore the obedience to the will of God that became the ultimate source of legitimization for any ruler. In that context, only a ruler who ruled in obedience to God should be followed: a situation that ruled out obedience to any who were not Muslim as far as al-Afghani was concerned.[20] In order to illustrate this, he uses the parallel of Indians being happy to be ruled by an Ottoman Turk, an obvious allusion to the Caliphate, or by a foreign regime, provided that they adhere to religious laws and precepts. What these 'precepts' are remains undefined.[21]

Thus, obedience to rulers was, for al-Afghani, limited purely to Muslim leadership of the state.[22]

Muhammad Iqbal

Muhammad Iqbal also expressed sentiments similar to Maududi, al-Afghani, Perwez and Asad on the question of why Muslims need a 'Muslim government':

> Is religion a private affair? Would you like to see Islam, as a moral and political idea, meeting the same fate in the world of Islam as Christianity has already met in Europe? Is it possible to retain Islam as an ethical ideal and reject it as a polity in favour of national politics in which religious attitude is not permitted to play any part?[23]

Perhaps this question was even more pertinent for him, than for Maududi, as he had witnessed the secularizing program that Atatürk had undertaken in Turkey, effectively removing Islam from life outside the mosque.[24] This was something that Iqbal could not countenance and in one of the most eloquent passages about the need for Muslim to have state apparatus of the modern period, Iqbal places himself firmly in the Maududi-Parwez-Asad school as he writes:

> [Islam] is individual experience creative of a social order. Its immediate outcome is the fundamentals of a polity with implicit legal concepts whose civic significance cannot be belittled merely because their origin is revelational. The religious ideal of Islam, therefore, is organically related to the social order which it has created … Therefore, the construction of a polity on national lines, if it means a displacement of the Islamic principle of solidarity, is simply unthinkable to a Muslim.[25]

Here, it is important to correctly understand Iqbal's final sentence, for it can easily be misinterpreted: he is not saying that the creation of an Islamic state which would break up the subcontinent would be anathema to a Muslim, for he is not concerned about the solidarity of Indians as a set of people. Instead, he is saying that the creation of a nation-state (independent India) would not allow Muslims to be Muslims properly because they would be absorbed into a larger whole. It is because of this he concludes that Muslims on the subcontinent require a separate homeland to be 'fully Muslim'.

As with his fellow 'visionary separatists', Islam to Iqbal is an all-encompassing social system, not merely a private faith, which could not function without the implementation of divine law and therefore needs some form of state apparatus to implement it, necessitating headship by a Muslim.

Muhammad 'Abduh

'Abduh's opposition to the British invasion of Egypt in the 1880s is well documented.[26] Indeed, one might argue that his experiences during that period were formative in developing nationalism that will be explored further in the following chapter. That said, once the British and French were in control of Egypt, he appears to have taken a more non-confrontational approach and begun to follow a path of obedience.[27]

This obedience was apparently pragmatic, rather than theological. 'Abduh believed that European influence could be beneficial for a time in terms of breaking out of the 'taqlid' that Egypt had fallen into.[28] However, this did not mean that he was happy for non-Muslims to rule Muslims, of course. His concern was for the long-term betterment of Egypt and Islam: if that meant a period of foreign rule then so be it.

Summary

The 'visionary separatists' base their requirement for Muslim leadership of Muslims on the principle that Islam is not just a faith, it is a whole social order, which cannot be made subordinate to the laws or system of any other cultural or religious group. In such a context, Muslims cannot allow any leadership over them, other than their own. One might say therefore that their understanding of Islam comes both from the 'golden era' [(when the Muslim Empire stretched from Spain and North Africa to Southeast Asia)] on the basis of shari'a as defined in the previous chapter.

Sayyid Ahmad Khan and the Pragmatic Philosophers

Unlike the 'visionary separatists', the 'pragmatic philosophers' are a group with diverse viewpoints, but they have
been grouped together as they all share one common char-
acteristic, a desire to deal in the present, and to make Islam
stronger through building on the past, rather than starting
again with an ancient 'Arab' model.

Sayyid Ahmad Khan

An alternative perspective to the one offered by the 'visionary
separatists' can be found in Sayyid Ahmad Khan's response
to the 1871 publication of a book by Dr William Hunter.[29]
Hunter's book, which was widely in circulation in India at
the time, strongly questioned the loyalty of Muslims as subjects of the British Crown.[30] It claimed that Wahhabi mis-
sionaries were stirring up Indian Muslims to rebel against
the British. This claim found receptive ears in the light
of the murder of Chief Justice Norman by a Muslim one
year before the book was published, and reflected a natural
suspicion of Muslims in general, whom many British felt
were behind the rebellion of 1857–58.[31] Khan's desire was
to quell this vicious rumour as quickly as possible before
it had a chance to take root in public consciousness. In the
course of his argument therefore, he systematically destroys
the fear of a widespread Indian Muslim plot to overthrow
the British government by showing Dr. Hunter's errors in
fact and understanding.[32]

In order to defend Muslim loyalty to the British Empire,
Khan omits discussion of Islamic scripture and focuses
instead upon a legal argument that centres around the definition of India as dar al-Islam rather than dar al-Harb.[33] In
adopting this line of argument, he deploys the essence of

the Hanafi shari'a code that would have been familiar to him. Because of this ruling, he argues, the British rulers had nothing to fear from Indian Muslims because, under such a definition, Indian Muslims had no right to rebel.[34] Thus his understanding of these terms and their implications are of particular relevance in relation to the question that is being explored here.

Having decided upon this legalistic argument, he therefore deploys the senior Islamic scholars of the day to lend weight to what he says, quoting the fatwas of Ahmad Bin Dahlan; Mufti of the Shaafi Sect of Mecca, Husain Bin Ibrahim; Mufti of the Maliki Sect of Mecca and the Law Doctors of North India, who all stated that India was not dar al-Harb. In fact, they also ruled that India was dar al-Islam and did not create the conditions under which rebellion against authority was lawful.[35]

It is interesting to note at this point that on the question of whether India under the British was dar al-Harb, not dar al-Islam, even Ahmad Riza Khan Barelwi agreed with Sayyid Ahmad Khan and the other Muslim clerics who said that India was not dar al-Harb, citing the very Hanafi fiqh that Khan's argument was drawn from.[36] The reasons given for India not being dar al-Harb were either that if any aspect of Islamic practice survived, then it was still dar al-Islam, or if there was religious freedom, then rebellion could not be justified. Sayyid Ahmad Khan himself, felt that the country was at an in-between state, where it was neither fully dar al-Islam or dar al-Harb and thus there could be no firm direction to rebel when the country was religiously and politically still in a state of flux.[37]

Such a 'legal' argument seems rather surprising in one sense, given that it would have been more difficult to argue that India was still Islamic, rather than to say, as he did in his Aligarh Gazette article of 2 February 1889,[38] that it was simply scripturally wrong for Muslims to engage in treasonous actions against British rule. Furthermore, there is no mention here in Khan's argument, of the example of Joseph in Egypt that McDonough cites as Khan's precedent for Muslims living under foreign rule.[39] Khan's argument therefore rests upon the authority of the 'ulama, rather than direct appeal to Islamic scripture himself. This is an interesting choice given that he was himself the author of a tafsir, and clearly therefore, an eminent Qur'anic scholar in his own right.[40]

Chiragh Ali

Chiragh Ali's inclusion would appear on one level to be slightly facile given the fact that he was a protégé of Sayyid Ahmad Khan, and his views were very similar to his master's. However, it is worthwhile considering some of his ideas in their own right for, although he is swimming in the same philosophical stream as his mentor, he does not by any means simply repeat his mentor's thoughts, but defines a clear position for himself. Not only that, but he achieved notoriety in his own right as a legal reformer in the late nineteenth century.

In the introduction to his book on Muslim legal reform, published in 1883, his credentials as a Muslim reformer are clearly established through his use of the classic reformist notion of the original ummah as the example and remedy for the Muslim world's strife.

> The idea that Islam is essentially rigid and inaccessible to change, that its laws, religious political and social, are based on a specific set of precepts which can

neither be added to, nor taken from, nor modified to suit altered circumstances: that its political system is theocratic, and that in short the Islamitic [sic] code of law is unalterable and unchangeable, have taken a firm hold in the European mind, which is never at any trouble to be enlightened on the subject ... I have endeavoured to show in this book that Muhammadanism as taught by Muhammad, the Arabian Prophet, possesses sufficient elasticity to enable it to adapt itself into the social and political revolutions going on around it.[41]

It is clear that he felt this 'original' form of Islam to be relevant to society at that moment, even though it was based on an Arab eighth-century model of political and social organisation. In so doing, he might easily have been placed within the 'visionary separatist' camp, however, he begins to significantly diverge from their position a few short phrases after the quotation just given, when he proposes that the first four Caliphs were essentially republican and democratic, rejecting the notion that the Islamic state was essentially theocratic as Maududi would later argue.[42] This somewhat surprising perspective is explained by a useful analogy in which he draws a parallel between the dictators of Rome and the pious Caliphs, based upon the fact that both were elected and under the authority of the law.[43] Unfortunately, his evidence is rather undermined by the fact that the pagan Roman leaders did not claim to rule over a community of believers at the behest of God as the Caliphs did. Nevertheless, the analogy is useful insofar as it displays Ali's desire to engage with non-Muslim references when seeking to make his case. Whether this renders him more or less valuable as an opinion-shaper will depend on the individual individual's perspective of a Muslim, however, the fact that Ali was willing to look outside of Islam for ways of developing answers to the difficulties Islam in India was undergoing at the time shows a openess to learn from non-Muslim cultures for the long-term benefit of the faith.

Whilst his use of non-Muslim examples to encourage Muslim revivalism or development might be questioned, his argument that the history of Islam in India was one of organic development, which needed to continue, strikes a far more resounding note.[44]

His message to Muslims is that, for Muslim rehabilitation to take place, it must change and adapt, as all systems must change and adapt.[45] For Chiragh Ali, shari'a has not been allowed to do that, causing Islamic thinking and cultural dynamism to fall well behind the rest of the world.

What he does not define is what the final goal or product of this reform will be, for nowhere is there even a hint that Islam should be a political power or state authority in the manner that Maududi would later argue. Perhaps he simply assumes it, for he was writing at a time when the Ottoman Caliphate (which he refers to several times) was notionally at least still a major power.[46] What is more likely though is that he saw religion and state separating in the same way that Khan did, for he says, towards the end of his introduction

> ... Muhammad never set up his own acts and words as an infallible or unchangeable rule of conduct in civil and political affairs, or, in other words, he never combined Church and State into one.[47]

This comes after he cites the example, attributed to Muslim, of Muhammad giving bad advice on tree husbandry, which he uses to illustrate his idea that Muhammad's opinions were valid only in spiritual matters.[48] From this, he draws the conclusion that Muhammad did not intend to set up a state or way of life, but only redirected people towards the true God. However, this line of argument does not take into account the evidence from the *Constitution of Madina*, where Muhammad specifically enters into a political agreement with other faith communities in order to develop his political and military power.[49]

Islam as the 'all-encompassing blueprint' of al-Afghani, Maududi, Iqbal and Asad is reduced by Ali to an evolving system which was never all encompassing, but mostly an administrative tool that changed to suit the time and location. In the past, shari'a had been the evolved law of the 'ulama of a particular area, but now it was the law of the ruled, who now had other laws to follow as well, and so Muslims would need to rethink their shari'a accordingly.[50]

Thus, even though Ali displays sound reformist credentials (harking back to the Medinan model), he displays an essentially pragmatic viewpoint that sought to rationalise shari'a as a body of law, removing its divine authority and placing it at the same level as any other civil code. As soon as he does that, it becomes a devise that can be changed and developed as the user desires: a dynamic that would be impossible if it retained its divine credentials.

Mohammed Arkoun

The eminent Algerian-born Ismaili philosopher Mohammed Arkoun expressed very similar sentiments to those of Chiragh Ali in his seminal work *The Unthought in Contemporary Islamic Thought*. For Arkoun, Muslims had no reason not to participate fully in non-Muslim citizenship. Arkoun himself had made the transfer from Algerian to French citizenship following Algeria's independence in 1954 and his writings display the lack of apparent struggle he felt as a Muslim living and participating in French life.[51] Indeed, Arkoun seemed keen to encourage equality for all religions even within Muslim majority states that would have been at complete variance with the views of fellow Algerians such as Ben Badis, in particular. Arkoun's goal was for Muslims to aspire to being 'trans-individual' subjects, where the 'trans' indicates an ongoing mentality of making and remaking perceptions of 'Islam' in new contexts.[52]

Syed Abid Husain

The views expressed by Khan and Ali in the colonial period have been have been redefined and developed in a new political context by Syed Abid Husain of the Jamia Millia Islamia.[53] He too was an avid Muslim reformer, but as he was partly educated at Aligarh University, so more hard-line Muslim scholars might reject his work on account of the Sayyid Ahmad Khan influence. However, his zeal for the resurgence of Islam cannot be doubted, as he was the founder of *Islam and the Modern Age Society*. The society sought to revive the fortunes of the faith in the subcontinent through attempting to build bridges into mainstream Hindu society, rather than through communal politics. For that reason, the society's stance brings them into direct conflict with the salafi accent on regeneration for domination.[54]

In his book *The Destiny of Indian Muslims*, Husain attempts to pull Indian Muslims away from the communal mindset that he believes they had, into full participation in main-stream Indian life.[55] His concern is to allay Muslim fears about living as Muslims in a country that did not impose shari'a, or even have a Muslim leadership.[56] As he was writing at the same time as Maududi's *Law and Constitution* was being published, it therefore it provides quite a useful contrast between the views at either extreme of Muslim religio-political opinion. It also is useful in terms of looking at the views of the generation of Indian Muslims who had gone through Partition and had aligned themselves with the secular state, thus providing a modern context for the views of Sayyid Ahmad Khan and al-Afghani who were writing in an imperial age.

What is most fascinating about Husain's views are the reasons that he gives for urging full Muslim participation in everyday secular society. The 'siege mentality', or 'desire for the recapturing of past Islamic glory', seem to have gone to be replaced with an encouragement to accept what is around them and to develop the cause of Islam by full, integrated participation in the life of the new nation-state.[57]

This is pragmatic advice for the advancement of Islam based on a present reality, not a yearning for recaptured glory, impossible to achieve without untold violence and suffering. The reasons he gives for his advice, however, would be more likely to repel the hard-line extremist, rather than encourage him:

> Indian national life itself is part of the modern world-culture, which India has adopted as the foundation of its social and political life, and to accept Indian nationhood is really to accept the general pattern of modern world culture.[58]

In expressing his view that Indian national life is the same as the rest of the world culture, he must be thinking of the adoption of parliamentary democracy as a governmental model. For, whether one was looking at very protectionist policies when it came to trade, or the separatism that was an integral part of the Non-Aligned Movement in the Cold War era, India could not be classed in the mainstream of world culture.[59] However, the point he was making – 'that India engages with the world around it and that Muslims should do the same in India' – is clear.

Later on, Husain explains his definition of 'world culture' as the foundation of his main argument concerning how Muslims should engage with the secular culture around them.[60] The thrust of his argument is to differentiate between 'scientific secularism' and 'political secularism'.[61] In the former, according to Husain, the scientific and religious communities separate amicably with mutual benefit in the stimulation of opposing viewpoints. In the latter, science and religion are at odds with each other, trying to prove each other wrong. Here Husain notes that, even under this assault, religion in Protestant countries has been able to adapt to this conflict.[62] The object of this slightly suspect reasoning is to make far more valuable points concerning the nature of the Indian Constitution and Muslim attitudes towards it: firstly that it is 'scientific secularist'; secondly, that it gives all religions freedom of worship; and thirdly that it has adopted many of the central Islamic values (such as universal brotherhood of man, social and economic justice and freedom of the human spirit) into the ideals of the Indian state.[63]

This belief in the inherent freedom for Muslims as a minority is shared by the politician and scholar Syed Shahabuddin, who sets the concerns of the Muslim community within the wider context of the country as a whole:

... Muslims are not the only religious minority for every religious minority and every linguistic group faces a minority situation in one or more states of the Indian Union ... . India is a land of minorities and needs a national norm to deal with minority situations at various levels of administration. The Constitution, therefore, provides many safeguards for the protection of minorities.[64]

Thus, Husain and Shahabudin are certainly articulating something that is entirely outside of the thinking of the 'visionary separatists': the concept of gratitude that the state of affairs are as they are, rather than an attitude of grief or victimisation that constantly complains about what has been lost, or not given. This is a valuable idea, which is not peculiar to the position of Islam alone, but applicable to any minority community living in what may be termed a 'free society'. It is a realisation that things could be a good deal worse and a gratitude that they are not.

After making this positivist plea, he moves on to one of his core themes: effective use of the democratic system to advance the cause of Islam in which he talks about the Indian Constitution specifically:

... as it is the constitution of a democratic state, it gives to Muslims, as Indian citizens, the right and opportunity to try and change anything in the national constitution or national life which appears to them to be in conflict with Islamic values and to advocate the adoption of more Islamic values.[65]

He encourages Muslims in India to engage in the democratic process in order to bring about any changes they feel are needed in the same way that any other group would do.[66]

He is, however, at pains to point out that the current Constitution is, in his view, perfectly compatible with Muslim life anyway.[67] Not only that, but because democracy naturally contains the elements of science, observation and reasoning, the democratic system itself is an excellent test for any belief.[68] Subjecting Islam to that process, he argues, would allow for the eradication of any elements, which are anomalous to the faith and would, in the end, produce a leaner, fitter religion. In this sense, Maududi et al. would support his reasoning although not, one suspects, in the context in which he is framing it.

Husain then moves on to the central question, which all Muslims in any non-Muslim or even Muslim state need to address:

> ... all Muslims in India have to ask themselves whether or not loyalty to the nation is prior to and more important than the loyalty they owe to religion.[69]

This is a key question and it is unfortunate that he fails to adequately answer it. Instead he hides behind an abstract argument in which he first outlines his definitions of what 'state', 'nationalism' and 'patriotism' are[70] before concluding

> Consequently loyalty to the State necessarily demands loyalty to the nation and country. So the Indian Muslims who have accepted loyalty to the state as a fundamental principle will have to accept nationalism and patriotism as necessary corollaries.[71]

Effectively, he passes the burden back to individual Muslims to decide for themselves. But he adds that, when nationalism and patriotism are used as political terms, perhaps almost rising to religions in themselves (he cites the example of extremist parties such as the Nazis in Germany), then this makes it more difficult for the Muslim to decide how to react. His concern is principally with what he saw as the rising tide of nationalism in India, making the issue all the more pertinent as its immediate consequence was heightening tensions with the Muslim country of Pakistan.

He is supported in his stance by Muhammad Munir,[72] who also argued that religious belief and political matters are two distinct domains and cited a Hadith, without attributing it, to lend weight to his statement.[73] This argument is somewhat difficult to sustain in the light of the discussion in Chapter One, however, Husain's desire to encourage participation in wider society presents a positive approach that seeks to shake off separatism and suspicion in favour of engagement.

Husain ends with a conclusion that attempts to delineate between a just loyalty to a 'healthy' nationalism-patriotism on the one hand and a 'feishist' one on the other, which elevates state loyalty to the level of religion itself. Unfortunately, it is hard to see how Husain's technically refined advice could be of much practical benefit for the practising Muslim in a predominantly Hindu state, which has three times been to war with a Muslim state.

One might say that Husain is making a very encouraging attempt at ending Muslim isolationism by arguing that the Indian state is worthy of loyalty simply because Muslims should be grateful that it is secular and not Hindu. The issue of secularism in a modern context has been the subject of much discussion and a useful contribution to the debate in a British context particularly came with *British Secularism and Religion* (edited by Yahya Birt, Dilwar Hussain and Ataullah Siddiqui) in 2011.

Whilst this in itself is a reasonable argument from a pragmatic standpoint, it does not solve the theological issues that need to be addressed if a Muslim is to feel that he or she can wholeheartedly give their loyalty to a non-Muslim authority.

Mushir Ul-Haq

One of Husain's contemporaries, ul-Haq, takes a slightly more sinister view of the same secularism that Husain urges the Muslims in their minority position to embrace. As such, his book acts as an answer to many of the points made by Husain. It is unclear who his target audience is, however, for the language is not that of 'appeal to fellow Muslims', more 'explanation for non-Muslims', which would seem to suggest that it was intended much more for the general Hindu public, rather than for his fellow Muslims. For that reason, it provides a useful insight into the way one Muslim viewed the mindset of his fellow believers and, although there are inconsistencies in his argument, his essential points concerning the invidious nature of 'secularism' for an Indian Muslim are very revealing.

He agrees with Husain's assessment that India is indeed a secular country, suggesting that Muslims did not welcome it for its own sake, but for the fact that they feared a Hindu state more.[74]

It is the nature of what constitutes a 'Hindu state' that focuses ul-Haq's attention once more upon the nature of an 'Islamic state'. In that context, he begins to think about the place of shari'a within any kind of state apparatus. What is illuminating in terms of his religio-political thinking is his definition of what shari'a is for an Indian Muslim:

> The Indian Muslims generally hold 'Islam' as 'faith' and 'Shari'a' or 'the practical exhibition of faith' to be inseparable. Faith must show in action. And action has to be strictly in line with the rules and regulations

formulated by the fuqaha' ('jurists') in the golden days
of Islam, chiefly on the basis of the Qur'an and the
Prophetic Traditions.[75]

Ul-Haq's definition of shari'a as the 'practical exhibition of
faith' is difficult to sustain in the light of the discussions
in Chapter One in this book. Nevertheless, his accent upon
the shari'a as a living, rather than simply legal code is useful in illuminating an understanding of shari'a as a 'lived'
element of Islam. That said, it would have been unlikely to
have found many fellow adherents willing to agree with his
perceptions: Khan and Chiragh Ali might very well disa-
gree with his definition of shari'a and Maududi would take
issue with the importance he ascribes to the opinions of the
jurists over that of the sunnah.

Whilst ul-Haq's line of argument appears to lead him
into somewhat hot water, the water begins to boil when
he attempts to delineate between 'the secular state' on the
one hand and 'secularism' on the other. For he argues that a
'secular state', which accepts religion as 'faith' and guaran-
tees religious freedom, can be acceptable to all Muslims. At
one level, ul-Haq's argument falls in line with the thinking behind the ruling of the North Indian 'ulama and the
then Ottoman Caliph-Sultan when they declared the British
Empire 'dar al-Islam'. But ul-Haq is not differentiating
between religious pluralism and secularism as a philosophy.
Consequently, ul-Haq's arguments are likely to be rejected
outright by Muslims who see 'secularism' as a 'poisonous
philosophy', which cannot, by definition, be acceptable, for it
undermines the shari'a.[76] If he had chosen instead to discuss
the pros and cons of religious pluralism, he might very well
have opened up a far more sympathetic hearing for himself.

Benazir Bhutto

In the more recent past, the autobiography of the former Pakistani Prime Minister, Benazir Bhutto, takes the foundational issues outlined by Husain and ul-Haq and seeks to offer a way forward for Muslims as Husain had done a generation before. She suggests that, for Muslims living under non-Muslim rule, the best way to understand and practise their faith whilst in the minority in the West would be through following the early Meccan surahs, ignoring the later Medinan ones.[77] Her argument is that, in the same way that when Muhammad was in a minority situation in the early Meccan years he sought to build bridges with the Jews, Christians and Pagans, Muslims should do the same once again in their current minority situations. The tone and style of Muhammad's revelations during that period tended to be conciliatory and peaceful, in sharp contrast to the later surahs from the Medinan phase, when he achieved political ascendancy and began to assert the power of Islam over other faiths.[78]

In principle, this argument has a strong theological foundation, although the question remains over the extent to which the early Meccan surahs in the Qur'an can still be seen as relevant when one applies the doctrine of abrogation. However, leaving aside concerns about the validity of this theological methodology, the relevance of Bhutto's message could not be more clear: whilst Islam is in a minority situation politically, it needs to adopt the methodology of Muhammad himself.[79] Bhutto's argument would find theological and legal affirmation in the Hanafi shari'a code and warm endorsement from the 'visionary separatists'.[80] This is because she implies not passive acceptance of Islamic subservience, but obedience to authority whilst at the same time, proactively engaging in raising the status of Islam within the state to the point at which it can assert its wishes more powerfully or influentially.

Bhutto's argument makes uncomfortable reading for Western governments searching for a formula which will keep Muslim communities forever as integrated elements of a wider cohesive society rather than its eventual dominating force as she describes here. However, Western democracies live within the tensions created by the competition between different ideologies and faiths. Bhutto's line of thinking simply encompasses one element of that non-violent competition and does so in a context that is seemingly scripturally founded. Thus, whatever concerns non-Muslims might have about her perspective, critiquing her reasoning from scripture is a harder task given the theology outlined in Chapter One.

Summary

Each of the five writers takes a slightly different approach to the question: Sayyid Ahmad Khan chooses to attack the idea of disloyalty through shari'a, but without reference to Islamic scripture. Instead he deploys the rulings of the major religious clerics of the day to lend weight to the idea that India under the British was dar al-Islam, therefore the conditions for rebellion did not exist. For Chiragh Ali, loyalty to one's rulers was correct because it did not interfere with the shari'a as it was an organic document which adapted through the centuries. Thus, every new ruler of the subcontinent added to a developing system, rather than it being immutable. Arkoun appeared to go further than even Khan or Ali and was willing to posit Islam as an evolving philosophy in which anything, including a Muslim's relationship with non-Muslim authority, was part of a continuous development. Husain was keen to end a Muslim culture

of separatism in India through encouraging active participation in the political process in order to change aspects of
national culture and legislation that might be deemed contrary to Islam. ul-Haq takes a slightly different line arguing
that, though generally suspicious of secularism as a political
force, was grateful that India was at least Constitutionally
secular rather than being a Hindu state. He, like Husain,
poses the difficult questions of loyalty and identity, but
fails to come to grips with them effectively. Finally, Bhutto
takes a similar line to Husain, arguing that loyalty to non-
Muslim leadership is obligatory, however, this does not
mean that Muslim should be forever submissive citizens;
instead, they should actively seek greater power to the point
at which they can exert real influence and eventually power.
Bhutto's thinking is entirely in line with classical Muslim
theologians who argued that any treaty with a non-Muslim
was only temporary.[81] However, she fails to acknowledge
the development in Muslim thinking that took place after
the Classical period.

Conclusions

The argument Maududi creates for himself – the enforced
removal of any government which is not shari'a based – is,
on the surface at least, appealing for Muslims insofar as it
is based strictly upon the apparent teachings of the Qur'an
itself. Fundamentally, it seems that for Maududi, there could
be no compromise in relation to Muslim rule over Muslims.
However, this rigid, seemingly theologically founded position is undermined by the assumptions he makes when
defining his terms at the opening of his argument. This is
seen particularly in his definition of 'diin' when applying it
to non-Muslim cultures. Essentially, therefore Maududi's is

a 'universalist' argument seeking to lay down fundamental principals which will speak to all Muslims, at all times and in all places.[82]

In sharp contrast to the apparent theological authority of Maududi's position, Khan's advocacy of loyalty to a foreign ruler rather than advocating a resurgent Islamic state would appear to be on somewhat softer ground. The evidence he presents to defend the need for obedience to non-Muslim rulers here is based purely on the current (for the time) opinions of admittedly eminent Islamic scholars and other culturally relevant historical evidence. He therefore omits to draw upon the Qur'anic sources, which would have lent greater religious authority to his words.[83] Even so, his characterisation of British India as dar al-Islam on the basis of shari'a ruling would certainly have carried very significant theological weight of its own in relation to its Hanafi basis, even though he did not quote directly from either the Qur'an or Hadith.[84]

Khan's contemporary, al-Afghani, refused to accept the principle of obedience to non-Muslim rulers; instead he advocated a patient waiting game for Muslims, studying the West and their ideas and learning from them as the launch pad for an eventual resurgence of Islam. Thus, al-Afghani's stance is one of temporary submission, whereas Sayyid Ahmad Khan saw loyalty to one's ruler as the guiding principle, with the renewing of Islamic strength purely within the context of that rule.

Chiragh Ali accepted the reality of secular or foreign dominance as his mentor did and, believing that it was a Muslim's duty to obey non-Muslim authority, he viewed the dominance of British law as an opportunity to continue the historical development of Islam on the subcontinent that had already been going on through many centuries.

In so doing, he was looking for a distinctive Indian Islam, rather than any form of trans-national ummah.

Husain, ul-Haq and Bhutto all pose the central question of how a Muslim in a minority status should engage with the question of obedient submission to them. In coming to their conclusions, Husain and Bhutto focus upon pointing the way forward, encouraging a positive response to the situation from Muslims. However, whilst Husain argues on the basis of philosophy and history, Bhutto argues more on the basis of theology. They both share the view that Muslim submission to non-Muslim authority in the short term does not mean that a Muslim cannot engage in the democratic process in order to change the position of Islam within society in the long term. In this respect, both of them find echoes in the sentiments of al-Afghani and the 'visionary separatists', although one would suspect that Husain particularly would have been less interested in such proactivism than Bhutto would. Ul-Haq begins in the same way, but ultimately leaves it for the readers to draw their own conclusions for his assessment of the situation, which, in general, is more suspicious of secular influence than Husain is.

Ultimately, what can be seen very clearly in the debates analysed here is the apparent irreconcilability of the two approaches and the quandary that faces the modern Muslim in a minority context. For they are trying to grapple with relative calls of a faith that appears to enjoin the interweaving of the sacred and secular, with a society around them that is not only non-Muslim, but sees no need for the kind of religio-political integration that they naturally understand to be the appropriate order of human life. That said, it maybe that the clear effect of the combination of church-state, public-private belief and secular culture of the West is having on successive generations of Muslims will change

the dynamics of the issue for Muslims going forward anyway. However, given that any attempt at prediction would
be foolhardy in the extreme, the issue of faith-state loyalty
is one that cannot be swept under the carpet in the hope
that it will eventually be washed away with the passage of
time.

Essentially the debate leaves the modern Muslim with
two questions, one for each side: to the 'visionaries' he or she
might ask why a faith that has developed so much tradition,
leadership and thought within each individual geographical context that it has inhabited requires 're-Arabisation'
in order to become powerful again? And to the 'pragmatic
philosophers' he or she might ask how an effective grasp of
the rituals and practices of his faith can be maintained in
the face of un-Islamic values in the society around him if
one does not find relevance for the shari'a.

It appears that these questions cannot be satisfactorily
answered until the connected issue of the level at which the
notion of the 'Muslim community' should function (including the question of the place of shari'a) has been answered.
And it is to that question that we will now turn.

CHAPTER FOUR

FROM IJTIHAD TO KHILAFAH STATE: ON WHAT LEVEL SHOULD THE NOTION OF THE MUSLIM COMMUNITY FUNCTION?

Introduction

As we have seen in the previous chapter, there is a very broad spectrum of opinion even within one small part of the Muslim ummah on the question of whether there is a necessity for Muslims to be ruled by Muslims in order to allow for full expression of Islam in society and individuals. This chapter now takes on the broad principles concerning Islamic governance discussed in the previous chapter and moves on to examine differing viewpoints on at what level the ummah should exist in relation to the functions of leadership and authority.

The question is prompted, not just from the issues raised in Chapter Three, but also from the argument presented in Faruki's book *The Evolution of Islamic*

Constitutional Theory and Practice, in which he proposes that effectively there were, prior to 1947, two distinct and separate groups living in India: Muslims and Hindus.[1] By this he meant that the two groups were identifiable because of the differing religious rules and practices they followed. Does Faruki's observation imply that the formal imposition of a state or ummah on a geopolitical basis is unnecessary as the need for a Muslim to live in a 'Muslim system' is already being fulfilled to the extent that they could be identified as a distinct group within an existent state? That is probably a leap too far, but the very ability to identify what makes a Muslim community without formal state-applied shari'a in effect does undermine those who would argue that shari'a and the state must incontrovertibly be intertwined for Islam to be fully expressed. This is something to bear in mind for Chapter Five as well as this one. However, it is enough for the present to simply see Faruki's comment and to have it in mind as the next two chapters unfold.

Whatever the truth of Faruki's observation, one senses that for some Muslims, Faruki's standard is not nearly high enough to feel comfortable, for it could be said that the issue is not simply about whether the community is 'identifiable' or not, but whether it can be 'Muslim', to the extent that the Qur'an and Muhammad would require it. The acid test therefore is whether a Muslim feels that the system in his or her home state permits the 'full expression' of their faith.

This essentially interpretive issue began to be examined in the previous chapter and this chapter will move further into that territory.

The chapter will begin with the 'visionary separatists' as their concept of Islamic government naturally leads them

towards the full state-religion inter-relationship exemplified in the Caliphate as the ideal for the ummah. From
that universal, all-encompassing standpoint, the rest of
the visions of the ummah gradually become less elevated,
thereby allowing for a discussion that encompasses many
alternative perspectives and their rationales.

Finally, it is worthwhile highlighting at this stage that
the amount of ink used surveying the position of either side
of the debate is almost completely the reverse of that of the
last question. For the 'visionary separatists' take up the vast
bulk of the survey and analysis in this section, as opposed
to the last in which the 'pragmatic philosophers' attracted
the most attention. For that, there is an entirely logical reason which will become apparent as the analysis develops. It
should also be said that the 'visionary separatists' include
one Ahmadiyya: Muhammad Ali, in their section. The reason for this is that, regardless of his beliefs, the views which
he expresses on this particular question places him within
the 'visionary separatist' stream of ideas.[2]

Maududi and the Visionary Separatists

Maududi

It is in his final section of *The Theory of the Caliphate and the
Nature of Democracy in Islam* that Maududi brings together
the Islamic political theory that he has been outlining
together with its outworkings, through a description of
the ideal Muslim state. In Maududi's idealised vision, the
ummah becomes a global geopolitical entity without borders, in which all are ruled by the shari'a, a shari'a that is
founded upon 'Quranic law'.[3] This law is juxtaposed with
the forms of shari'a that include 'Western philosophies'

which have been, therefore, corrupted in Maududi's eyes. Here it is likely that Maududi was taking a swipe at the Ottoman 'Majalla',[4] which was a hybrid of shari'a and Western civil code.[5]

The functioning of Maududi's ummah-state is not detailed, but it would not be unreasonable to suggest that it would find a strong resonance in the detailed 'Caliphate state' that is found on the Hizb ut-Tahrir website www. khilafah.com, whose vision of the universal ummah-state strongly echoes that of Maududi himself.[6]

As shall be seen, Maududi's seductive vision leaves unanswered many of the fundamental questions about his ideal shape of Islamic government. His desire is to lay out fundamental principles rather than to plan a pragmatic workable state. To this end, his consistent underlying principle is the sovereignty of God, which he is at pains to keep at the forefront of the reader's mind. Maududi's reasoning links the sovereignty of Allah with the necessity of the ummah-state; as Allah is sovereign, so the governance of the earth should reflect that sovereignty. All Muslims are vice-regents of Allah's earth and should therefore have a say in the governing of that earth.

It is the delegation of the authority of God that brings Maududi to focus on the nature of the ummah in relation to the remit of the Caliph. Maududi's vision of a universal Caliphate state was already touched upon in the previous chapter and here, Maududi takes the vision of a global ummah without borders as read and instead turns to fleshing out the detail of participation within the global state. In seeking theological foundations for his more detailed picture, he turns to Q24:55, where he interprets the ayah to mean that all Muslims are the 'vice-regents of God' and their job is to enforce God's law on earth.[7] He then clarifies whom this is notion is applied to:

> ... the power to rule over the earth has been prom-
> ised to the whole community of believers; it has not
> been stated that any particular person or class among
> them will be raised to that position ... The Caliphate
> granted by God to the faithful is the popular vice-
> regency and not a limited one.[8]

He strongly argues that everyone in this society – by which
he means all Muslims – are equal and should participate in
the task of ruling that has been assigned to them. In this
context, he specifically argues against the primacy of the
Qurayshi tribe, going so far as the parallel their hegemony
with Brahmin power in India.[9] He follows that with the
historical example of slaves and their descendents who were
appointed to high posts in the Medieval Islamic Empire,[10]
employing the Ibn Kathir reported Hadith concerning
obedience to masters, even if slave or negro, to add further
weight to his case though he fails to attribute it.[11]

Maududi's vision for the ummah here is therefore of a
globalised religio-state where there is full representative
participation for Muslims within the necessary instruments
that would be needed to sustain such a state.

Finally, he turns upon those who would wish to see autocratic rule:

> There is no room in such a society for the dictatorship
> of any person or group of persons since everyone is a
> caliph of God herein. No person or group of persons
> is entitled to become an absolute ruler by depriving
> the rank and file of their inherent right of caliphate.
> The personal position of a man who is selected to con-
> duct the affairs of the state is no more than this: that
> all Muslims (or, technically speaking, all caliphs of

God) delegate their caliphate to him for administrative purposes.[12]

Maududi appears to be advocating rule by a single person,
which he differentiates from autocracy by observing that
the leadership of this individual is given to him by his fellow Muslims, rather than being taken forcefully. In this
idealised vision, the power of this individual is limited by
two things: firstly, rule through Divine Law and secondly
by what Maududi sees as the necessity in Islam of individual Muslim freedom to pursue their own priorities.[13] This
'individual Muslim freedom' is not explained but one might
see it as a reference to the doctrine of ijtihad being applied
in a wider sense of 'ingenuity' rather than in its classical
application in relation to the interpretation of shari'a.[14]

Perwez supports Maududi's position. The essential difference between the two is that Perwez favours the idea that all
political structure in the Islamic state should be based upon
the Qur'an alone, on the basis that the Sunnah is too confused to interpret. However, he reaches much the same conclusions about the supremacy of Qur'anic law as Maududi[15]
and is keen to reject any 'Western political philosophies'.

Several assumptions are built into the ideas of Maududi
and Perwez. Principal among them is the notion that
Muslims should rule over Muslims,[16] and that leadership
is indeed reposed in one man who becomes not a religious
leader, but an 'administrator'.

Whatever the theoretical underpinning of this governmental concept, Maududi must have been aware of the
abuses of power that had existed under so many of the
Caliphs. Abuses that took place under the very system that
he was now proposing and one can therefore only assume
that he believed that would not happen if a pious enough

man were found who did indeed live under the law as he suggested.[17]

He concludes with the notion that Islam allows for democracy in its purest form, where individuals are safe-guarded, but where

> ... the individual does not exceed his bounds to such an extent as to become harmful to the community, as happens in Western democracies[18]

Clearly what is being proposed is a 'democracy' with a new definition, for Maududi is clearly keen to exclude the kinds of political freedoms that are available in the West. Maududi's ideal ummah is not a place where there is dis-cussion about government policy, or even a say about who the leader should be, but where the 'burden of governance' is removed from the people and placed in the hands of an individual, however limited his authority might be under the 'Divine Law'.

The main criticisms of the position that Maududi takes here is that there is no discussion as to who decides the leader and on what basis they rule the Islamic world. Furthermore, there is no answer to the issue raised by Q3:26, which shows that all government on earth, whether Muslim or not, is raised up, or brought low at Allah's behest. So if it is 'Allah's will' for this state of affairs to remain the case, what need is there for the kind of ummah-state that Maududi is proposing?[19]

Thus, from the arguments outlined above, Ahmad's criti-cism of Maududi's approach appears to be entirely accurate.

> In Maududi, the effort to retain the supremacy of orthodox Islam is accompanied by selective dissocia-tions with traditional absolutism.[20]

For Maududi is repackaging absolutism with a universal Muslim suffrage, explaining it in terms that are rooted in the Qur'an, but whose outworking would still call for autocratic rule.

Maududi's leader has a wider remit than the Pope insofar as his would be a rule to include legislative power and executive authority, not just spiritual guidance. However, translating this leadership into reality is impossible unless some guidance as to the shape of the ummah can be explained. Maududi is very happy to point Muslims back towards Muhammad's Arabia for their inspiration, but he fails to engage with the reality of the world's geopolitical climate of the time. He contents himself with outlining the principles that should be adhered to, without explaining the detail about how this could operate in actuality and at what level of society – local, national, trans-national or global – it should be manifest. He appears to favour 'consultative' leadership to a point, but, in the context of the question posed at the beginning of this section, he leaves only more questions, rather than viable answers.

Perwez is much clearer, explaining ideas which very much fall into line with Maududi, but specifying that there would be an elected assembly of Muslims with government at a global level, which could create an administrative assembly with limited powers in the realm of administration. That said delineating where administrative power ends and the remit of the clerics begins in Islam has been a source of internal conflict since the early years of the faith when the Caliphs and the clerics wrestled over control over dogma.[21] Furthermore, he does not specify a level either: he assumes, in the same way that Maududi does, that the ummah is united on a global geopolitical level before any of the administrative and executive functions he outlines come into existence. Thus, whilst it provides a framework for a global power and a possible model for any individual nation-state that may wish to adopt it on its own, it fails completely to deal with the 'possible' and the 'current'. Neither do Perwez or Maududi seek to provide a 'roadmap' which would lead from the current geopolitical situation to their politically and geographically 'unified ummah'.

Thankfully, some of the questions that Maududi and Perwez leave hanging are addressed by al-Afghani's work, which concerns the need for Islamic solidarity. For it begins to try and give shape to the eventual form of an Islamic state through the definition of Islamic 'nationhood' that was picked up by Qutb particularly in later years.

Al-Afghani

The notion of 'nationhood' based on religious belief rather than geographical boundaries is explained in 'Islamic solidarity', where al-Afghani's reasoned argument for the notion of pan-Islam comes through very clearly.

He begins with a survey of the whole course of human history as he saw it, in which he argues that society began to organise itself along tribal lines for mutual protection, gradually evolving to become nations until they reached a point where

> Each of these groups, thanks to the combined strength of its members, was able to preserve its interests and safeguard its rights from any encroachments from another group. Moreover, they have gone even further than necessary as is common in the evolution of man: they have reached a point where each group is bitter if it falls under the rule of another. It believes that domination will be oppressive even if it is just ...[22]

This quotation suggests that al-Afghani somehow feels that concerns about the domination of one nation by another are minor squabbles. If this interpretation of his tone here is accurate, it is somewhat confusing, for this was written by the same man who spent considerable energy attempting to unite the Iranian Imamate and the Ottoman Caliphate as one Empire, whilst at the same time decrying the impact of European hegemony in Islamic lands.[23] Indeed, al-Afghani wrote at length about learning from the West in order to eventually defeat it.[24] As such, the 'petty squabbles' he appears to be describing here actually formed an important element of his writing and thinking. Perhaps more extraordinarily, he did not seem to see the ambiguity in his defence of Ottoman power against that of European power. Of course, the major difference was that the Ottomans were 'Islamic rulers' (however that is defined) whereas the Europeans were not. Therefore, al-Afghani's argument would appear to need a lot of qualification when trying to shore up the foundations of his position.

However, whatever the inconsistencies of his position, he skirts lightly around issues of Muslim rule versus non-Muslim rule in order to get to the core of what he wants to say. It seems clear that Afghani is not worried about the leadership of individual nations.

> [Racial] solidarity can disappear just as quickly as it can arise. Such can take place when an arbiter is accepted and the contending forces are brought together ... .This arbiter is the Prince of all things, the Conqueror of heaven and earth ... .When men recognise the existence of the Supreme Judge ... they will leave it entirely

to the possessor of sacred power to safeguard good and repel evil.[25]

It is in this context, he proposes that Muslims should put aside ethnic issues in favour of relationships with other believers, including clan issues. This is the theology of 'tawhid' overwhelming the developing philosophy of nationalism.

Al-Afghani's vision of universalism trumping narrow ethno-centrism points towards another universalist mindset. Like Maududi and Perwez, he does not define the level that he is calling for people to live 'under God' at: it could be anything from personal faith through to global political unity. Unlike Maududi or Perwez, however, he does not describe the executive structure of this 'super-state', for there is no direction as to whether this state should be ruled by one or many. What is likely is that al-Afghani was not particularly interested in any of this detail; for him the important essential was that 'God' was somehow supreme and that Muslim powers should join together against the onslaught of European encroachment.[27]

Muhammad Ali

Maulana Muhammad Ali's inclusion in this discussion is based on his place as the founder of the Khalifat Movement. He has been placed on this side of the debate, in spite of a more moderate approach to the whole question of what level the ummah should work at, compared to Maududi/Perwez standards. For whilst he was supported in the movement by many prominent Hindus such as Mohandas Gandhi, he was a keen advocate of Muslim separatism in the years before Iqbal, Jinnah and others began to seriously call for a Muslim homeland on the subcontinent. His speech, given shortly before the Abolition of the Caliphate in 1924, is examined here in order to understand the level and shape of Islamic political authority that this highly influential scholar desired.[28]

His main contention is that the British should not interfere in religious matters in general and certainly not abolish the Caliphate. The basis for his argument comes from a proclamation, which he says was issued by Queen Victoria, in which religious freedom would be respected.[29] He felt betrayed by the British as he considered that they had gone against this by perpetrating the act of abolition. This sense of betrayal is heightened by the fact that many Muslim Indians had fought and died whilst fighting the Caliph in the First World War's Mesopotamian campaign on the side of the British.[30] Thus, having proved their loyalty to their immediate rulers, Ali now felt that their religious convictions had been snubbed by the removal of the supreme head of their faith.

The close relationship that existed between the Indian Muslims and the Ottoman Caliphs has been described in some detail by Özcan, and it is clear from his work that any action taken against the Ottoman Caliph was going to be felt very keenly on the subcontinent. But what is particularly interesting in relation to the question posed at the opening to this chapter is that he deliberately goes out of his way to tie all Muslims into the Caliphate and in so doing shows, not just what the institution meant to Muhammad Ali himself, but also what form of government he believed equated most closely to the Muslim ideal:

He [Khalifa] was the Commander of the Faithful, the President of our theocratic Commonwealth, the leader of all Muslims in peace and war, though he could neither claim to be infallible like the Pope, nor could he in all circumstances exercise unquestioned authority, for Allah was the only sovereign, and in cases of dispute Muslims were bound to refer back to the Holy Qur'an and to the Traditions of the Prophet whose successor the Khalifa is.[31]

Clearly, this was a man who was thoroughly familiar with Q4:59 and the exegesis of it. However, what is particularly interesting about the above passage is some of the assumptions that he makes, which raise more questions that they answer. The most pertinent of these relates to the way the Caliph could be seen as 'the leader of Muslims in peace and war',[32] particularly as Ali had already said himself that Indian Muslims had fought against the Caliph in the First World War. What form does this leadership take therefore?[33] This question remains frustratingly unanswered, yet it is clear that, whatever other roles and duties Ali equates with the Caliph, Ali's understanding of idealised Islamic government includes the sense that there is a single ruler in-charge of all Muslims, but that his power is limited by virtue of the supremacy of shari'a as the expression of the sovereignty of Allah. This is pure Maududism from an Ahmadiyya.

> The claim put forward is a simple claim. It says that it is one of the fundamental doctrines of Islam, absolutely unalterable, that there should always be a Khalifa, and that the Khalifa should have temporal powers at all times adequate for the defence of the Faith ... The second claim is that the local centre of our Faith, the land known as the Island of Arabia, should be free from non-Islamic control in any shape or form.[34]

The second 'claim' is more straightforward insofar as it is not an unreasonable request and is based on his well-founded belief that Britain was making a play for the oil fields of Iraq and Arabia just at that time. It also carries the notion that the natural home for the Caliph would be in Arabia rather than Turkey and, as he nowhere requests the reinstatement of a specifically Ottoman Caliphate (or one based in Constantinople at least), it must be assumed that that Ali's ultimate aim would be to see a Caliphate installed in Arabia, which would be given a geographically defined boundary. This then is a slightly more pragmatic vision: it mourns the passing of the Ottoman Caliph, but sees also an opportunity to supplant it with a more ideal Caliph.[35]

Ali's desire for a single, unified Caliphate under the rule of a pious leader with real power (in whatever form that may take) showed his desperate desire for the Muslim world to be seen as great once again. It also showed his harking back to the original ummah for inspiration was both natural but also ill-thought out: for he lived in an age where such demands were not feasible, not just because of foreign rule, but also because the ummah itself, as the single entity he was describing, had long since ceased to exist.

His conclusion has an ominous modern ring to it:

> If we want to threaten you we obviously cannot threaten you with Howitzers and Dreadnoughts and Aeroplanes and Tanks: but we possess a thing that is unconquerable; our determination to die true to our Faith.[36]

What is clear here is the desperation to see Islam holding some kind of power once again, united under the leadership of an office which goes back to Muhammad himself. What is less clear and what has dogged all the arguments for Islamic state authority is how far that authority should extend and in what form.

Muhammad Iqbal

It seems that Iqbal ran into the same problem as those already described when attempting to fix a level and identity for the ummah. For his philosophy describes a unity under Islam, a unity which does not recognise national boundaries, yet, he became famous for his call for Pakistan. The central problem in reading Iqbal is therefore reconciling his apparent universalist vision with the call for a self-contained homeland for Indian Muslims only. This accusation of inconsistency would seem to be evidenced by Muhammad Munawwar's essay on the contribution of Iqbal to Islam in India in which he describes Iqbal thus:

> As a poet, Iqbal thought, his work was to guide the Muslims of the Subcontinent and through them to transmit his message to the Muslim Ummah, which for him, was neither a racial nor a territorial and linguistic entity.[37]

Munawwar's assessment of Iqbal paints the poet as an almost messianic prophetic figure, calling, through his poetry for the kind of tawhid ummah that sits snugly next to Maududi's thinking. Indeed, Munawwar's assessment fits well with Mir's analysis of Iqbal's broad understanding of the nature of society.[38] Perhaps therefore in this context, Iqbal's call for 'Pakistan' can be seen as a blueprint, an archetype that other Muslim groups could follow and that would lead to a consolidated pan-national super-state.[39] This would be a plausible explanation, but is there evidence for this in his writings? Iqbal justifies the call for a separate state in North West India on the grounds that

> The life of Islam as a cultural force in this country very largely depends on its centralisation in a specific territory.[40]

His words therefore have the ring of defence, rather than promotion and advance. Perhaps then, Iqbal's position shift comes in response to his observation that Islam would have been in some trouble on the subcontinent if there was not some form of homeland created to 'protect it' from the huge Hindu majority. This defensive mindset would not have been an unreasonable position, given the encroachment of imperial powers into Islamic states and the disassembly of Islamic authority under the Tanzimat reforms in Turkey that he had witnessed in his lifetime. In this time of change therefore, his primary concern was Islam's preservation in his homeland. This reasoning is both rational and pragmatic, but it does display Iqbal's Indian heart, for even though he had a vaulting ambition in relation to the worldwide ummah, when the possibility of threat arose, he focussed on his homeland and in so doing showed that he was, despite his own reasoning, an Indian Muslim, rather than simply a Muslim.

In his lectures for Sophia University, Christian Troll offers a fascinating explanation for Iqbal's shift from pan-nationalism to nationalism, painting Iqbal as the politician, rather than the poet philosopher, experimenting with different ideas and revising his aims as he saw what was happening in the rest of Asia.[41]

Was the threat-induced pragmatic reasoning outlined above was the reason for his apparently anomalous thinking? Iqbal's conclusion to his famous 'Pakistan' speech shows once again the apparently pan-Islamic nature of his beliefs, into which his call for an Islamic state looks like a rock in a swirling river, obstructing its natural path:

> The truth is that Islam is not a church. It is a state, conceived as a contractual organism long before Rousseau ever thought of such a thing and animated by an ethical ideal which regards man not as an earth-rooted creature, defined by this or that portion of the earth, but as a spiritual being understood in terms of a social mechanism and possessing rights and duties as a living factor in that mechanism.[42]

In his lengthy article on Iqbal's philosophy, Shaida characterizes Iqbal's attitudes to nationalism and patriotism thus:

> ... .we find that Iqbal moved between dogmatic territorial nationalism and an enlightened Internationalism interspersed with his emphasis on the possibility and realisation of the Universal Islamic Community, i.e. the Ummah.[43]

Given the evidence from Iqbal's writings above, this assessment appears to be accurate, though it is fair to say that his movements shifted more towards universalism as Iqbal grew older. Iqbal's position is essentially pragmatic Islamic nationalism whilst longing for a geopolitical ummah that has no boundaries. In relation to the question therefore, Iqbal's heart remained firmly in the Maududist universalist vision of a global ummah. That said, he was content for the ummah to operate at a local state level in the short term, both to preserve it and in the long term, to create the building blocks that would lead to the global ummah he desired. As a philosopher Iqbal was therefore a universalist, as a politician, he was a nationalist.

Muhammad 'Abduh

Since Muhammad 'Abduh shared many philosophical viewpoints with Sayyid Ahmad Khan as well as al-Afghani's theories, it might very well have been that this major influence on the reformist movement could have been grouped in a separate category outside of both the 'visionary separatists' and the 'pragmatic philosophers'. However, there were elements of 'Abduh's work that placed him firmly in the 'visionary separatist' camp in relation to this question, even though, as Malise Ruthven points out, 'Abduh did accept British rule on a temporary basis.[44]

'Abduh's book, *Risalat al-Tawhid* (The Theology of Unity) has become a seminal work in the Islamist canon. Yet it is steeped in a rationalism that belies the utopian yearnings of works such as Maududi's and instead focuses upon the recapturing of Muslim intellectual and spiritual vigour.[45] 'Abduh spent only a little time involved in political theology, spending his post-exilic years focussing on education as a way of raising Muslim society once again. That said, his brief engagement with the field saw one particularly important principle proposed.

'Abduh's perception of the ideal of the ummah is perhaps best expressed in the yearning evident at the beginning of his chapter 'Islamic Religion or Islam':

It [Islam] was actively followed among them for a period without schism or deviations in interpretation or sectarian tendencies, ...[46]

'Abduh is immediately setting out a vision of the early ummah as a community that had no division of any kind. As has been seen, this is not necessarily an accurate picture, but it is one upon which 'Abduh built his vision of the ideal of the ummah. However, where one might logically expect 'Abduh to follow the line of al-Afghani and Maududi, he departs from them quite radically in his proposed outworking of the principle above, for he argued that people should be free to choose their own government which best suited them.[47] This principle was articulated and developed in relation to the definition of 'al-watan' in an article entitled *al-Hayah al-Siyasah* (The Political Life) in 1881.

> The word al-Watan as used by those who study politics means the place after which you are called, where your right is safeguard, and whose claim on you is known, where you are secure in yourself, your kin and possession. It has been said: there is no al-Watan without freedom.[48]

For 'Abduh, 'al-watan' was a physical place of safety where there was a sense of common belonging. That sense of belonging crossed the religious divide to include Jews and Christians as well, and is one of the main reasons both why he engaged in inter-religious work and why his ideology was at variance with the other universalist ideologues.

The exact nature of citizenship for other faiths within 'Abduh's vision of an Islam reborn is difficult to ascertain, especially given the clear superiority of Islam he expressed in *The Theology of Unity*; however, there can be little doubt that 'Abduh's desire for Muslim renewal had led him to the belief that, however the unity of the ummah might be expressed by Muslims, the nation-state should be the central unit that bound people's together.

Albert Hourani summarises 'Abduh's ideology thus:

> ... the common history and interests of those who lived
> in the same country created a deep bond between them
> in spite of differing faiths. The sense of the importance
> unity, which affected his view of Islamic reform, col-
> oured also his view of the nation. Unity, he maintained,
> was necessary in political life, and the strongest type of
> unity was that those who shared the same country –
> not only the place they lived in, but the locus of their
> public right and duties, the object of their affection and
> pride. Non-Muslims belonged to the nation in exactly
> the same as Muslims, and thus should be good relations
> between those who differed in religion.[49]

Therefore, for 'Abduh, the ummah could not replace the
state as the vehicle for an Islamic superstate; whatever
the ummah had meant historically, its definition did not
include a shari'a global superstate – a Caliphate. In this, his
thinking was at variance with Iqbal who saw the Islamic
nation-state as the stepping stone towards the global super-
state. For 'Abduh, it was an end in itself.

'Abd al-Hamid b. Badis

Badis stands at once separate from, but in the broad camp
of the 'visionary separatists' in this area.

He believed absolutely that Muslims should govern
themselves in all things, as such, the ummah was a geopolitical entity; however, he differed slightly from both Ali and
Maududi in relation to his perceptions of the nature and role
of the 'Islamic state.' For Badis, independent states could be
created in which Muslims could rule themselves in parallel

with the broader state, through a jama' and connected to
the wider Muslim community.[50] This was different from the
pragmatism of Iqbal, for Iqbal saw the creation of a Muslim
state as a step along the road to a Maududist utopia, whereas
for Badis, the state was a legitimate final goal in itself and,
as such, he falls much more within the flexible doctrines of
'Abduh.[51] Universality of faith did not, for Badis, translate
into a state without borders and his Algerian heritage was as
integral to him as his Islam: 'Islam is my religion, Arabic is
my Language, Algeria is my country'.[52]

Lapidus sums up Badis thus:

> His thinking distinguished the cultural from political
> nationality, and thus allowed for a conception of a Muslim
> community as universal in principle and yet divided into
> politically and culturally distinct regional groups.[53]

Badis therefore conceived of an ummah that did not attempt
to cut through ethnic loyalties as Muhammad himself had
done, but saw the ummah as both universal and ethnically
defined at one and the same time. As such, 'Abduh and
Badis were the forefathers of the modern nationalist movements such as Hamas and the Taliban. But in relation to
this chapter's question, it meant that 'the ummah' could be
allowed to be an umbrella under which nations, or locali-
ties, could operate as they saw fit.

Summary

We have seen clearly coming through in the opinions of all
the writers outlined above the separatism mooted by Shah
Wali Ullah in the eighteenth century.[54] However, in all cases,
they fail to come to translate their broadstroke thinking into
a workable reality that took account of the different shari'a

schools and ethno-cultural differences across the spectrum of Muslim communities. The use of state instruments is a common element of the vision of the ummah as a religiopolitical entity but the exact nature of a geopolitical ummah at the level of transnational or national levels remains unresolved.

Sayyid Ahmad Khan and the Pragmatic Philosophers

As was mentioned in the introduction to this chapter, the pool of opinion in this camp is much smaller than it was for the last question. This is because the question itself is less relevant for them insofar as the concept of a universal Islamic nation-state and leader does not exist within the realms of possibility. The relative lack of comment by Husain, ul-Haq and others can be seen as a tacit admission that the ummah cannot be defined in these physical, geographical terms, hence their urging of identity through faith and active engagement in the states that Muslims are part of already. What remains to be seen is whether these writers are willing to place themselves nearer to the positions of 'Abduh and Badis, or whether they reject any form of formalised arrangement for Muslims including some community role for shari'a or not.

Sayyid Ahmad Khan

Let us first turn to Sayyid Ahmad Khan: he makes clear his disregard for the notion of Muslim religious states and single global leadership through a pamphlet published in 1920.[55] In the course of his argument, he deploys both theological and historical evidence, though his factual understanding in both areas on this matter could be called into significant question as can be seen in his opening statement:

> He literally means succession, and the person who succeeds is khalifa. But the word Khalifa has now

assumed a religious significance and the khalifa is now looked upon as a person holding a religious office. The origin of the khalifa may be traced back to the Roman Catholic religion. The head of the Roman Catholic church is regarded as the successor to St. Peter, a disciple of Christ and is styled as the Pope.[56]

The most breathtaking aspect of this statement is the fact that any Muslim reformer, even one as sympathetic to Western imperialism as Sayyid Ahmad Khan, would even think of suggesting that one of the most important symbolic institutions in Islamic culture was copied from such an apparently inferior faith. Evidence for such a claim is impossible to find, particularly when trying to find a chain of transmission of the idea from Roman or post-Roman Europe to the Arabian peninsula. The Church historian Chadwick, for example, is very reluctant to name even a rough date for the inception of the title 'Pope' or his assumed leadership of the Western church.[57] However, even omitting this blunder, the opening couple of lines alone show a very limited understanding of the office and the role that it played as both a religious and temporal guardian of the faith.

Khan continues to move through a history of the office of Caliph, in which he hammers home the point that it very quickly became, not a religious office, but an administrative one. He refutes the notion of the universal authority of Caliph through the example of the Caliph only being recognised as such within their territorial area.[58]

Khan moves on to translate this argument into a call for loyalty to the British, even though, at the time, they were supporting the Greeks in their war against the Turks.[59] For Khan therefore, the very notion of any form of Pan-Islamic unity or identity was antithetical to his understanding of

Islam and the role of the ummah. In his thinking, the Ottomans were just another dynastic monarchy.[60] This lack of geopolitical attachment to his notion of the ummah permitted him the opportunity of exhorting and encouraging the development of Muslims within India alone, without having to work towards a far-off ideal. This stands as a parallel, yet paradoxical approach to that of Iqbal, for, whereas Iqbal was indeed a universalist at heart and was essentially motivated by perceived threat to focus upon India alone, Khan stepped outside of a single geopolitical unity in order to be able to focus on Muslims in India.

Khan concludes his discussion with a typically bold and unreferenced statement:

> The contention that there should be one khalifa or Imam for the whole world does not find any support from the Quran or Hadis. Such a khalifa has never existed in the world and when they live in countries ruled by non-muslims, no musalman can be khalifa over them, nor a universal Imam ...[61]

Clearly for Khan, the question of Muslim political authority was very straightforward: for him, the ummah existed on a universal faith level only. His very lack of reference to shari'a is itself an indication of the lack of relevance he felt it had in a climate where non-Muslims were ruling Muslims. Indeed, under Hanafi shari'a, he was not wrong. Yet it is a shame that Khan did not seek to explain what place shari'a had within more localised Muslim community life. Again, his very silence might be an indication of a lack of relevance for the subject, but his actions suggest otherwise, for he spent considerable energy into securing a ruling on behalf of the North Indian 'ulama that under Hanafi shari'a, the

British Empire was dar al-Islam. This indicates that the role of shari'a was a live one for him, yet there is nothing in his argument here to suggest an engagement with it.

For Sayyid Ahmad Khan, Muslim faith is personal, not even communal: any form of community definition for Khan is therefore invalid. His stance is logical in relation to his views of nature of the Caliphate, yet his lack of engagement with the role of shari'a in a period in which he was trying to secure the loyalty of Muslims in India with a shari'a ruling is somewhat frustrating. For his actions clearly display a recognition that shari'a was indeed important for Indian Muslims but there is no direction from him as to what role it should play in the day to day lives of Muslim communities within the subcontinent.

Muhammad Mujeeb

Mohammad Mujeeb, once Vice Chancellor of Jamia Millia Islamia, argued that rather than conform to its original Arabian model, Islam in India should be Indian. For there was no sense, according to Mujeeb, in attempting to forge a global Muslim shari'a state, when Indian Islam had its own identity and history.[62] For him, Islam in India had taken on a syncretism through the influence of the Hindu culture around it that was to be valued, rather than eroded in the quest of a 'super-state' based on an idealised Arabic model. In such reasoning, the notion of a single ummah on anything other than a 'personal belief' level was not just unrealistic, but was not even to be desired. As a consequence, national identity became important, not just in terms of being one facet of a person's identity, but in defining that individual's religious identity as well. In this respect, he differs from 'Abduh who appears to separate the need for a secure space for all, from his desire to see Islam resurgent once again. There is no sense in 'Abduh that religious identity is formed within cultural frameworks, even though the evidence of the local custom elements of shari'a, were familiar to 'Abduh.

Mujeeb went further than 'Abduh did, locating even his religious beliefs within his cultural framework. As such, 'India' could become a religious, as well as a national identity.[63] Consequently, for Mujeeb, the nature of any concept of an ummah had to be at most localised and any shari'a observance had to be personal, based around schools that were inherently woven into the developing fabric of Indian Islam such as the Hanafi code in the north and the Shaafi code in the south.

Summary

In arguing against the need for an 'Islamic state' at any level, Sayyid Ahmad Khan and Mujeeb cast doubt on the notion that Islam had ever been a unified ummah, other than in the earliest years of its inception, and chose to highlight instead the changes that Indian Islam itself gone through. Effectively, they argue an alternative Islamic nationalism based not on a desire to look back at Arabia, but to look back at Muslim India and to reform and develop as Indian Muslims and not just pan-nationalists. That said, their stance is not a homogeneous or even consistent one: it does not, for example, explain why the ummah should exist at a national level rather than a transnational or local community level. Their response to the question is therefore as frustratingly inconclusive as that of the visionary separatists, yet, its core appeal lies in foundation within the stream of what 'is' rather than 'what might be'. In this sense, theirs is a more positive view of organic evolutionary narrative-based solution finding, rather than a more Cambodian style 'Year 0' that had become the outworking of the 'visionary separatists'.

Conclusions

The writings surveyed and analysed above show that the Indian Muslim reformers addressing the subject of political Islamic leadership are not clear about the level of society at which the ummah should exist.

There is no agreement amongst even the 'visionary separatists', who had appeared more united on the question of the necessity for Muslims to rule Muslims. The essential difficulty, which none of them were able to satisfactorily come to terms with, came in translating their antiquated, idealised model into a modern, globalised context. This appears incomprehensible given that Maududi, al-Afghani and Perwez in particular were preaching a clear universalist message in what was an increasingly global era. Yet it is both the pragmatics and the problems of theological interpretation that hamper any attempt to flesh out the broad-stroke utopian vision they espouse.

Essentially they appear to misunderstand what the original ummah really was; this seems extraordinary given the level of combined knowledge within the group. But their characterization of it as a fully functioning and identifiable nation in terms of geography, leadership and laws bears little resemblance to what it was at its inception. Watt characterised the early ummah as being based upon the substitution of loyalty to Muhammad and Allah for traditional clan ties.[64] What Maududi and his fellow visionaries are looking for is not a return to the ummah of Muhammad, it is the power of the Abbasids they desire. Their 'salafism' is aimed about a hundred years after Muhammad, not to Muhammad himself. Ironically this period, though seeing the high point of geopolitical power for the Islamic Empire, also saw the break-up of the Empire into myriad kingdoms who fought one another.

SECTION THREE

ISLAM IN MINORITY: SHARI'A AND THE STATE

Introduction

The two preceding chapters have examined the issue of citizenship, loyalty the place of shari'a and the level of the ummah from the perspective of the Muslims themselves. The following two chapters shift focus from the ruled to the rulers in order to understand the complete range of issues involved in matters of citizenship and the place of shari'a in a Muslim minority context.

We shall do this by examining two specific events that highlight the considerations of the rulers in relation to this issue. For the British, the focus is upon the passage of the *Shariat Act 1937* and for the French, it is the motivations behind the development of the *Code Morand*.

As was stated in the Introduction to this book, the primary focus is upon the writings and issues thrown up by the British interaction with Islam in India. For that reason, Chapter Five, which looks at the *Shariat Act,* is considerably longer than Chapter Six, which examines the *Code Morand*. Even so, the French colonial experience and policy-making in Algeria provides a useful foil to the analysis of the British experience. The differing experiences of Islam from two nations that had such differing approaches to both the goal of Empire and the place of religion within their own cultures serves to highlight the pitfalls and positives in either's methodology.

Before embarking on this phase of the analysis, it is worthwhile noting that there has been a previous contribution to this comparative work in the shape of David Powers' 1989 article.[1] However, whilst Powers' study was focussed on comparing the impact of each of the imperial powers on the Muslim societies they ruled, this study is concerned with the methodology and reasoning behind the events for the purpose of understanding the key issues that arise from their efforts to fuse two apparently differing legal cultures in the context of citizenship and integration issues. These case studies raise the important questions to be asked when such issues are being examined once again in the present.

CHAPTER FIVE

THE INTRODUCTION OF SHARI'A INTO BRITISH IMPERIAL INDIA: ISSUES AND QUESTONS

In order to facilitate this shift in focus, from the ruled to the ruler, the chapter will focus upon a case study that serves to illustrate the approach to and engagement with matters of Islamic identity and citizenship. The case study chosen for this purpose is file IOR L/P&J/7/43; it is the India Office file which contains all the debate that lead up to the *Shariat Act* of 1937. It is an Act that still resonates for Muslims in India to this day as it passed into the body of Constitutional law for post-colonial India as well.

In 1998 the *Indian Express* carried an article about the divorce of a Ms. A S Parvin Akthar, a human rights activist, whose husband had pronounced 'talaq' three times whilst she was away, thereby being able to divorce her. The article mentioned that it was the 1937 Act under which this was done.[1] More recently, *The Hindu* carried an article in October 2003, which discussed the *Shariat Act* in relation to other similar acts such as the *Hindu Succession Act 1956*.[2] A more in-depth article comparing the Hindu and Muslim situation was written for the *Indian Express* by Bina Agarwal, which, although praised some aspects of the 1937 Act, also expressed a desire for further developments to take place.[3]

For women living in India today therefore, the *Shariat Act* is not simply history; it is part of their lives. As such, it makes the perfect bridge between historical critique and modern policy-making issues.

Of course, the *Shariat Act* was by no means the only act of its kind during the period of British rule in India as was seen in Chapter Two. However, it was debated and adopted at a time when the broader question of independence in India was very much alive. In that context, it provides the perfect case study because of both its timing and its content, for, it sought to engage with Muslim identity at a time when 'identity' was the central issue in British Indian politics.

Before delving into the case study itself, it is worth spending a few moments looking specifically at the role of shari'a in British India historically.

The European powers began to encounter it in relation to their administrative responsibilities as the burgeoning East India Company administration was brought into contact with the Hanafi shari'a system imposed by the Emperor Aurangzeb.[4] Therefore, as Company and then direct imperial rule came to pass, the issue for the new rulers centred around three primary questions: firstly, to what extent did the system currently in place need to be amended to suit the new masters? Secondly, how much compatibility was there between the system that the British brought with them and the system imposed on

India by its Mughal rulers? Lastly, what political impact would these changes made?

Britain had a very high proportion of the global Muslim population living within its imperial borders, therefore, it was keen to keep such a large and recently disempowered group on its side for the sake of imperial longevity.[5]

It was out of these core issues that the eventual adoption of elements of shari'a into the imperial code were born.

Thus, even as early as 1772, when the East India Company began to claim taxation rights outside of their facilities, they quickly adopted elements of shari'a to ease their administrative pathway into broader power. The Company did replace qadis with magistrates even in 1772, but until 1864, they worked alongside muftis who frequently encouraged the magistrates to impose shari'a punishments.[6] Furthermore, it was not until 1872 that shari'a laws of evidence were superseded by the English civil system.[7]

Over time, an increasing number of India's civil magistrates did come from the country's Muslim population. The situation therefore arose where Muslim lawyers received training in English Civil Law, whilst they were still interpreting law that was ostensibly shari'a derived.[8]

Even so, the move was consistent and yet piecemeal. Different parts of India applied local law in relation to their religious custom and practice and the Muslims within India experienced this in much the same way as both Hindus and Christians. Thus, even coming into the period of the Independence Movement, when 'identity' became important both communally and nationally, a combination of dynamics were concurrently on display. On the one hand, the *Congress Party* had attempted to unite both Hindu and Muslim against British rule, but at the same time the growing possibility of home rule was increasingly causing the question of identity to be asked on all sides. Both the British themselves and politicians on all sides were attempting to use the issue for their own purposes, but for Muslims calling for a land of their own, the principal political consideration became how to identify an issue around which Islamic identity could reassert itself over local identity in order to provide the negotiators and politicians with the authority to speak on the behalf of the whole Muslim population. The question of shari'a and the specific area of personal law provided the perfect tool for such identity-shaping to take place, for it appeared progressive in relation to the rights of women, and it was a legitimate area of debate for the whole Islamic community as it was both religiously obliged and universally recognised as distinctively Islamic.

File IOR L/P&J/7/943 opens with an extract from the Legislative Assembly Debates at Simla on 26 September 1935 in which one of the delegates from the Punjab, a Mr. Abdullah, requests the opportunity to introduce a Bill for the purpose of applying Muslim Personal Law throughout India to all Muslims.[9] It is the same Bill that had been passed into law one month before by the Legislative Assembly for the Northwest Frontier Province.[10] The motion was adopted without any reason being given or sought, although the folio which follows it set out the 'Statement of Objects and Reasons' why the Bill should be considered and it is worthwhile drawing out a few of the central themes and issues that arise from it.

For several years past it has been the cherished desire of the Muslims of British India that Customary Law

should in no case take the place of Muslim Personal
Law. The matter has been repeatedly agitated in the
press as well as on the platform. The Jaimat-ul-Ulema-
i-Hind, the greatest Moslem religious body has supported the demand and has invited the attention of
all concerned to the urgent necessity of introducing
a measure to this effect. Customary Law is a misno-
mer inasmuch as it has not any sound basis to stand
upon and is very much liable to frequent changes and
cannot be expected at any time in the future that certainty and definiteness which must be the characteris-
tic of all laws. The status of Muslim women under the
so-called Customary Law is simply disgraceful. All
the Muslim Women's Organisations have therefore
condemned the Customary Law as it adversely affects
their rights. They demand that Muslim Personal Law
(Shariat) should be applicable to them. The introduction of Muslim Personal Law will automatically raise
them to the position to which they are naturally entitled. In addition to this the present measure, if enacted,
would have a very salutary effect on society because it
would ensure certainty and definiteness in the mutual
rights and obligations of the public. Muslim Personal
Law (shariat) exists in the form of a veritable code and
is too well known to admit any doubt or to entail
any great labour in the shape of research, which is the
chief feature of Customary Law.[11]

Abdullah's first hypothesis is that customary law is not
adequate as a basis for law for Muslims insofar as it is subject to change and is not consistently applied.[12] By implication therefore, the suggestion is that what is being proposed
corrects that error and can be seen as both immutable and

consistent. As was seen in Chapter One, one might argue that Abdullah's argument here is in line with the theory of the shari'a.[13] However, the proposition that shari'a has been somehow immune to the vagaries of human tampering is one that flies in the face of historical fact as outlined in Chapter One.

Secondly, the school of shari'a being proposed is never discussed. Thirdly what is perhaps more alarming is the clear implication in the first sentences that customary law, agreed and developed by society over time, is an insufficient basis upon which to found law. Abdullah's statement of "Objects and Reasons" carries with it the implicit concept that shari'a, which is founded upon God himself, is a much firmer basis upon which to found it.[14] It therefore becomes necessary to implement the law for its own sake, but also to provide Muslims with the stability in law that can only be guaranteed by this code alone. This significant premise – that customary law does not carry sufficient sustainability – is not explored and it is unfortunate that no one thinks to ask whether that same principle applied to any other non-Muslim law.

Further on in the document, customary law in India is accused of being particularly hard on women. Here the document has touched upon a valid observation, for there is widespread agreement that customary law as it stood in India at the time disadvantaged Muslim urban women particularly.[15] From a political standpoint therefore, the proposed law had the advantage of being seen as both progressive and necessary. However, Deputy Commissioner Akola of the Central Provinces takes a different view of the Bill when his views are elicited:

Does the sponsor of the Bill desire that Shariat should be made into immutable law, secure against all onslaughts by progressive and reformist minds? In my opinion ... the door should not be closed to all reform, as appears to be the intention of the mover.[16]

Thus, although the Bill has the appearance of progressive thought, for Akola at least, the Bill was designed to do the opposite. The argument provides an interesting perspective and suggests a deliberate attempt by those Muslims sponsoring the Bill to elevate the status of Islam back into apparatus of government in which it had been present through the Mughal and early East India Company periods. As there is no document which can show that such was the aim of the proposer, the opinion cannot be verified, but it is an interesting perspective that has the circumstantial evidence of shari'a theory, as outlined in Chapter One, behind it. Certainly it cannot be doubted that such a political move would be in keeping with the philosophy of Maududi et al., whose perceptions were examined in the previous two chapters. It would also be in keeping with the recently published work of the *Tablighi-Jama'at*, whose founder had been calling Muslims back to piety since the late 1920s.[17]

Whatever the underlying drivers behind the Bill's proposal, its language is articulated in such a way that both appeals to Muslims craving identity and progressive-minded people who wanted to see the status of women properly raised and defended.[18]

One further point needs to be made. If one were being generous, one might reasonably argue that there was an assumption that the shari'a being discussed was in fact the Hanafi madhahib. That being the case, the issue that was noticeably absent from the discussion was the reason for imposing that rule across the whole of India, when the South Indians followed the Shaafi code.[19] Clearly the vagueness is an aid in the political aims of the Bill. Moreover, the final sentence of the Bill appears to be a deliberate avoidance of detailed discussion and investigation as being 'unnecessary' as it is all so familiar.

Following its proposal, the Bill is then published as widely as possible and sent all over India for expert comment from all the different provinces: a process which took eight months to carry out.[20] This was entirely standard practice when important Bills were being introduced.

There was clearly great interest in the Bill and even though a significant number of the British officials took the line that it was generally a matter for the Muslims alone to decide, more detailed comment did flow from some Hindus, a few Britons as well as other Muslims.[21]

Many of the British governors and administrators sound a note of caution in their covering letters to the advice they attach.[22] Broadly speaking, they bow to the legal expertise of the Muslim lawyers they have canvassed, as do Hindu colleagues. However, it is clear from the language in their correspondence that they do have some caution and reservation which they seem to be either unwilling to fully explain or lack the confidence to articulate.[23] What can be ascertained from the comments was that whilst the Bill was not something to be opposed, there was a constant request for exemptions to be made for their own local conditions. Clearly, this would have been something that Abdullah and Jinnah (who vociferously supported the passage of the Bill) would have strongly fought against, for it not only undermined the very core of the reason for the Bill's proposal in the first place, but it would have propagated the localised nature of Islam that they were so desperate to end.[24]

The principle objections to the Bill are reflected in the concerns raised by the Additional District Judge (ADJ) of

Ajmer-Merwara, who was concerned that the wording of the Bill would actually negate a lot more law than was at first realised insofar as it was deliberately worded to supersede previous customary law, a situation that could potentially affect more than just Muslims.[25] Given the discussion at the beginning of this chapter, this objective seems likely, even probable.

The ADJ of Ajmer-Merwara's objection was also reflected in the somewhat alarmed note from the President of the Durgah Committee in the same area, who believed that the law would change the broader legal status of Muslims enormously,[26] and his alarm was also reflected in the response from the Governor of the Punjab, who was particularly concerned that the Bill would produce a fragmentation of holdings in his district. As such, he argued that the Bill would be regressive, rather than progressive.[27]

For the Bill's supporters, it is interesting to note that, in language that is reflected in the correspondence from all over India, the Muslim associations, parties and individuals who support the Bill were keen to highlight that the Bill did indeed have broad support from Muslims all over India. Their language therefore deliberately isolated the voices of those Muslims who did want to object to the Bill and builds a perception of consensus that belies the substantial body of alternative opinion that came from within the Muslim communities themselves.[28]

In this connection, the observation made by several of the respondents from the Central Provinces and the United Provinces are of particular interest: they all argue that there is no necessity for the new legislation as the existent legislation already covers the ground that the new code will also cover.[29] The Governor of Bengal is one among many who point out that Act XII of 1887 already covers the aspects of the application of Muslim Personal Law covered in this Bill.[30]

This observation, raised initially in isolation, becomes more widespread over the course of the passage of the Bill and becomes one of the contributing factors in the amendments that eventually serve to blunt its impact. It also provides the strongest evidence to hand of the Bill's essentially political nature.[31]

Apart from the issue of local exemptions, the belief of widespread support among Muslims, the concern about the negation of existent legislation and the lack of confidence of British officials in tackling the issue, the other key issue revolves around the Bill's suitability for both urban and agricultural Muslims. The main support for and origins of the Bill seem to have arisen from urban Muslims rather than agricultural Muslims. Space constraints do not permit an examination of the underlying causes of the disconnect between the two groups, this book will need to be content itself with the observation of the dichotomy of interest between the two groups rather than a discussion of the legalistic dynamics. It is important to note however, that, in view of the fact that the weight of legal correspondence from many sides consistently opines that the Bill will significantly disadvantage those Muslim women particularly in agricultural situations, the purpose behind the Bill must itself be highlighted afresh. For, given the fact that the Muslims drafting the Bill must have been aware of its implications, the net loss under this Bill for a sizable minority of the population must have been calculated.

This perhaps uncomfortable observation returns us to the question of the motivation behind the Bill, which the Governor of the United Provinces believed he had the answer to:

It is inevitable that Muslim sentiment as a whole should favour a Bill which asks that the Muslim

Personal Law should override customary law especially since the Shariat [sic] is considered to have high
religious sanction.[32]

This categorical statement shows perhaps an over-reliance
on the validity of the claims of mass support being received
from the Anjumen and others, for he also acknowledges
that the majority of Muslim legal advice he has received is
against the Bill. Indeed, the majority of advice received that
was strongly in favour of the Bill put forth the argument
not in terms of righting the social inequality that had been
the basis for its proposal in the first place, but in relation to
its benefit for Muslim identity.[33] This is echoed by Maulari
Hafiz Miran in Madras who opines that

it [the Bill] is necessary to clear the way for the
advancement of the Muslim community in India.[34]

What was noticeably absent in the discussion thus far was
the total lack of engagement with the theological aspects
of a Bill that had, at its heart, a proposal relating to the
practice of faith.

That said, however, it appears that one or two of the
responses from advisors did attempt to engage with religious issues.

Two deputy commissioners (DCs) in Punjab province
seemed to be alone in taking on the theological considerations that point to the central flaws that would undermine any attempt to implement the Bill: firstly, the DC
of Gurdaspur notes that it will be difficult to decide on
which interpretation of shari'a to use. Secondly, the DC of
Gujranwala points out that shari'a has not been defined
in the Bill. These concerns were noted at the beginning

of the chapter and there is no point repeating them again
here, but it is worth noting that nobody else had sought to
examine the fundamental problems that lie just beneath
the surface of the Bill until more than a year had elapsed
since the Bill's passage elapsed.[35] The fact that these objections came from within the Indian legal community, rather
than from British officials, perhaps illustrates the lack of
confidence felt by other British officials in asking the fundamental questions which would have teased these issues
out for themselves.

Having absorbed the comments, the Bill is debated the
following year at another session of the Legislative Assembly
at Simla in which an amended version of the Bill (whose
principal change is an exception for agricultural inheritance) is discussed in relation to whether it should be sent to
a Select Committee for further work. It is in this discussion
that the principal proposers of the Bill have an opportunity
to underline and clarify their stances in relation to every
proposed amendment.[36] It is therefore important to spend
some time examining the arguments they marshal, for participants include Shaukat Ali, Muhammad Jinnah and the
Bill's chief opponent, Sir Henry Craik, who was the Home
Member in the Legislative Assembly.

The discussion began with the proposer, Abdullah, making a statement concerning the Bill in which he acknowledges the amendment in relation to agricultural land,
although he believes it undermines the Bill as a whole, and
reiterates the belief that it is only non-Muslims who are
opposing the Bill. All Muslims are, according to Abdullah,
behind the Bill, 'as they should be.'[37] There are then a series
of Muslim speakers who all endorse Abdullah's motion and
emphasize the constant and trustworthy nature of shari'a
as a direct comparison to customary law. The words of

Faal-i-Haq Pircha (NW Punjab) encapsulate the tenor of all the remarks by these speakers.

> I am one who conscientiously believes that most of the present degradation of the Indian Muslims in social and spiritual sphere is due to their progressive abandonment of the social code of Islam.[38]

Clearly present in the minds of the proposers therefore are the familiar reformist themes of lack of purity and downtrodden Islam that was being echoed by *Tablighi Jama'at*, Muhammad Ali, Jinnah and Sayyid Ahmad Khan on the subcontinent, and by Badis, 'Abduh and al-Afghani elsewhere in the former Muslim Empire.[39] Fundamentally, the remarks serve to highlight once more the inherently political nature of the Bill and the desire for strength through unity that underlined it.

Amongst the speakers is Muhammad Yakub (Rohil Kamaan), who points out that the Bill's implementation would, in effect, simply fulfil a promise to the Muslim community made by Queen Victoria to have shari'a govern in this particular field. Evidence of such an undertaking is difficult to obtain and it is possible that Yakub may have been liberally interpreting the Proclamation made by Queen Victoria in 1858 in which she promised religious freedom for all.[40] This is the same Proclamation Muhammad Ali referred to in Chapter Three. It is therefore worth noting that terms such as 'religious freedom' have to be carefully considered before employing them, for phrases that are understood in one way within a particular cultural milieu will resonate differently outside it.

However, whatever the truth of Yakub's claim, it is clear that the Government of India had told the Bill's proposers that it would not oppose it. Both the delegate from Agra, Muhammad Yamin Khan and the Home Member, Sir Henry Craik, refer to the fact in their remarks.[41] The political and administrative reasoning behind such a stance can only be guessed at as there is no evidence of discussion on the file. This harks back to the comments made around the religious objections raised in the consultative phase by the ADJ of Gurdaspur and offers circumstantial evidence of deliberate complicity in the Bill's passage, even though there is nothing in government files to suggest such a ploy. An explanation of timidity, or lack of knowledge and insight, will probably have to suffice. But it is curious that the British officials felt no compulsion to raise concerns expressed in their opinion gathering before deciding to either step back or fight it. One might indeed argue that such a lack of investigation could be seen as a dereliction of duty in relation to protecting their imperial citizens. Politically however, it was advantageous to have an empowered Muslim community in order to undermine the work of the *Congress Party*.[42]

In opposition, Sir Henry Craik is keen to highlight what he felt to be the lack of necessity for the Act at all. In his speech, the final one before the motion to put the Bill to a Select Committee was adopted, he pointed out that the Act XLVI of 1920 already covered the required areas. He also advocated that Muslim groups who wished to opt out of the Bill should be allowed to do so on the grounds that they might prefer custom to shari'a.[43] Craik's argument here would have been strengthened by the deployment of the arguments of the Deputy Commissioners in relation to the concerns over which shari'a system should be employed. By arguing on behalf of custom, he was speaking up on behalf of a system that, to those he was opposing, was either inferior or completely discredited.

The minutes are therefore useful in shining a light into the principles and considerations of the proponents of the Bill, whilst, at the same time, illuminating the passive role of the British colonial government insofar as they had been given plenty of advice that raised important concerns, but seemingly did little about them.

As the Bill emerged from the Select Committee phase, there is one last debate that examined all the proposed amendments.[44] This debate is of particular significance as some of the amendments that had been tabled go right to the heart of the issue of identity. Of particular interest is the fact that Muslim members of the Legislative Committee had clearly held a separate meeting to discuss the Bill at which one dissenting Muslim voice had been deliberately excluded as shall be seen below.[45]

The principal revision to the wording of the text as announced by Muhammad Ali Jinnah was that Muslim women would now be able to apply to the district court on any grounds recognised by shari'a.[46] This had the effect of connecting the shari'a courts to the civil administration. Theologically, given the theory of shari'a, the foundation for such an accommodation is difficult to find, however, from a pragmatic point of view, it raises the prospect of a very close working relationship between Muslim courts and the broader British civil legal system.

One might argue that this could be seen as a return to the early years of British involvement in India, when they ruled via shari'a anyway.[47] This closer relationship between shari'a and the governmental code would bring the system back to the dar al-Islam that it had been characterised as already, yet it had the appearance of a regressive step which seemed to turn the tide of inexorable shift away from shari'a, back towards it. Furthermore it was a move that flew in the face of the gradual replacement of that system with a civil system over the previous one hundred and fifty years.

It is in the final debate on 16 September, when the Bill passed, that the central discussion of the broader principles of the Bill were once again analysed. Several of the participants expressed concern at the principle of passing religious legislation at all and another expressed concern at the lack of definition offered by the term 'Shariat' in the Bill.[48] The strident response to these concerns by Zafir Ali Khan and Ghulam Bhik Nairang provides the reader with the most fascinating exposition of the underlying motivations for the Bill in the entire course of the debates.

Nairang begins once again with the Proclamation by Queen Victoria, highlighting the use of her phrase 'promoting religious liberty'. He argues that in order for Muslims to have religious liberty, shari'a must be adopted and that, 'until this Bill is passed, there is a community living in India as Muslims who cannot be Muslims'.[49] A view that speaks clearly into the opinions expressed by Maududi et al. in the previous chapter, and which takes no account of the alternative opinions expressed by the pragmatic philosophers who were offering a progressive approach to the issue.

Nairang's view is endorsed by Zafir Ali Khan, who points out that *Congress* has mobilized mass support through identity calls and it seems only natural therefore that Muslims should do the same. This perspective ignores the fact however that *Congress'* identity politics were specifically upon nationalistic lines, rather than religious ones. Indeed, Gandhi had made considerable effort to speak on behalf of both Muslims and Hindus alike.[50] Whether such a policy was advisable is not under discussion here, but it is important to note that the term 'identity' was being invested with different meaning in each case. It is very likely that it was precisely this dynamic that was concerning the Muslim proposers of this Bill: at the root of everything for them was the fear that the concept of any form of homogenous 'Islamic community' would disappear under a wave of patriotic fervour. It is perhaps this concern that underpinned Khan's most concise articulation of the Bill's motivations:

> This [shari'a] is a sort of domestic law for us and unless we come under this law there is a great danger of the Moslems [sic] losing their national solidarity and unity.[51]

It is interesting therefore that the Hindu members of the legislative Assembly are generally happy to support the Bill as a way of showing solidarity with Muslim colleagues at a time of communal violence and tension, whilst, at the same time expressing concern about the regressive nature of the law being enacted. For example, M.S. Aney of Berar poses a fundamental question.

> Hindus would not re-introduce old Vedic law to solve modern problems, why therefore are Muslims going back to arcane law to address women's issues?[52]

Even so, he does not oppose the Bill when it comes to the vote and, although his point has some validity, the repeated statements by Jinnah, Ali and others in the debate must have shown Aney the underlying motivation of the Bill. His concerns might have been better directed towards the issue of identity rather than seeking to make a point about regressive legislation.

It is then that another Home Member of the Legislative Assembly, R.F. Mudie, who is the nominated government official, moves to limit the scope of the Bill by replacing the word 'shari'a' with 'Law'.[53] His main concern was to ensure that the Bill would not override provisions in the criminal procedures code. Not surprisingly, this draws a strong response from Jinnah and the other proposing delegates in the Assembly. Their counter-argument was that such an amendment would muddy the waters that were otherwise clear in the current wording. Ziauddin Ahmad further asserted that, without the word 'shari'a' in, the Bill would change nothing for Muslims. Jinnah added that local custom is not shari'a, therefore the term has to remain. This of course omits the argument that shari'a already incorporated local custom in its codes as was seen in Chapter One.

The amendment remained, much to the frustration of Jinnah et al., yet, the fact that it remained should not remove focus from the fact that none of these Muslim politician's statements is challenged by any of the members present. Even Jinnah's assertion about custom being anomalous with the shari'a is left unquestioned. Perhaps the other delegates were unaware that the Shaafi particularly, as well as Hanafi and Maliki systems, all incorporated custom and validated it.[54]

This point is driven home by Muhammad Yamin Khan, who seems to have been excluded from the discussions that the other Muslim delegates held outside of the debates in the chamber. His strongly worded response to the inclusion of the word 'shari'a' places him firmly in the camp of the 'pragmatic philosophers' and, in so doing, throws light on the practical outworking of the two differing perspectives, in this case, in relation to law-making.

The Bill is not being brought in the language of Arabia, nor in the language of Persia or in Urdu. This Bill is introduced in the English language and therefore we must try to understand it as such. Personal law is understood now as administered by the courts. If a Muhammadan belongs to the Sunni Jamaat, Sunni Law applies to him: if a Muhammadan belongs to the Hanafi Jamaat, then Hanafi applies to him ... .There is no one law as far as the Muslims are concerned.[55]

This central point is somewhat lost as the debate moves on, but its inclusion is worth noting not simply for the reasons mentioned above, but also for showing that the British officials who had stepped back from the process had heard, through the debates, the thinking of the Muslim community in India on this issue. They had seen the differing philosophical approaches and the underlying reasons for the Bill's proposal as well as hearing the problems that it entailed, yet, their limited intervention had the tone of mild concern rather than the deeper concern at the motivation and implications of the Bill that it perhaps should have engendered.

The Bill was passed with the amendments that had been suggested, much to the frustration of Abdullah, Jinnah and Ali. The remainder of the file shows the discussions surrounding and eventual adoption of some relatively minor amendments in 1943.[56]

Summary

From its proposal through to its adoption, the *Shariat Act* displays some key aspects of identity politics with regard to the role of minority identity formation, the actions of government and the aims of politicians. It also displays the interplay of language and expectation in relation to minority aspiration along with the complexity of engaging effectively when theology is pushed into the political arena. For those reasons, this episode draws out significant issues for the present day as several Western states re-explore a possible role for shari'a in their civil codes.

On the government side, two dynamics come through very clearly: a failure to ask effective questions when examining the Bill and a desire to avoid interfering in the Bill's passage. Whether one wishes to adopt a more conspiratorial theory to explain the British government's actions in this, or whether one chooses to see it as an extension of the principle of religious liberty, the underlying lack of investigation must be characterised as a failure to adequately protect the interests of its citizens.

As far as Muslims in India are concerned, it shows clearly both the differing perspectives of the community at the time and the outworking of the theoretical positions of the 'pragmatic philosophers' and 'visionary separatists' seen in the previous two chapters. It therefore highlights the fact that the theoretical positions examined in Chapters Three and Four have direct application into the political and cultural life of the state in which they exist. Of fundamental importance is the motivation behind the introduction of the Bill, for it shows the more separatist-minded politicians using an issue to bind a community that had been disparate together and to position themselves as the spokesmen for that group.

In his important chapter on Islamic interaction with the British administration, Anderson summarises the *Shariat Act* as

The culmination of the scripturalist influence on law … .which originated in the efforts, primarily among

some of the 'ulama to secure statutory enforcement of
the Shari'a.[57]

Whilst this observation is useful, as we have seen, this
reading omits the political ramifications and issues of identity that underpinned much of the motivation for the Bill's
proposal and passage. Perhaps therefore, it is Muhammad
Iqbal's observation on the place of shari'a within modern
Muslim reformism that serves to provide a deeper insight
into the desire of some Muslims to seek shari'a within the
legal code of the state:

> ... partly owing to a misunderstanding of the ultimate
> motive of Rationalism and partly owing to unrestrained
> thought of particular Rationalists, conservative think-
> ers regarded the movement as a force of disintegration
> and considered it as a danger to the stability of Islam
> as a social polity. The main purpose, therefore, was to
> preserve the social integrity of Islam and to realize that
> the only course open to them was to utilize the bind-
> ing force of the Shariat and to make the structure of
> their legal system as rigorous as possible.[58]

For Iqbal therefore, the threat of the very notions that
were being proposed by Muslim rationalists such as Sayyid
Ahmad Khan caused a turn towards shari'a to 'protect'
Islam.

Iqbal's observation certainly provides a logical and non-
political explanation for the drive of Jinnah and his companions, but, given that those who were calling for the
Shariat Act came from very diverse religious backgrounds,
Iqbal's explanation of fearful religious orthodoxy about

internal Muslim movements cannot fully account for the active pressing for the establishment of shari'a in law. In this, religious explanation can only go so far, and where Iqbal's explanation falls short (though providing a fascinating insight), the political explanation outlined earlier makes more sense in the context in which the Bill was being proposed.

From the point of view of government engagement and policymaking therefore, the passage of the Act highlights the need to heed expert advice and to do 'due diligence' for the sake of al its citizens rather than simply seeing the short-term political gain. The Act was unnecessary and potentially regressive although it served a political purpose in strengthening the hand of Muslim politicians who could divide the opposition to the British rule in the short term. Moreover, it gave a political voice to a group of Muslim politicians who did not speak for all the Muslim communities on the subcontinent.

* * *

Having examined some of the effects of the theoretical positions seen in Chapters Three and Four in this case study, it is worthwhile spending some time looking, albeit briefly, at the development of the *Code Morand* in French Algeria at the turn of the nineteenth to twentieth centuries. This provides a foil to the discussion above insofar as it both broadens the scope of the discussion of the effects of the different Muslim perspectives on non-Muslim rule, and also provides the opportunity to analyse whether the same issues also manifest themselves in a parallel, but distinct cultural setting.

CHAPTER SIX

FRENCH IMPERIAL INTERACTION WITH SHARI'A[*]

From the outset, the French approach to their colonies differed from that of the British. For the British, the sheer size and complexity of the administrative task facing the rulers, as well as an eye for profit margins, engendered a desire to allow for a minimal layer of governance to be laid over whatever local systems were in place. This is not to say that the British were content to leave local administration untouched, but rather through a focus on education, infrastructure and national-level management, it could be said that they were content to allow change to come gradually. By so doing they put aside any residual desire to turn all colonial possessions into mirrors of Britannia and did not engage in questions of identity and citizenship.

---

[*] Much of the research for this chapter is based upon the excellent work of Oussama Arabi's exposition of Morand's work. However, whereas Arabi's focus is upon the methodology and outcomes of Morand's work, my engagement is with the implications of the work.

This was not so for the French who, from the early years of their North African expansion, attempted to bring the people of the newly annexed territories not simply under the administrative umbrella of France, but also into full citizenship of that country. Thus, one might talk of a conscious act of cultural imperialism in French North Africa in a way that we could not under British imperial rule.[1]

This policy became explicit following the revolutions of 1848 in France when some of the revolutionaries were sent across to Algeria to build villages that were deliberately designed to mimic urban France in culture, law and architecture.[2] This went against the express wishes of the French military, who were keen to allow the Arab population to remain under their Maliki shari'a code so as not to enflame anti-imperial feeling.[3] They had had frequent experience in engaging with the rebellions that flared between the 1830s and the late 1840s and therefore understood the importance of shari'a in maintaining identity.

As was discussed in the earlier historical section, the French had taken a different cultural approach to their colonies than the British had, encouraging a concept of 'France overseas' in Algeria. Consequently, little attempt was made by successive French authorities to try and find a conjunction between their civil code and the indigenous Maliki shari'a. Indeed, there appears to have been a conscious effort to remove shari'a and replace it with what the French believed to be a more enlightened form of legislation as part of their 'civilizing mission'.[4] It is an attitude that is sharply highlighted by Paul Silverstein in his book *Algeria in France: Transpolitics, Race and Nation*, in which he records the words of the French senator M. Sabatier during a debate about possibly naturalising all

Algerians, whether they renounce their religion or not, on the grounds that it

> would implicitly condone Coranic [sic] civil and family practices from feudal land tenure to polygamy which escape French laws, not to mention French morality.[5]

French civil law was therefore offered to Algerians as an opportunity to adopt a more enlightened government such as in the *Senatus Consulté* of 1865. That said, by the late nineteenth century and early twentieth century, a more integrated approach to legal governance in the area of family law was proposed by Jean Luciani, the Director of Indigenous Affairs in the Government of Algeria.[6] The Decree of 17 April 1889 had regulated that all Algerians would be governed by French law, except in relation to personal status, inheritance and specific areas of property law.[7] It was under this remit that Marcel Morand conducted his research and drafting in the fields of inheritance and endowments property, evidence and personal status. His work mirrored that of David Santillia, who was producing a code for Tunisia.[8]

Of central importance in relation to this study is the question of why both Morand and Santillia only engaged with formulating personal status and family law issues, rather than engaging with the penal aspects of shari'a.[9] Arabi suggests that

> [i]t is not surprising therefore, that when considering the domain of applicability of Islamic legal norms in Algeria … Morand sees with a sympathetic eye the wisdom of maintaining Islamic jurisdiction over the basic spheres of family and inheritance. [For] In Morand's eyes, it would be politically unwise to

upset the religious Islamic feelings underlying these rules.[10]

She goes on to quote Morand, who is explicit in assigning very pragmatic political motives to the framework of his codification.

> The basic principles of Islamic law being proclaimed in the Qur'an, the legislator wanted, by maintaining the benefit of their law and customs to our Muslims, to demonstrate his respect for their religious beliefs and secure their sympathies, or, at least to disarm their hostility and make them more easily accept our domination.[11]

This fascinating insight from a man who was at the heart of the French colonial administration at the time begs a whole series of questions, most of which are simply unanswerable. However, what is displayed here is an explicit policy of expediency in order to gain political advantage. This was not peculiar to the French by any means; the British had used the Ottoman Caliph to their own advantage in securing the peace of their Muslim subjects on more than one occasion.[12] However, whereas the British had desired to manage their empire in order to gain the wealth that could only be fully exploited in peaceful conditions, the French were using the adaption of Islamo-French law in these particular spheres in order to bring a peace that would enable a deeper cultural assimilation.[13]

As a central cog of the legal machinery of the French colonial administration, one might expect Morand to have used his opportunity to create a new hybrid legal fusion to imprint the perceived superiority of French legal theory upon the Algerian shari'a code. However, this does not appear to play a part in his thinking. Indeed, Arabi suggests that Morand was concerned with defending the importance of maintaining as much of shari'a as possible, not just from a pragmatic point of view of not upsetting the Algerians further, but also from a personal respect for the theory that underpinned it.[14] This is important to remember when reflecting on his conclusions, for, in Morand Algerian Muslims had an ally, rather than a foe.

Other than the opposition that Morand faced from his colleagues, his principal problem concerned how he could legitimately create a modern code whilst being seen to remain within the confines of usul ul fiqh. The crux of the problem is articulated by Arabi:

> Not much in the way of reform could be done if the anachronistic elements in Islamic law were upheld as binding, regulating its more progressive aspects to oblivion.[15]

The central issue in this circumstance was reconciling the European need for equality for all under the same law against the classical Muslim position of the dhimmi status.

In seeking to find a way through this, Morand sought for answers in both the Ottoman Majalla of 1876 and in the Maliki doctrine of maslaha.

The Ottoman Majalla provided a recent blueprint for the work that both Morand and Santilla were undertaking. Moreover, it had the added benefit, from a legitimizing perspective, of having been executed by the leading Sunni authority in the Muslim world at the time.

To facilitate this use of the Majalla, Morand's gateway for innovation lay in the work of Ali Haydar, who was able to quote the work of the early Hanafi jurist Abu Yusuf (d.798 C.E.) Abu Yusuf articulated the principle that 'custom is binding' and Haydar incorporated that into Article 36 of the *Ottoman Hanafi Civil Code*. Haydar's conclusion expanded his three-word statement:

> Custom and Practice become legally binding when there is no textual support for the intended ruling; if there is a text it should be followed because believers have no right to change the texts and the texts legally overrules the custom It should be noted however that Abu Yusuf ... said that if the text was derived from customary practice it could be ignored and the new practice of the changing times becomes binding: the Majalla adopts the position of Abu Yusuf.[16]

However, whilst this provided an opening, Morand still faced the problem that he was engaging with Maliki, rather than Hanafi shari'a and further that discerning what aspects of shari'a were based upon customary practice that could therefore be overturned was a mammoth, indeed, near impossible task.

Given the discussion in the opening chapter concerning the adoptive role that custom played in developing shari'a in the early phase of Islamic jurisprudence, Ali Haydar's argument here appears to be in keeping with that principle. However, it also potentially becomes the door through which any innovation, no matter how radical, could come. It therefore seems to be a mechanism that would be fraught with multitudinous potential pitfalls and therefore, to be used only with extreme caution.

Nevertheless, for Morand's purposes, it was the perfect device, although it effectively meant that he adopted Hanafi shari'a rather than Maliki, an ambiguity that Morand both recognised and accepted.[17] This is remarkable from a multitude of differing perspectives, but chief among them is the fact that the Code Morand continued to be the key legal text in post-colonial Algeria long after independence, although it was never formally adopted into Constitutional law.[18] That being the case, the observation of the centrality of a Muslim's shari'a identity discussed in Chapter One would seem to stand at odds with this dynamic. However, it is worth noting that the Algerian regime, in common with many of the modern states in North Africa and the Middle East, have been characterised as un-Islamic by those jihadi-salafi groups who have been seeking to overthrow them and establish a more 'Islamic' government. In this context, it will be interesting to see how the new governments formed in the aftermath of the 'Arab Spring' will engage with this area as they develop new Constitutions. This lack of Maliki identity in the legal construct of the state would be another contributing factor to the anti-government propaganda and, in that light, it could be said that, for all his desire to construct something beneficial, Morand's work in relation to the Majalla ultimately served to inadvertently undermine the state.[19]

One might argue that Morand's search for the tools with which to frame his codification had already been fulfilled within the Hanafi mechanisms he adopted, but it is interesting that he felt the need to further justify this switch by the adoption of another legal mechanism: maslaha.[20] Maslaha was the doctrinal device which essentially permitted what might otherwise be un-permitted in the interests of the 'public good'. For Morand therefore, it was the perfect tool to accomplish his purpose.

In her article *Maslaha in Contemporary Islamic Legal Theory*, Felicitas Opwis argues that ever since classical times the concept of 'public good' has been interpreted according to education, historical setting, expediency and cultural background. Thus, of the various reformers and theorists she analyses such as al-Ghazali, Fakhr al-Dn al-Razi, al-Tufi and al-Shatibi, there is considerable variation in the role each assigns to maslaha in determining doctrine and law.[21] This observation is also evidenced in the work of Khadduri, Ramadan and Olidort who all seek to show the theological validity of this ultimately pragmatic doctrine in similar terms.[22]

It would therefore not be unreasonable to see the work of Morand as entirely in keeping with that stream of doctrine and, as such, validating the action that he took.

Certainly, it gave him the opportunity to create his Code and in that context, it served its purpose. However, even though the Code remains a remarkable achievement, the necessity to employ tools such as the ones Morand had to in order to achieve his goal points to the underlying difficulty in creating a cohesive code from such different legal cultures.

From the perspective of the French rulers therefore, Morond's task was necessary in relation to blunting the fears of Algerian opposition to French assimilation. But Morond's exhaustive efforts did not manage to find a formula for civil-shari'a harmony, rather, it highlighted the essential incompatibility of the two systems.

Summary

For Morand himself, although he had invested so much of his energy in carrying out the work, he was able to recognise that the French engagement in the legal life of Algeria pushed the boundaries of cultural engagement further than those of their contemporaries.

> Of all the Muslim countries governed by a Christian power, Algeria is perhaps the place where the heavy hand of the occupant was at its greatest; for France not only demanded the recognition of its authority by the vanquished it also undertook to govern them and impose on them its own institutions.[23]

Thus, whereas the British had encouraged the concept of freedom of religion upon its imperial subjects, the French approached the issue through the lens of nationalism as cultural identity. To be a French citizen was to renounce the centrality of shari'a in one's life and to turn instead to loyalty to the country. In so doing, it asked of its Muslim citizens a mono-loyalism that was absent in the British Empire, yet this same approach avoided the demands from her Muslim subjects that came through Britain's seemingly open-handed approach.

CHAPTER SEVEN

THE NEW WORLD: CITIZENSHIP, IDENTITY AND THE NEW EUROPE

Introduction

Thus far the book has focussed upon historical and theological analysis; however, if meaningful and relevant conclusions are to be drawn in the final chapter, acknowledgement of and reference to policymaking in response to the current debates need to be made.

Britain

Evidence of the relevance of the identity and citizenship issues grappled with by Muslim reformers of the nineteenth and twentieth centuries are not hard to find. Perhaps no other event in recent history encapsulates the sensitivities that surround the issue than the international furore that greeted Rowan William's Royal Courts of Justice lecture in 2008 . Earlier that day, he had given an interview to British Radio 4's *World at One* in which he had outlined the broad themes of his speech.[1]

The Archbishop's desire had been to examine what accommodation might be made for religious conscience within the existing legal framework.[2] On a broader level, he was interested in opening a discussion on the rights of religious groups within a secular state.[3] As an example of that his conclusion focused on the particular place of shari'a within British Law.

> If we are to think intelligently about the relations between Islam and British Law, we need a fair amount of 'deconstruction' of crude oppositions and mythologies, whether of the nature of shari'a or the nature of the Enlightenment.[4]

Although there was support for the Archbishop's remarks, his nuanced argument was quickly drowned out in a 'chorus of disapproval' as many politicians, journalists and clergy condemned what they understood Dr. Williams to have said.[5]

The then Prime Minister Gordon Brown rejected his comments saying that British law should be based on British values, although he did not entirely rule out the possibility of 'some accommodation'.[6] Baroness Warsi, the Conservative spokesperson for cohesion at the time, said that the Archbishop's comments were 'unhelpful'.[7] *The Times* rejected Williams' views and said that he was out of touch.[8] The comments of Trevor Phillips, Chairman of the *Equality and Human Rights Commission*, were along the same lines, characterizing the Archbishop's views as 'muddled and unhelpful'.[9] Some Muslims such as Khalid Mahmood the Labour MP for Birmingham Perry Barr, criticized the Archbishop's views, saying that 'Muslims do not need special treatment or to be specially singled out. This would not contribute to community cohesion.'[10]

Perhaps surprisingly, given the near-universal furore and condemnation, the Lord Chief Justice, Lord Phillips, revisited the topic a few months later and came to similar conclusions. In a talk entitled 'Equality Before the Law' at the East London Muslim Centre, Lord Phillips cited his own grandparents' Jewish heritage and used that as the foundation for arguing that there did need to be some accommodation of minority systems within British law in order to permit freedom to practice faith and custom. He cited the Archbishop's argument and broadly agreed with the points Dr. Williams had been making.[11]

Once again, there was strong (if not quite so aggressive) resistance to the argument, with virtually every commentator who remarked on the speech refuting the idea that any exception to British civil law could be made for any group, including Muslims.

Charles Moore in *The Daily Telegraph* commented that both Islam and shari'a need different treatment to other religions, such as Judaism or Christianity, because neither of these desire to establish religious states in the way that some Muslims do.[12] In a similar vein, Matthew Parris, writing in *The Times*, called aspects of Lord Phillips' speech 'a charter for cultural bullying; for peer-group pressurizing; for self oppression ... a charter against women and teenagers ... a charter for discreet duress.'[13] Writing in her *Spectator* blog, Melanie Philips suggested that the Lord Chief Justice's comments proved that he was 'ignorant and confused about Islam'.[14]

On the other hand, Madeleine Bunting, in *The Guardian*, agreed with Lord Phillips' 'sensible comments' and suggested that the accommodation of shari'a within arbitration law would force current shari'a councils into a position of more open scrutiny.[15] But she was clearly in a minority. However, her comment reminded a public that otherwise might not have been aware of it that shari'a councils were already operating in this country. Indeed, it was in September 2008 that the *Sunday Times* 'revealed' that shari'a councils had been set up and were operating in England. This story was quickly picked up by other press and media, many of whose stories gave the impression that Britain was now operating under shari'a.[16]

The influence of shari'a in the UK was something that had been the subject of intense speculation in the press following the July 2005 attacks, with the *Daily Telegraph* publishing on the front page a survey in the wake of the London bombings, which claimed that 32 per cent of British Muslims thought that western society was decadent and immoral, 16 per cent felt no loyalty towards Britain and 24 per cent of British Muslims sympathised with the motives of the bombers.[17] Furthermore, there were also numerous editorials and articles in all the newspapers expressing concern about the preaching that was apparently being done in some mosques discouraging loyalty to Britain.[18] A poll of 1,000 Muslims commissioned by Channel 4's *Dispatches* program following the 7/7 attacks found that 54 per cent of their sample wanted to live under British law, rather than shari'a, but that a higher percentage of 18- to 44-year-olds (33 per cent as compared to 23 per cent) said that they would like to live under shari'a. The poll therefore suggested an increasing rather than decreasing desire for shari'a identity amongst younger Muslims, which lent fuel to the concerns expressed by Andrew Brown amongst others in his article 'How British Can a Muslim Be?'[19]

These small-scale surveys were unlikely to produce meaningful data in a population that is over two million strong. However, what was perhaps more telling were the results of an Department of Communities and Local Government's internal survey in 2009, which took a sample of over 10,000 in various faith communities within the country and asked them to rate how important their faith was in terms of their identity, ten being not important and one being the most important. Significantly, the non-Muslim respondents overwhelmingly rated their faith at around 'seven', whereas Muslims overwhelmingly responded at around the 'three' mark. If nothing else therefore, such a wide-reaching sample showed the contrast between Islam as an identity marker in contrast to any other faith.[20]

The implications of this finding are significant insofar as they show that Islam, even in a minority situation where some of the respondents were third and fourth generation immigrants, was an important identity marker and therefore that questions of 'citizenship' were likely to have more relevance for them than the believers of other faiths.

Useful as this data undoubtedly is to the outsider there is a chance that it can lead to a skewed perception of Muslim attitudes for any rounded analysis should not neglect the vigorous debate on the nature of 'citizenship' taking place across the Muslim communities in the UK. Some of the arguments are strongly reminiscent of those of their imperial forebears so, as the strengths and weakness of differing positions from that period were probed in Chapters Three and Four, it is important to engage with these modern Muslim's positions. That said, however, many of the points that they make are already covered by their Imperial predecessors, so, rather than exhaustively laying out the position of each one, we will explore two publications that exemplify the dynamics we are analyzing.

In 2008, Muhammad Anwar published an article in the *Journal of Muslim Minority Affairs* that surveyed the status of Muslim minorities in Europe and North America, drawing in to focus on the UK.[21] Anwar made a number of useful observations, but perhaps most importantly, he laid out clearly the principle concerns of the Muslim communities in Britain; he cited housing, unemployment, political representation and religious discrimination amongst the chief barriers to building a cohesive society. According to Anwar, such issues prevent the inculcating of a sense of a belonging that feeds citizenship.[22]

The list of grievances is a useful one and it raises legitimate issues, but it is noticeable that the article did not contain any theological discussion on ideologies pertaining to the role of shari'a, the nature of the ummah and the understanding of 'citizenship' in a civil society at all. The questions posed in his article would be common to many minorities, but what about dealing with the ideologies that might impede integration? How does a Muslim seek to be a contributing member of civil society whilst remaining rooted in their faith? This was not engaged with.

A deeper engagement with the issues of integration and citizenship for Muslims in the UK came with the publication in 2009 of the *Contextualising Islam in Britain: Exploratory Perspectives,* which was the outcome report of a series of research gatherings at Cambridge University under the project leadership of Professor Yasir Suleiman.[23] The report covered the same opportunity and empowerment that Anwar's article had highlighted, but it went on to

actively engage with more ideological and theological questions relating to citizenship. In its conclusions, it drew out
some important principles for UK Muslims in their present
minority status:

> It is important to avoid the confusion, to which many
> young Muslims have fallen victim, between the sover-
> eignty of God as a metaphysical and theological con-
> cept and the discussion of issues relating to human
> political authority. Some do not make this distinction,
> which is the fundamental basis of democracy. The
> invocation of notions of divine sovereignty by politi-
> cians is problematic in practice since it can be used by
> individuals or groups 'to play God'. Muslim think-
> ers have done some important work critiquing these
> notions of 'divine' sovereignty that are misapplied to
> politics, but further detailed reflection is needed.
>
> For Muslims living as a minority in a secular lib-
> eral democracy, applying the Shari'ah is a matter
> of personal conscience or communal moral suasion
> rather than legal sanction. It is important to reclaim
> the original meaning of khilafah – as a code of eth-
> ics of individual and collective moral responsibility
> ("vicegerency") rather than as a structure of political
> authority ("caliphate").[24]

As was discussed earlier, there are strong echoes of the arguments seen in the imperial context here. Reading this document, the impression that is given is of a desire to move
forward in a pragmatic manner without a sense, present in
the opinions of Bhutto for example, that participation and
minority citizenship should only be temporary, as in classical fiqh.[25]

As such, it is a constructive and thought-provoking attempt to engage with the thorny issue of citizenship in doctrine and theology, the logical place for such an engagement since the issues relate to religious dogma. Indeed, the only criticism one might make of the paper outside of doctrinal debate would be that it is unfortunate that this paper for British Muslims has a foreword written by a non-British Muslim.

The paper does contain a very useful critique of the development of the dar al-Islam and dar al-Harb that has a direct bearing on the British context, although it unfortunately fails to engage with the fact that there are multiple Muslim communities with differing shari'a and cultural backgrounds.

Aside from these doctrinal and stylistic criticisms, perhaps the principal criticism would be a relative lack of Qur'anic quotation in a context where the document is seeking to create an alternative, positive narrative from extremists. This is a shame because one of the principal reasons that 'extremist Muslims' have been able to draw people into their worldview has been the aura of doctrinal purity they have created that remains largely unchallenged simply because they quote selectively, but extensively, from scripture.

The two publications above are examples of the differing forms of engagement with issues of citizenship from within the UK Muslim communities.

Shifting focus from the ruled to the rulers: for the vast majority of the period since the 9/11 attacks, the Labour Party has been in government. Their response to the concerns over the conflict of loyalty and issues of citizenship that have been the focus of so much political attention over that period has been the initiation of CONTEST and its public face: preventing violent extremism (PVE).[26] The PVE strategy has been widely criticised, particularly with regard to the underlying philosophy at the heart of the strategy that focuses on the implied concept that only Muslims can de-radicalise their own community.[27]

As part of the early development of the PVE strategy, Sir Keith Ajegbo was asked to write a report entitled *Diversity and Citizenship Curriculum Review* in which he analysed how the school curriculum might strengthen a drive towards integration and shared citizenship.

Sir Keith Ajegbo's report focussed instead upon inculcating a sense of shared 'Britishness' based around values, rather than any ethno-centric narrative. In so doing, it engaged with a debate that had been quietly buried for forty years: what does it mean to be British? The perceived threat of Islam (as well as the growth of the European Union institutions) had brought it to the surface again.

Unfortunately, it seemed that noone either knew the answer to that question, or was prepared to say so in a public forum, for there was little offered by way of an answer other than a few general mutterings about 'freedom' and 'tolerance'. However, the search for a definition of 'Britishness' as a 'stakeholder' concept, rather than a tepid framework of rejectionism of past identity formulas did not die with the end of the Labour government. Rather, the new Coalition government has sought to build a sense of identity at a local level, which it has developed into a new narrative concerning 'Britishness'

David Cameron announced in 2010 a new scheme to encourage a sense of community, part of the wider 'Big Society' proposals, in which school leavers would be involved in community projects aimed at encouraging a sense of contribution to society, rather than taking from it.[28] This concept of relational activity in connection to developing a sense of belonging to society has been one element of a developing promotion of a 'citizenship as participation' definition of the concept. The possible benefits to inter-community and inter-religious relations are clear, yet at the same time, one might argue that this is a form of homogenous citizenship which lacks any sense of national identity within its definition. This could be deliberate, but the sense that came out of David Cameron's speech in Munich on combating extremism on 5 February 2011 suggested that a more British-specific, British-bound definition of 'citizenship' is what the current Prime Minister seeks.[29] That strong hint was given greater credence with the Communities' Secretary's announcement of a new cohesion strategy on 21 February 2012, which made an explicit break with multiculturalist policies and identified the English language and the Christian religion as central pillars of British identity.

David Cameron is the latest in a line of Prime Ministers, including his two predecessors, that have engaged in finding positive definitions for 'British citizen' that avoided falling into the negative definition: laying out what Britain's are not. This is a Herculean task, for the concept of what it means to be British is fraught with difficulties.

In his article in *Modern Intellectual History*, Peter Mandler seeks to summarize and develop the work of social scientists in the realm of 'national identity'.[30] According to Mandler, who is basing his argument upon Anderson, 'national identity' is something unique from generalized understanding of the nature of individual or group identity[ies].[31] Mandler quotes Benedict Anderson's hypothesis that it was the

formulation of print and other communication technologies [that] made it possible for the first time for individuals scattered across distances to feel themselves strongly and simultaneously part of a single 'imagined community'. The modern state developed new technologies of its own to build-up, configure, manipulate and mobilize that sense of 'national identity'.[32]

Anderson was proposing that once that has been achieved, then 'national identity' becomes the identity to which all others are subordinated.

This argument is not new; it has been used particularly by historians seeking to explain such diverse events such as the Reformation and the Indian independence movement.[33] However, this theory does not completely explain the dynamic, for, in order for print and communications to help bind a series of communities into a wider whole, there needs to be some form of commonality upon which to base their 'identity'. For McGrath, the glue that bound communities together in the Reformation period nationally was supplied by common faith along with their defence against a common enemy: in that case, the Papacy and the Catholic Church.[34] McGrath's findings were also in line with the research of Linda Colley, who observed in her book on the shaping of 'Britain' as an entity, that 'national identity' was shaped against another, in Britain's case, against the French during the Napoleonic Wars.[35]

What the whole issue of shari'a, citizenship and integration has highlight for the UK therefore is that it has arisen at a time when 'Britain' as an entity has been struggling to decide what it is and what it stands for anyway. The 9/11 and 7/7 attacks have, in this context, become a useful catalyst for facilitating the discussions that were both necessary and avoided.

As a result, the issues of integration and citizenship for Muslim and non-Muslim alike have been bound together within a wider debate about the impact of immigration to this country.

It s against this changing political and social landscape that there has been a growing furore over the aims of the 'prevent' strategy and apparent waste of money in its implementation. For that reason, the new coalition government, produced a new strategy in June 2011 which sought to re-focus the 'prevent' strand of CONTEST.[36] At this early stage, it is unclear whether the Muslim anti-radicalization elements of the new strategy will focus on jihad (the methodology) or the Caliphate-ummah (the ideology). However, the new strategy appears to actively promote an engagement with ideology that appeared to be less explicitly detailed in the previous incarnations of the strategy. The core of the ideological engagement will need to bridge the gap between those who believe in the sovereignty of God and those who are convinced about the sovereignty of the people to find a way of co-existing that permits the expression of both.

France

The French engagement with issues of identity politics and policy-making has taken a different route to that of the UK for a series of historic and cultural reasons, some of which have been touched upon already.

Concerns about the effects of mass migration in France have been growing over a number of years. The seminal 2007 book, *God's Continent*, by Professor Philip Jenkins of Penn State University brought to broader public attention the discussion of France's demography that had begun over a decade ago in articles such as Michal Gurfinkiel's (the then Editor-in-Chief of the conservative *Valeurs Actuelles*).[37] Whilst some in both the UK and continental Europe dismissed the concerns Gurfinkiel and others had expressed as no more than customary conservative bugbears, the 2009 elections in Europe and the sharp swing to the political right that it brought suggested that Gurfinkiel's concerns were shared by many. This served as a sharp reminder to

the political establishment that such concerns not confined
to a narrow few for whom worries of immigration were a
constant concern anyway. As a result, a series of flagship
issues have provided the vehicle for the public polity to
discuss questions of identity, and particularly questions of
integration over assimilation, more openly. Central to this
whole discussion has been 'veiling'.

Amélie Barras highlights how the debate over the headscarf has become a symbol for a wider discussion on the
role of *laïcité* in contemporary French culture. Perhaps
Barras' most significant point is that the headscarf debate
has afforded the French elites the opportunity to 're-brand'
laïcité as more than simply a legal principle, but develop it
into a term that can describe the 'ethic' of French living.[38]

The trigger for the debate was the banning of 'ostenta-
tious tokens of faith' by a secondary school headmaster at a
school near Paris in 1989. Although he was seeking to target
Jews observing the Sabbath, as well as Algerian girls wearing a headscarf, it was the headscarf that attracted national
attention.[39] The public debate, overwhelmingly in favour of
the banning of the headscarf, encouraged the French government to ban it from schools in 2004 and in May 2010, the
Government passed a resolution banning the 'Islamic veil'.
As this is written, legislation has been passed to ban full
veiling in public with a penalty of euro symbol 150 for the
wearer and up to a Euro symbol 15,000 fine, or prison term,
for the spouse of partner who forced them to wear it.[40]

The reason for such extreme actions are not difficult to
find: the French state has had a long history of struggle with
the Church over its role in public life and one might argue
therefore that the entrée of Muslims into the state in significant numbers has simply broadened that ongoing secular-
religious conflict in a changing demographic situation.[41]

However, this logical conclusion has been challenged by the American Professor of Anthropology John Bowen, who was in France during the passage of the 2004 legislation. Rather than laying all explanation of French reaction at the feet of *laïcité*, Bowen points out that the French state has funded a significant number of mosque-building projects and further argues that the absence of the term from the important French law on religion in 1905 as evidence to suggest that a different catalyst needs to be sought out.[42] Instead, Bowen argues that it is the deeper underlying concern about terrorism and immigration as a threat to the 'French way of life' that lies at the heart of the matter.[43] Essentially therefore, Bowen is arguing that the concerns of France mirror those of the rest of the politicians and public figures in the UK and elsewhere in Western Europe.

> What ensures there were tempestuous debates about what *laïcité* should be and how Muslims ought to act not in the light of a firm legal cultural framework, but in the light of a the disappearing sense of certitude about what France is, was, and should be.[44]

The theme is a common one and the sense of rapid, perhaps uncontrolled change is palpable in the growing separation amongst French society.

> The growth of 'communalism', at the expense of social mixing, the increasing influence of international 'Islamism' in France and the denigration of women in the poor suburbs.[45]

Bowen's contribution to the analysis of French concerns around the veil is valuable both in relation to encouraging a more refined discourse of the issue for academics and commentators alike, yet his observations do miss some of the issues that are rigorously analysed in articles such as Cécile Labourde's in the *Journal of Political Philosophy*.[46]

> ... *laïcité* offers a distinctively republican interpretation of the requirements of liberal neutrality, which notably emerged as a response to the bitter conflicts between French republican institutions and the Catholic Church. In broad terms, republican *laïcité* endorses a more expansive conception of the public sphere than political liberalism, as well as a thicker construal of the 'public selves' which make up the citizens of the republic. So, crucially, state schools are seen to be part of the public sphere and pupils, as potential citizens, are required to exercise restraint in the expression of their religious beliefs.[47]

Patrick Weil has given the French integration debate the title *'nouvelle synthèse républicaine'*.[48] Its essential character is the remarkable continuity that has been seen from socialists through to the moderate right, both politicians and commentators, in articulating what the goals of integration should be in the French context. In particular, two sets of documents formed the core of the debate, each of which were the results of two committees which contained both lawyers and historians who focused around the question of what it meant to be French both at the time and into the future.[49] The commission asked over 100 prominent French persons from many and varied walks of life these two questions and the collected responses were published in a report, which was titled after the questions themselves.[50] The report's conclusions were followed up in 1990 by a commission that was tasked with examining the mechanics and processes of integration. Their conclusions, as with the previous commission focused around an historical under-standing of France as republican, coming together as a nation under the Revolutionary Wars and defining, in that period, what it meant to be a citizen within clearly deline-ated national boundaries.[51] Thus, France could call itself identifiably French from that period in much the same way as British did in the same period, according to Colley. In this context therefore, immigrants to France become 'inser-tions' and as such are seen as having to adopt the 'French way of life' in a way that is not a natural outworking of British integrationist philosophy. Therefore, the institution of the French 'Muslim Council' (now largely discredited) could be seen as an attempt to create a form of Islam in France that conformed to 'French life'. Indeed, the Council's creation gave the Interior Ministry the right in law, at least in theory, to remove any persons who might cause trouble religiously.[52] This has been the framework within which French integrationist debate has taken place and is the underlying cause of their early move to ban headscarves.[53]

That said, however, whilst the French are keen to assert the veil ban in an attempt to preserve 'the French way of life', this has not stopped them encouraging the adoption of shari'a finance products as a way of boosting cash flow into the country. According to *The Economist*, the French govern-ment had been taking an active interest in the pursuit of shari'a finance products.[54] Nicholas Sarkozy's attachment of an amendment to an unrelated piece of legislation that opened the way for shari'a finance products, particularly the sukuk bonds, has caused a major row between the political establishment and French financiers.

Therefore, although the French concerns with integration have a similar look and feel to those in Britain, the French

have wedded themselves to a certain construct of identity
that allows little room for natural evolution.

Summary

The decades since the end of the European Empires have
seen Europeans reflect in earnest upon their values and identities in a rapidly changing world. This has been fuelled by
both the shift to trans-continental organisations and vastly
improved communication, along with a growing concern
about the effects of immigration at a time when identity
is largely undefined and, until recently, little talked about.
The outworking of the reformist engagement in the Muslim
diaspora has forced Western governments and opinion-
formers to confront the issue of identity systematically once
again. In this context, the place of shari'a within this new
milieu has become the catalyst issue when discussing such
questions, just as it was in the days of the European Empires.
The reason is that shari'a, with its religio-legal structure,
stands as an obvious alternative to western legal norms. As
such, it becomes a metaphor for all that is apparently "alien"
to western culture about immigrants generally and highlights the "otherness" at a time when western politicians and
commentators are struggling to articulate who "we" are

* * *

Having outlined the current state of the debate in Britain,
and France, the final chapter will now draw together the
discussion in a series of observations.

CONCLUSIONS

In 2001, the second edition of Adrian Favell's *Philosophies of Integration: Immigration and the Idea of Citizenship in France and Britain*, was published.[1] It set itself the task of reviewing the methodology and approaches of the two states in relation to cultural, racial and religious issues and outlined the key area of contention:

> ... there has been a spate of public and intellectual debate across the Western world about the meaning and content of citizenship. Everybody is talking about citizenship because these problems pose very fundamental questions about the unifying values, cohesion and identity of liberal democratic states.[2]

For Favell, the question of citizenship in an era of immigration goes to the heart of the burgeoning question of developing identity in a post-colonial era. The aim of Favell's study therefore has been to measure the success or otherwise of integration policies in these two states as a way of analysing the strength of democratic principles in the current era. This is made explicit further on in the book's first chapter.

> ... there ought to be a way of reading the policy challenges that ethnic dilemmas pose – and the applied

solutions found by different liberal democratic states –
as a kind of litmus test of the nature of liberal democracy generally. The reaction of liberal democracies to
these problems will reveal the grounds upon which
they may fairly claim to have political legitimacy as
tolerant, open or pluralist states.[3]

Whilst the study has value, one would suggest that it
puts an unrealistic onus upon the role of the 'host state' to
adapt to the immigrant, leaving aside completely the role
and desire on the part of the immigrant to adapt to their
adopted land. This book has aimed to encapsulate both
sides of this complex issue as it relates to one particular
group. What follows now therefore is a summary of the key
findings from the diverse facets of the argument that will
lead to the observations and recommendations that close
the body of the book.

Summary of Key Findings

Muslim Perceptions

The question of 'citizenship' and 'identity' for Muslims
has undergone something of a traumatic change over the
past 150 years, although the relationship between Muslim
and non-Muslim could be said to have been under fairly
constant renegotiation since the time of the Constitution
of Madina itself. The theological and historical discussions in the early chapters demonstrated that the place
of shari'a for Muslims defines the nature of a Muslim's
relationship between their faith and their government.
Shari'a is indivisible from doctrinal Islam insofar as it is a

pathway along which the adherent must pass in order to stand any hope of passing successfully through the Day of Reckoning and into Paradise. The fact of its gradual emancipation from its central role in the life of the Islamic state as the nature of the Empire changed over time does not alter its fundamental importance in the practice of Islam for practicing Muslims in any geopolitical situation. One might say therefore that, whilst the nature of what it means to be an 'Islamic state' has undergone considerable metamorphosis, the status of shari'a itself has remained unaltered. The central issue for the Muslim in a modern minority situation is therefore predicated upon their understanding of the place of shari'a and ummah in a community setting rather than upon its validity as a system. For that reason, in the debates in Chapters Three and Four concerning the nature of the ummah and the possibility of loyalty to a non-Muslim authority, the argument is framed within the principle that adherence to shari'a in some form must continue.

In essence therefore, when a Muslim is being asked their opinions in surveys about the place of shari'a the respondents are revealing what they understand to be true about the relationship between their faith and the state. The concerns and concepts that they attempt to engage with are precisely those that are now being examined by Muslims all over the world and as such, provide a valuable insight for the ongoing discussions that have taken place in the wake of the London bombings and 9/11.

Within that context, there are several clear patterns that have emerged from the study now completed: firstly and most obviously, is the clear divide on the subcontinent in the way that the reformers wished to identify themselves. These fed into the solutions for Islamic 'malaise' that they were advocating, for, there were those such as Maududi, Parwez, al-Afghani, Iqbal and Abduh who saw themselves as Muslims first and foremost and therefore chose to advocate a universalist solution in the shape of an 'Islamic state' however broadly or narrowly defined, based around what they characterised as the 'early ummah' (but should be more accurately described as the early Muslim Empire). It is a concept that is not confined to any one sect of Islam as was shown by the inclusion of Shi'as, Sunnis and Sufis in the debates.

One could argue that this ideology could be characterised as Arab-centric rather than universalist given the cultural roots of the faith, but, quibbling aside, the fact remains that the intention was for universalist appeal, rather than pan-Arab cultural imperialism.

On the other hand, there were those such as Sayyid Ahmad Khan, Mujeeb and ul-Haq who identified themselves as 'Indian Muslims' and were keen to propose a road to Islamic resurgence based upon the particular line of evolution undergone by Islam on the subcontinent. This was a regeneration of faith leading to social participation, rather than power, although their final goals differed somewhat.

Their approach could be seen as a more positive engagement with the society and problems that modern Muslims found themselves in at the time of their writing. As such, they were focused less on quoting the Qur'an, Hadith, Sunnah or fiqh in the course of their analysis and advice, but rather on providing what they felt to be practicable suggestions alongside interpretations of Islamic writings in order to encourage Muslims to be Muslims in the situations they were in. As for the need to alter the 'world order' of the time through trying to create a geographically defined pan-Islamic state, they made no attempt to engage in a struggle which, they believed, was not even to be contemplated insofar as it involved disloyalty to their current rulers. This was something that Sayyid Ahmad Khan particularly could not countenance, even though he vigorously defended Islam from outside attack and strove to see a resurgent religion once again participating actively in the nation.

Khan himself differs in outlook from the more modern 'pragmatic philosophers', failing to engage in the kinds of debates that others such as ul-Haq and Husain did, as they devoted pages trying to define the extent of Muslim loyalty to faith and state. Instead, he longed to see an intelligent, articulate and identifiable Muslim community actively participating in the affairs of the nation, integrated and trusted by the wider national culture and so able to have a voice. There was no need, for him to split hairs over dual loyalties, as the issue simply did not exist for him. He was an Indian and Muslim, and proud to be both.

Faruki's ability to identify Muslims as separate would probably have pleased Khan and he would have been all for Husain and ul-Haq's urging of Muslim participation, though perhaps not the tortuous arguments about 'secularism', its definition and dangers, that they articulated with it.

As for Maududi, it was clear even from his translation and exegesis of Q4:59 that his sentiments were very different to those of Khan. But it would be simply wrong to say that this was due entirely to the changed historical circumstances in which he lived, for his thinking was similar to that of al-Afghani who lived and was in India, in precisely the time period of Sayyid Ahmad Khan. What else could account for the different conclusions? Historical setting, the ending of the Caliphate and the move towards Pakistan must certainly be taken into account, but above all it was a desire, not just to reinterpret Islamic scripture, but to rely on it completely, ignoring the rich Islamic heritage in India itself that drove him along such a different path to that of Khan. For Maududi, the idea of an Islamic state, physically existent, may not have been a possibility, but it was something that should be strived for because it would, according to him, allow Muslims to be 'fully Muslim' once again. To Maududi, a Muslim required the state as well as the individual to come under the direct sovereignty of Allah in the manner he describes in *Islamic Law and Constitution*. That said, he struggles to define what constitutes an 'Islamic state'.

Whatever the inconsistencies and basic problems of accurate definition that undermine Maududi's position, he is consistent in his universalism. It is a universalism based on a perceived requirement to reflect the 'Oneness' of God embodied in the concept of 'tawhid' as a geopolitical reality. In this, al-Afghani and Badis join him, though Muhammad Ali and Muhammad Iqbal expressed similar ideas but fell short of the global view that these expressed. These last two showed the same desire as Maududi and the others, but displayed a pragmatic streak that was incongruous, yet revealed the politician in them.

The second point that emerged very clearly from the survey was a lack of any definitive direction for Muslims as to what the ummah should be in practice. Given the points already highlighted above, this is not surprising. However, even leaving them aside for a moment and accepting the 'visionary separatists' model of the late Muhammadan and classical ummah as a geopolitical entity, definable within geographical boundaries, they are not able to satisfactorily detail how such a model is transferable to the modern times, particularly when it comes to defining the level in society that such an ummah would work.

The debates in the subcontinent and North Africa can therefore be seen as part of the process of a transition from what might be described as 'Imperial Islam' to 'ijtihad Islam'. In this light, the two groups identified (the 'visionary separatists' and the 'pragmatic philosophers') are indicative of the desire of reformers to adapt to the new world or to reject it for a 'purer model'.

In order, therefore, to resolve this divergence, Muslims need to decide on whether they want to build on what they have already built, or tear it down and start again. They will also need to decide whether they will do this as one body, or as regional groups. In doing this, Muslims in the Western world will get to the heart of the underlying issue: to define what the ummah is truly to be. In that context, the changing nature of what it means to be a citizen in any state is also significant, for, as has been seen, it has already gone through significant metamorphosis in the light of expediency. In this innovative spirit, where abrogation and apostasy doctrines are, by necessity, subsumed within pragmatism, the adaption of Muslims to this new reality becomes possible if a willingness to work with the mindset offered by the pragmatic philosophers is adopted.

The revivalism that is everywhere evident in the writings of the various Muslim ideologues can be seen as a process of engaging with present reality and in so doing, choosing to accept it, or reject it. In this context, the nature of 'citizenship' for a Muslim living under non-Muslim rule as well as the role of the ummah and shari'a in this minority context have become the central theological issues for Muslims living in Britain, France or the rest of the Western world.

For this reason, the arguments over the place of shari'a within any Western society can be seen as a catalyst for the wider discussion on what 'doing Islam' looks like in an alien environment. The discussions in Chapters One Three, Four and Five have shown that any argument for the 'necessity' for having shari'a incorporated into Western civil codes has no theological foundation and that the use of shari'a as a political device can be divisive rather than constructive.

As things stand at present, it seems unlikely that there will be significant support for the formal incorporation of the personal and family elements of shari'a into either French or British society. That said, both governments have sought to open the doors to shari'a finance products that could produce, in the long-term, a far greater influence for shari'a in Western society than has previously been seen.

The political impact of shari'a aside, Muslims in the UK, France and the rest of the Western world face the choice of constructive identity-building or regressive identity reconstruction. Citizenship, even within the Muslim world, has had multiple definitions over the centuries and Muslim communities have an opportunity to write a new chapter in that evolving narrative.

The Public Polity in France and Britain

It is clear that the British and French approached their imperial possessions with a rather different set of governing principles. The desire to extract economic gain was the same for both, and both struggled with groups that opposed them, sometimes cracking down on them with great ferocity as in the 1857–58 Indian rebellion for the British or the Kabylia rebellion in French Algeria. However, whilst the British shied away from a policy of cultural assimilation, the French threw considerable resources into making Algeria an integral part of France until the late nineteenth century.

One might argue that ultimately, neither policy was successful insofar as both the British in India and the French in Algeria were ejected from their respective holdings by popular anti-colonial movements. This observation, however, whilst not inaccurate, does not encapsulate the nuances of the narrative, for both states at differing points in their colonial periods did attempt to accommodate the Muslim populations in order to help maintain the peace and, in Britain's case, help them politically in relation to the *Indian National Congress*. Of course, the two situations were different insofar as the Muslim population of India was a minority, whereas the Muslim population of Algeria constituted virtually the whole population. Nevertheless, taking these situational differences into account, the research did unearth some fascinating dynamics within both milieus that are worth highlighting before the conclusions are drawn.

Firstly, the British government was either naive or culpable in relation to allowing the *Shariat Act* passed unopposed through the Legislative Assembly and onto the statute books in spite of the very clear advice concerning the implications of the Act from officials from many religious backgrounds and none. Muslims such as Jinnah and Ali had chosen an issue that had the appearance of progressive policymaking as a vehicle for rallying a previously disparate Muslim community behind a single leadership team. That team successfully manoeuvred dissenting Muslim voices out of the frame and was, from then on, empowered to negotiate on behalf of an Indian ummah in a way that it had not been before. If this was an example of the British using Muslims to break the momentum of the Independence Movement then one might argue that it was a clever piece of politicking but also a substantial causal factor in the communal violence that accompanied the creation of Pakistan at one and the same time.[4]

The case study also made clear that there was a substantial lack of understanding of the terms being used and their implications. Nowhere is this seen more clearly than in the lack of definition sought over the term 'Shariat', when the Bill was going through the house. Certainly individuals, Muslim, Christian and Hindu all questioned this wording to the extent that it was amended in the final act, but one would argue that the lack of proper questioning represented a failure to protect the citizens under its care. It is important to note therefore that for any government engaging with cross-cultural issues, particularly ones which will lead to legislative Acts, appropriate understanding of the terms are vital. Frequently, this will involve expert analysis from several differing perspectives in order to ensure that no one sectarian view is being advocated.

This dovetails into the third point: the belief in a single, mass, homogeneous viewpoint. Time and again, those Muslims who were advocating on behalf of the Bill were at pains to argue that there was mass Muslim support behind it and, as such, those that were advocating on its behalf were indeed speaking on behalf of that overwhelming voice. Clearly, there was evidence to the contrary even in the words of the advocates themselves who mentioned that the Bill was necessary to unite a community that was currently not united. Nevertheless, the perception of a single community speaking with a united voice appears to have been successfully created.

The development of the *Code Morand* showed that, even in a context where Islam is the only faith of the ruled, there are enormous practical difficulties in attempting to fuse Western legal thinking with Islamic religio-legal theory insofar as the fundamental premises are different. For, in the Western codes the people are sovereign and the legal text is changeable as necessary, when circumstance dictates, by the representatives of the people themselves. In shari'a, the rulings of the codes are established as doctrine as well as legal precedent and are seen as immutable and unchangeable unless by the ruling of a scholar or practicing Muslim jurist. By incorporating shari'a into Western legal code therefore, sovereignty in judicial affairs passes from the people to the clerics.

At their root therefore, the discussions around both the development of *Anglo-Muhammadan Law* more broadly and the *Code Morand* in its case study demonstrated that the corpus of shari'a as a whole was not compatible with Western civil codes. This study has shown that, in the context of shari'a theology, the question of whether a fusion of Western civil codes and shari'a can and should be attempted becomes fundamental. Clearly some think it can be, but the British and French case studies would suggest that the task is fraught with such difficulty as to render the effort unnecessary, especially when there is no theological necessity for it.

Conclusions

The issue of citizenship and minority status for Muslims is a delicate and fundamental one. It is bound up in an understanding of 'identity' and the nature of the ummah in a post-Muslim imperial world. Above all, it is bound up with a conscious choice that the Muslim communities in France and Britain need to make for themselves: the choice to build something new that is free from the constraints of dogma, perhaps feeling free to develop new dogma under a reconstituted doctrine of abrogation in which the necessity of change (which already exists in shari'a) can fuse with abrogation to create the space to go forward towards developing French, British or European Islam. The Swiss scholar Tariq Ramadan has already explored this process and it seems appropriate that the new generations of Muslims in Europe should be able to write their own chapter in this evolving narrative.

For the policymakers and opinion-formers in both France and Britain, the central issue concerns the necessity for shari'a and the type of accommodation that is felt to be required. The practice of shari'a is absolutely required for a Muslim to progress in the afterlife, yet the question of whether this must have the force of state law behind it is a different consideration entirely. Chapters Three and Four showed that there were many differences of opinion amongst Muslims themselves concerning the nature of the relationship between the state and shari'a, which centred around what is understood to be the nature of the ummah itself. What is clear is that creating a place for shari'a within the law of a non-Muslim state, particularly if its terms and parameters are not minutely specified, risks elevating a group of Muslim lawyers, jurists, politicians or scholars to be the representatives of a community that might not want to be identified with them.

Muslim communities in both Britain and France (as elsewhere) are not homogenous, and experience over the last decade has shown that there is no single Muslim who can speak with authority on their behalf. Incorporating shari'a into the law of the land gives opportunity for that to happen.

NOTES

Introduction

1. Online version of the *EB*, http://library.eb.co.uk/eb/article-9082718-?query=citizenship&ct= accessed 2 June 2010.
2. For a deeper analysis of the ethnic and sectarian populations of the UK, see P. Lewis, *Young British and Muslim. London*: Continuum, 2007.
3. The French Interior Ministry in *l'Islam dans la République* published figures from 2000, giving ethnic breakdown. Haut Conseil à l'intégration, November 2000. p26.
4. With so many excellent histories already written, there seemed little point providing another apart from the need to provide the briefest of historical contexts for the debates.
5. This wider context will be discussed in Section Four of Chapter Seven as examples of practice in other states frequently become the tools for modern policymakers.
6. A. Favell, *Philosophies of Integration and the Idea of Citizenship in France and Britain (Migration, Minorities and Citizenship Series)*. 2nd ed. Basingstoke: Palgrave, 2001. Favell's work will be discussed in the final chapter.
7. K. Moore, *The Unfamiliar Abode: Islamic Law in the United States and Britain,* New York: Oxford University Press USA, 2010; W. B. Hallaq, *Shari'a: Theory, Practice and Transformations,* Cambridge: CUP, 2009.

8. D. Hiro, *Islamic Fundamentalism*. London: Paladin, 1988; G.W. Choudhury, *Islam and the Modern Muslim World*. London: Scorpion Publishing Ltd, 1993; F. Burgat, *Face to Face with Political Islam*. London: I.B.Tauris, 2003. cf. E. Burke III, and I. Lapidus, (ed.) *Islam, Politics and Social Movements*. London: I.B.Tauris, 1988; R. Schulze, *A Modern History of the Islamic World*. London: I.B.Tauris, 2000.

9. I. Ahmed, *The Concept of an Islamic State, An Analysis of the Ideological Controversy in Pakistan*. London: Frances Pinter [Publishers], 1987.

10. A.M. Zaidi, *Evolution of Muslim Political Thought in India. Volume 1, From Syed to the Emergence of Jinnah*. New Delhi: Indian Institute of Applied Political Research, 1975.

11. B.D. Metcalf, *Islamic Revival in British India: Deoband, 1860–1900*. Princeton: Princeton University Press, 1982.

12. S.H.H. Navdi, *Islamic Resurgent Movements in the Indo-Pak Subcontinent during the Eighteenth and Nineteenth centuries: A Critical Analysis*. Durban: Academia, the Centre for Islamic, Near and Far Eastern Studies, Planning publication, 1987.

13. R. Ahmed, (ed.), *Understanding the Bengal Muslims*. New Delhi: OUP, 2001.

14. Examples would be: M. Hasan, *Islam and Indian Nationalism: Reflections on Abdul Kalam Azad*. New Delhi: Manohar, 1992; D. Pandey, *The Role of the Muslim League in National Politics*. Delhi: Tiwari,1991; K.H. Ansari, *The Emergence of Socialist Thought among North Indian Muslims (1917–1947)*. Lahore: Book Traders, 1990.

15. S. McDonough, *Muslim Ethics and Modernity: A Comparative Study of the Ethical Thought of Sayyid Ahmed Khan and Maulana Maududi*. Montreal: Wilfred Laurier University Press, 1984; A.A. Rizvi, *Shah Wali-Allah and His Times: A Study of Eighteenth Century Islam, Politics and Society in India*. Canberra: Ma'rifat, 1980.

16. J.M.S. Baljon, *Reforms and Religious Ideas of Sayyid Ahmed Khan*. Leiden: E.J. Brill, 1949.

17. Academics such as Professor Jonathan Fox have also spent considerable time explaining the necessity of faith perspective in policymaking (Professor Fox's particular field has been Foreign Policy). Too often, policymakers examining the Israel-Palestine question, or the Kashmir issue, have ignored the theological aspects of the issues. See also S. Oliver-Dee, *The Caliphate Question: British Government and Islamic Governance*. Lanham, MD: Rowman and Littlefield, 2009.

18. N. Gonzalez, *The Sunni-Shi'a Conflict: Understanding Sectarian Violence in the Middle East.* Anaheim, CA: Nortia Books, 2009.
19. V. Nasr, *The Shia Revival: How Conflicts Within Islam Will Shape the Future.* London: W.W. Norton and Company, 2007.
20. In the early part of 2010, with the instability and toppling of many Middle Eastern regimes, the struggles of the ruling family of Bahrain against its active Shi'a population has featured prominently.

Chapter 1   State, Citizenship and the Law: Islamic Theology and History

1. Oliver-Dee, *The Caliphate Question,* Appendix A: See also the work of Bernard Lewis, Patricia Crone, Wilfred Madelung, William Montgomery Watt, Anthony Black, Henri Laoust and Ann Lambton.
2. A.A. an-Na'im, *Islam and the Secular State: Negotiating the Future of Shari'a.* Cambridge, MA: Harvard University Press, 2008.
3. When an-Na'im cites the Qur'an for example, he cites it as a book, rather than giving specific ayahs.
4. A glance at the material found on the Hizb-ut-Tahrir portal www.khalifah.eu would give a good entré on to the essential doctrines of this political theory for the Sunnis, whilst those wishing to understand the modernist global Imamate doctrine could read chapter 22 of Mansoor Moaddel and Kamran Talattof's *Modernist and Fundamentalist Debates in Islam: A Reader.* New York and Basingstoke: Palgrave Macmillan, 2002. The chapter is a translation of Khomeini's 'The Nature of the Islamic State and the Qualifications of the Head of State'.
5. T. Fatah, *Chasing a Mirage: The Tragic Illusion of an Islamic State.* Toronto: Wiley, 2008.
6. Oliver-Dee, *Caliphate Question.* pp. 16–22.
7. It is accepted that the period of the Umayyad Caliphate has been characterised as Arab imperialism rather than the 'Islamic imperialism' instituted following the successful Abbasid coup of 743–750. See I. Lapidus, *A History of Islamic Societies.* Cambridge: CUP, 2002. pp. 19–22.
8. See R.B. Serjeant, 'The Constitution of Medina.' *Islamic Quarterly,* Volume 8 (1964).
9. The exact nature of this 'state' is contested amongst scholars, however Patricia Crone's *Medieval Islamic Political Thought.* Edinburgh: Edinburgh

University Press, 2004 offers an excellent analysis of the developing Islamic Constitutionalism. See also A. Lambton, *State and Government in Medieval Islam.* Oxford: OUP, 1981; W.M. Watt, *The Formative Period of Islamic Thought,* Edinburgh: Edinburgh University Press, 1973.

10. Some of this is discussed later in Chapters Five and Six, but it is worthwhile flagging up the contributions of H. Gibb, *The Formative Period of Islamic Thought*, Edinburgh: Edinburgh University Press, 1973; T.W. Arnold, *The Caliphate,* with a Final Chapter by S. Haim. London: Routledge and Keegan Paul, 1965.

11. See M. Prawdin and G.Thailiand: *The Mongol Empire: Its Rise and Legacy.* New Brunswick, NJ: Transaction Publishers, 2006. p436.

12. H. Janin and A. Kahlmeyer, *Islamic Law: the Sharia from Muhammad's Time to the Present.* Jefferson, NC: McFarland and Co. Publishers, 2007. p79. Ibn Taymiyya was a complex theologian. See Ibn Taymiyya, *Kitab al-Iman (Book of Faith)* Trans. S. H. Al-Ani, Shadia Ahmad Tel. Indiana: Iman Publishing House, 2009; Y. Rapoport and S. Ahmed, *Ibn Taymiyya and His Times.* Oxford: OUP, 2010.

13. K.H. Karpat, *The Politization of Islam. Reconstructing Identity, State, Faith and Community in the Late Ottoman Period.* Oxford: OUP, 2001. pp19–31.

14. B. Lewis, *The Emergence of Modern Turkey.* 3rd ed. New York, London: OUP, 2002. pp71–83. See also A. Ozcan, *Pan-Islamism: Indian Muslims, the Ottoman Empire and Britain, (1877–1924).* Leiden, New York, Koln: Brill, 1997; A. Palmer, *The Decline and Fall of the Ottoman Empire.* London: John Murray, 1992; C. Kinkel, *Osman's Dream: The Story of the Ottoman Empire 1300–1923.* London: John Murray, 2005.

15. Kedourie, E., *The Chatham House Version and other Middle Eastern Studies.* London: Weidenfeld and Nicholson, 1970. pp85–91.

16. See Oliver-Dee, *Caliphate Question.* pp126–140.

17. Ozcan, *Pan-Islamism.* p36.

18. The Caliphate had become a major rallying point for the Indian Independence Movement of the 1920s. See N.M Qureshi, *Pan-Islam in British Indian Politics: A Study of the Khilafat Movement, 1918–1924.* Leiden: Brill, 1999. pp88–173. See also A. C. Niemeijer, *The Khalifat Movement in India 1919–1924.* s-Gravenhage: Nederlandsche Boek – en Steendrukkerij and Smits, 1972.

19. In many respects, this would be a natural place for a discussion of Apostacy as treason in theology and political theory. However, this complex issue would need the kind of in-depth treatment that is not

available here. Therefore, those wishing to explore the issue further should go to A. Saeed and H. Saeed, *Freedom in Religion, Apostasy in Islam.* Aldershot: Ashgate Publishing, 2004, or R. Peters and G.J.J. de Vries, 'Apostasy in Islam', *Die Welt des Islams,* New Series, Vol. 17, Issue 1/4 (1976–1977), pp1–25.

20. U. Davis, *Citizenship and the State.* Reading, MA: Ithaca Press, 1997. pp4–6. See also B. Lewis, *The Political Language of Islam.* Chicago and London: University of Chicago Press, 1988. p61; M. Durie, *The Third Choice: Islam, Dhimmitude and Freedom.* n.p: Deror Books, 2010.

21. Davis, *Citizenship.* p7

22. H. Wehr, *Arab-English Dictionary,* 4th ed., J. Cowen (ed.), Urbana, IL: Spoken Language Services, 1994. p109. Wehr enlarges upon the definition thus: 'subordination, subjection; subordinations, dependency; state of being subject, of pertaining to or belonging to, affiliation, citizenship, nationality.' On the Kurdish party see S.N. Eisenstadt and L. Roniger, 'Patron–Client Relations as a Way of Structuring Social Exchange'. *Comparative Studies in Society and History,* Vol. 22, Issue 1 (1980). pp42–77.

23. See M. al-Rasheed, 'The Shia of Saudi Arabia: A Minority in Search of Cultural Authenticity', *British Journal of Middle Eastern Studies,* Vol. 25, No. 1 (May 1998), pp121–138.

24. Wehr, *Dictionary.* p167.

25. Davis, *Citizenship.* p7. Israel is one country that has this two-tiered system. 'Muwatana' itself is based upon the Arabic word for 'state' – 'al-watan', although the term has been used with different definitions by many of the Muslim reformers such as Qutb and Abduh See Lewis, *Political Language.* pp63–64. In the modern period, the *Universal Islamic Declaration of Human Rights* has sought to enshrine the principles of Islamic citizenship in a global context. The UIDHR has both an Arabic and English version, which vary. See A.E. Mayer *Islam and Human Rights: Traditions and Politics.* Boulder, CO: Westview Press, 1999. p260. Another brief commentary on the different versions can be found in E. Bems, *Human Rights: Universality and Diversity.* Leiden: Martinus Lindhoff Publishers, 2001. p256.

26. J. Schacht, *An Introduction to Islamic Law.* Oxford: Clarendon Press, 1964, p1.

27. D.B MacDonald, *The Development of Muslim Theology, Jurisprudence and Constitutional Theory.* Exeter: Wheaton and Co. Ltd, 1902 pp66–67.

28. Lewis, *Political Language.* p19.

29. E. Lane, *Arabic-English Lexicon, Book I, Vol. 5.* Beruit: Libraire du Liban, 1968. First Published London: 1881. pp1534–1536.

30. Ibid.

31. See, for example, Q3:26, Q2:255 and Q28:88.

32. *The Holy Quran,* Yusuf Ali Translation, Birmingham: IPCI, Islamic Vision, 1999. p2–3.

33. Ibid. p1780.

34. See Oliver-Dee, *The Caliphate Question.* pp 15–17.

35. N. Calder, 'Shari'a' *EI2,* Vol. 8. p322.

36. Ibid.

37. Penrice, *Dictionary.* p76.

38. In his section on 'The Origins of Shari'ah', Mohammed Kamali also discusses Q45.18. He transliterates shaî'atan rather than sharî'atin. M.H. Kamali, *Shari'ah Law: An Introduction.* Oxford: Oneworld, 2008. p2.

39. Ibid. Kamali's characterization of the nature of this 'desire' as 'whimsical' is not immediately observable in Quar'anic dictionaries, but the transitory nature of one against the eternal solidity of the other is a useful contrast to make, even if it does nothing more than shine a light into an understanding of Islamic law vis-à-vis other codes.

40. 'The community shall remain on the shari'a as long as it does occur in it three things …' A. Ibn Hanbal. *Al-Musnad.* Vol 2. A. Shakir and H. Ahmad al-Zayn (eds.). Cairo: Dar al-Hadith, 1995. p183.

41. Calder, 'Shari'a', *EI2,* Vol. 8, p321.

42. Schacht, *Introduction,* pp15–16; K. Viktor, *Between God and Sultan: A History of Islamic Law.* London: Hurst and Company, 2005. p20.

43. In his book on the development of Islamic law, Knut Victor points out that delineating clear the definable streams of fiqh that this section describes is somewhat misleading as the grouping were not as clear-cut as is made out here and in other works. However, given the focus of this book, rather than spending extensive time picking apart this detail, the broad-stroke concepts and principles described here are felt to be accurate in relation to the purpose of this book. See K. Victor, *Between God and the Sultan: A History of Islamic Law.* London: Hurst and Company, 2005. p94.

44. Statistically, the overwhelming majority of Muslims in the UK come from the Mirpur region in Pakistani Kashmir. Although this group are predominately sufi in their faith, their shari'a is Hanafi. See P. Lewis, *Islamic Britain: Religion, Politics, and Identity among British*

Muslims, London: I.B. Tauris, 2003; K.H Ansari, *Muslims in Britain,* London: Minority Rights Group, 2002: S. R. Ameli, *Globalization, Americanization and British Muslim Identity;* London: Islamic College for Advanced Studies Press, 2002; R. Ballard, *Popular Islam in Northern Pakistan and Its Reconstruction in Urban Britain* on CASAS site December 2004, http://www.art.man.ac.uk/CASAS/pdfpapers/popularislam.pdf and R. Geaves, *The Sufis of Britain: An Exploration of Muslim Identity.* Cardiff: Cardiff Academic Press, 2000.

45. A translation of the brief work was done by William Montgomery Watt. *Free Will and Predestination in Early Islam.* Chicago: Luzac, 1948.
46. See Oliver-Dee, *The Caliphate Question.* p51.
47. Trans. M. Khadduri, *The Islamic Law of Nations: Shaybani's Siyar.* Baltimore, MD: John Hopkins Press, 1996.
48. Ibid. 21–23. See also J. Rahmen and S.C. Bureau (eds.), *Religion, Human Rights and International Law: A Critical Examination of Islamic State Practices.* Leiden: Martinus Nijhoff Publishers, 2007. pp81–114.
49. M. Shatzmiller (ed.), *Nationalism and Minority Identities in Islamic Societies.* Quebec City: McGill University Press, 2005. p16. See also A.El Fadl, 'Islamic Law and Muslim Minorities: The Juristic Discourse on Muslim Minorities from the Second/Eighth to the Eleventh/Seventeenth Centuries'. *Islamic Law and Society,* Vol. 1, No. 2 (1994), pp141–187.
50. Y. Dutton, *The Origins of Islamic Law: The Qur'an, The Muwatta, and the Madinan 'amal.* London: Curzon, 1999. p181.
51. Imam Malik Ibn Anas, *al-Muwatta,* Book 55: Book of Allegiance. Trans. M. Rahimuddin. New Delhi: Kitab Bhavan, 2000. p281.
52. M. Litvak, *Middle Eastern Societies and the West: Accommodation or Clash of Civilization?* Tel Aviv: Tel Aviv University, 2006. p204.
53. See discussion on Q4:59 in Oliver-Dee, *The Caliphate Question.* pp42–51.
54. Watt suggests that the majority of the ayahs that contain the phrase 'Obey Allah and Obey the Messenger ...' were given during the period of Muhammad's growing political power in Madina. Watt, *Muhammad.* p33.
55. A Maududi, *Towards Understanding the Quran* (trans. and ed. Z Ansari) Leicester: The Islamic Foundation, 1989. p50.
56. A full set of translations, as well as the original Arabic in transliterated form is to be found in Oliver-Dee, *The Caliphate Question.* pp42–45.
57. M. Asad, *The Message of the Qur'an: Translated and Explained.* Gibraltar: Dar al-Andalus, 1980. p115.

58. R. Bell, *The Qur'an Translated*, Volume I. London: T and T Clark, 1937. pXIX, and G. Sale, *The Koran Translated into English from the Original Arabic.* London: Frederick Warne and Co. Ltd, 1764. pp14–15.

59. A sample of anti-Islamic polemical material from the eighth to the sixteenth centuries can be found in J.V. Tolan, (ed.) *Medieval Christian Perceptions of Islam. NewYork* and London, 1996.

60. Sale, *Koran.* p81.

61. Bell, *Qur'an.* p122.

62. Ibid.

63. Maududi, *Qur'an.* p51.

64. Ibid. p52.

65. Ibid. p52.

66. S. Qutb, *In the Shade of the Qur'an, Volume III, Surah 4* (trans. and ed. A. Salahi and A. Shamis). Leicester: The Islamic Foundation, 2001. p192.

67. Ibid. p192.

68. A.Ali, *The Holy Qur'an, Text, Translation and Edited.* Isfahan: Tahriki, Tarsih Quran Inc, 1982. p382 and, S. Berrigan (ed.) *An Enlightening Commentary into the Light of the Holy Qur'an by a Group of Muslim Scholars.* Isfahan: Imam Ali Islamic Research Center, 2000. p75.

69. Imain and Scholars, *Holy Quran.* p76.

70. Ibid. p76, Point 11.

71. For an excellent description and analysis of the organic nature of the 'Muslim state', see M. Rodinson, *Mohammad* (Trans. from French by A. Carter). London: Penguin, 1961. p215.

Chapter 2   Anglo-French Imperial Interaction with Islam: Historical Contextualisation

1. See C. Finkel, *Osman's Dream: The Story of the Ottoman Empire 1300–1923.* London: John Murray, 2005. pp221–223.

2. Histories and views about on issues and event in both contexts, however A. Black, *The History of Islamic Political Thought.* Edinburgh: Edinburgh University Press, 2001. pp56–62 provides an excellent overview from the Muslim side, whilst M. R. Thorp and A. J. Slavin (eds.) *Politics, Religion and Diplomacy in Early Modern Europe: Essays in Honour of De Lamar Jensen.* London: Sixteenth Century Journal Publishers, 1994 examines the activity in Europe during the Reformation.

3. See J. Shotwell, *Turkey at the Straits*. London: Macmillan, 1940. pp12–14.

4. M. Khadduri, *The Islamic Law of Nations: Shaybani's Siyar*. Baltimore, MD: John Hopkins Press, 1966. p62.

5. Ibid.

6. See K.A. El Fadl, 'Islam and the Theology of Power'. *Middle East Report*, No. 221. 2001. pp28–33.

7. H.M. Wood, 'The Treaty of Paris and Turkey's status in International Law', *American Journal of International Law*. Vol. XXXVII (1943). pp262–274.

8. For a detailed breakdown of the terms of the Vienna Settlement, see A. Zamoyski, *The Rites of Peace: The Fall of Napoleon and The Congress of Vienna*. London, New York: HarperCollins, 2008.

9. For a fuller account, see L. James, *Raj: The Making and Unmaking of British India*. London: Abacus, 1998. pp3–79, See also K.P. Mitra, *Indian History for Matriculation*. Calcutta, Bombay, Madras and London: Macmillan, 1933. pp246–261. The acquisition and impact of the French Empire in North, West and Sub-Saharan Africa in the nineteenth century is articulately assessed in B. Singer and J. Langdon, *Cultured Force: The Makers and Defenders of the French Colonial Empire*. Madison, WI, London: University of Wisconsin Press, 2004. pp47–53; M.E. Lorcin, *Algeria and France, 1800–2000: Identity, Memory, Nostalgia*. Syracuse, NY: Syracuse University Press, 2006. pp133–146.

10. See D. Judd, *Empire: The British Imperial Experience from 1765 to the Present*. London: Fontana Press, 1997. p66; J. Dueck, 'The Middle East and North Africa in the Imperial and Post-Colonial Historiography of France'. *The Historical Journal* (2007), 50:935–949; A.F. Clarke, 'Imperialism, Independence, and Islam in Senegal and Mali'. *Africa Today*, Vol. 46, No. 3 (Summer 1999). pp149–167; E. Burke, 'Pan-Islam and Moroccan Resistance to French Colonial Penetration, 1900–1912'. *Journal of African History*. Vol. XIII, No. I (1972). pp97–118.

11. P.M.E. Lorcin and P. Sanders, 'France and Islam: Introduction', *French Historical Studies*, Vol. 30, No. 3 (Summer 2007) pp343–349; J. Bowen, 'Does French Islam Have Borders? Dilemmas of Domestication in a Global Religious Field'. *American Anthropologist*, Vol. 106, No. 1 (2004) pp43–55.

12. H. Enyat, *Modern Islamic Political Thought*. Basingstoke: Macmillan Education, 1982. p57.

13. It is accepted that the Mughal Sultans also styled themselves as caliphs, but for the purpose of clarity it seems appropriate for the differential to be maintained.

14. See M.R. Anderson, 'Islamic Law and the Colonial Encounter in British India' in C. Mallat and F. Connors (eds.) *Islamic Family Law*. Leiden: Brill, 1990.

15. A. Schimmel, *Islam in the Indian Sub-Continent*. Leiden-Koln: E. Brill, 1980. p216.

16. For an analysis of Wali Ullah's influence on Khan, Barweli and Iqbal, see J. M.S. Baljon, *Religion and Thought of Shah Wali Allah Dilhawi 1703–1762*. Leiden: E.J. Brill, 1986. pp166–168.

17. Barelwi's 'jihad' is said to have been directly inspired by Wali Ullah. See U. Sanyal, *Devotional Islam and Politics in British India, Ahmad Riza Khan Barelwi and His Movement, 1870–1920* Delhi: OUP, 1999. p32.

18. 'His Role was Greatly Misunderstood by His Contemporary Muslims in India.' In G.W.Choudhury, *Muslim World*. p90.

19. Sayyid Ahmad Khan, *Tafsir al-Quran*, 7 Volumes. Agra and Aligarh, 1885–1906.

20. Sayyid Ahmad Khan, in H. Malik (ed. with notes). *Political Profile of Sir Sayyid Ahmad Khan*. Islamabad: Institute of Islamic History, Culture and Civilisation, Islamic University, 1982. chapter six.

21. Sayyid Ahmad Khan, *The Truth about the Khaliphat*. K Ahmed (Comp). New Delhi: Khosla Bros, 1920.

22. James, *Raj*. p481

23. See P. van der Veer, *Religious Nationalism in India: Hindus and Muslims*. Berkley, CA: University of California Press. 1994. p21. See also S. Sarkar, 'Indian Democracy: The Historical Inheritance' in A. Kohli (ed.), *The Success of India's Democracy*. Cambridge: CUP, 2001. pp23–46.

24. The myth of the 'two nation theory' as a long-term desire of the Muslims in India was explored in A. Majid, *Hindustan or Pakistan: Partition or Unity*. Lahore: Ilami Markaz, n.d.

25. *Report on Indian Constitutional Reforms 1918,* Montague/Chelmsford Report. p1.

26. In his book, Das describes the galvanising effects of the Montague Chelmsford Report in more detail. H. Das, *The Constitution of the Indian Republic*. New Delhi: Chaitanya Publishing House, 1971.

27. See N.C. Chaudhuri, *The Autobiography of an Unknown Indian*. New York: Macmillan,1951. p227.

28. B.L. Grover and R.R. Sethi, *Studies in Modern Indian History: 1707 to the Present Day.* New Delhi: S. Chand, 1963. pp395–398.

29. Schimmel, *Subcontinent.* p226.

30. H.A.R. Gibb, *Modern Trends in Islam.* Chicago, IL: University Press, 1945. p61.

31. S.M. Ikram, *Modern Muslim India and the Birth of Pakistan.* Delhi: Renaissance, 1950; C.M. Ali, *The Emergence of Pakistan.* New York: Columbia University Press, 1967; A. Jalal, *The Sole Spokesman: Jinnah, The Muslim League and the Demand for Pakistan.* Cambridge: CUP, 1982; K. Sayeed , *Pakistan: The Formative Phase, 1857–1948.* London: OUP, 1968; F. Robinson, 'Islam and Separatism' in M. Hasan (ed.), *Communal and Pan-Islamic Trends.* New Delhi: Manohar, 1981.

32. For useful insights and perspectives on the 1935 Act, see M.R. Palande, *Indian Administration and the British Constitution.* New Delhi: OUP, 1936.

33. See O. Verkaaik, *Migrants and Militants: Fun and Urban Violence in Pakistan.* Princeton: Princeton University Press, 2004. A thoughtful and imaginative presentation of the case for Muslim Sindh independence is made by Sayed himself in *The Case of Sindh: G.M. Sayed's Deposition for the Court,* published shortly before his death in 1995, in which Sayed argues his case before an imaginary court.

34. M. Hasan, *Legacy of a Divided Nation.* London: Hurst & Co., 1996. pp100–112.

35. K. Sharma, *Ambedkar and the Indian Constitution.* New Delhi: Ashish Publishing House. 1992. pp180–181.

36. P. Spear, *Oxford History of India.* Oxford: OUP, 1964. p807.

37. Hasan, *Nation.* p128.

38. A detailed history of the internal Muslim debates can be found in M. ul-Haq, *Muslim Politics in Modern India,1857–1947.* Meerut: Meenakshi Prakashan, 1970.

39. See J. Esposito (ed.), *Islam in Asia: Religion, Politics and Society.* Oxford: OUP, 1987. pp55–56.

40. Maulana A'la Maududi, *Islamic Law and Constitution.* Lahore: Taj Company, 1960.

41. A. Husain, *The Destiny of Indian Muslims.* London: Asia Publishing House, 1965.

42. The pre-French history of North Africa is summarised by Charles Robert Ageron in *Modern Algeria: A History from 1830 to the Present.* London: Hurst and Co., 1991 (French original, 1964) pp 2–5.

43. Christopher Harrison has an excellent summary of early French–Muslim interaction in West Africa in *France and Islam in West Africa, 1860–1960*, Cambridge: Cambridge University Press, 2006. pp1–6.

44. M. Hiskett, *The Course of Islam in Africa*. Edinburgh: Ediburgh University Press, 1994. p25.

45. Ibid.

46. The importance of the widely held eschatological yearning over all of the North Africa, which flowed from several bouts of bubonic plague and major earthquakes at the turning of the thirteenth century following Hijra cannot be overestimated. It engendered the belief that such natural disasters were heralding a new age in Islam. However, this book's focus lies elsewhere and so time cannot be given to it here. See B.G. Martin, *Muslim Brotherhoods in Nineteenth Century Africa*. Cambridge: CUP, 2003. pp36–43.

47. For an in depth account of al-Qadir's life and work, see R. Danziger, *Abd al-Qadir and the Algerian Resistance to the French and Internal Consolidation*. New York: Holmes and Meier, 1977. See also Ageron, *Modern Algeria*, pp 11–12 and A. Nouschi, 'North Africa in the Period of Colonialisation' in Holt et al (eds.) *The Cambridge History of Islam*. Cambridge, New York: CUP, 1983. p92.

48. Hiskett, *Islam in Africa*. p26.

49. He based this tactic upon the hijra of Muhammad in 622. However, one might argue whether this could be classified as a strategic withdrawal or simply a fresh start in the face of stubborn resistance. See Watt, *Muhammad*. p42.

50. M. Emerit, 'Algeria' in *EI2*, Vol. 1. pp 367–370. See also Danzinger, *al-Qadir*, pp72–83.

51. Al-Qadir was forced to fight Muhammad 'Abd Allah who styled himself mahdi and instituted a rebellion against him for raising taxes. See J. M. Abun-Nasr, *Muslim Communities of Grace: The Sufi Brotherhoods in Islamic Religious Life*. New York, Chicester, UK: Colombia University Press, 2007. pp204–205.

52. T. Smith, *The French Stake in Algeria 1945–62*, New York: Cornell University Press, 1976.

53. See, for example, Paul Silverman's article on the Kabylia uprisings: 'Martyrs and Patriots: Ethnic, National and Transnational Dimensions of Kabyle Politics' in *The Journal of North African Studies*, Volume 8, Issue 1 Spring 2003. pp 87–111.

54. P. Shinar, 'A Controversial Exponent of the Algerian Salafiyya: The Kabyle Alim, Imam and Sharif Abu Ya'la Sa'id B. Muhammad al-Zawawi' in D. Ayalon and M. Sharon (eds.), *Studies in Islamic History and Civilization: In Honour of Professor David Ayalon.* Jerusalem: Cana Ltd, 1986. pp 267–290.

55. Shinar, 'Algerian Salafiyya', p268.

56. Ageron, *Algeria.* p33.

57. Emmit, 'Algeria'. p638.

58. Hiskett, *Islam in Africa.* p27.

59. Ibid. pp27–28.

60. As cited in M. Brett, 'Legislating for Inequality in Algeria: The Sénatus-Consulté of 14 July 1865.' *Bulletin of the School of Oriental and African Studies,* Vol. 51. No. 3 (1988) p455. Brett's premise is opposed by Preistley, whose view of French interaction with shari'a is more pragmatic. H.I. Priestley, *France Overseas: A Study in Modern Imperialism.* London: Routledge, 1967. pp140–141.

61. See M. Bennoune, *The Making of Contemporary Algeria, 1830–1987.* Cambridge: CUP, 1988. pp36–42.

62. This enduring and explicit attempt at assimilation as a policy is discussed in M.D. Lewis, 'One Hundred Million Frenchmen: The "Assimilation" Theory in French Colonial Politics'. *Comparative Studies in Society and History,* Vol. 4, No. 2 (Jan., 1962). pp129–153.

63. Benounne, *Contemporary Algeria.* p41. For a broader understanding of the theory of French assimilation policy see R.F. Betts, *Assimilation and Association in French Colonial Theory, 1890–1914.* New York: Columbia University Press, 2005 (originally published 1961).

64. Emerit, 'Algeria', *EI2*, Vol. 1, p370. See also J-L. Triaud, 'Islam in Africa under French Colonial Rule' in N. Levitzon and R. L. Randall (eds.), *History of Islam in Africa.* Athens, OH: Ohio University Press, 2000. pp169–187.

65. G. Tillion, *France and Algeria: Complimentary Enemies.* Charlottesville: Greenwood Press, 1976. pp63–65.

66. Ibid. p66.

67. P.M.E. Lorcin, *Algeria and France 1800–2000: Identity, Memory, Nostalgia.* Syarcuse, NY: Syracuse University Press, 2006. pp164–167.

68. Ibid. p182. See also P.C. Naylor, *France and Algeria: A History of Decolonisation and Transformation.* London: Routledge, 2007. p49.

69. Kurzman, *Modernist Islam.* p93.

70. Lapidus, *Muslim Societies.* p592.
71. M. Willis, *The Islamist Challenge in Algeria: A Political History.* New York: Ithaca Press, 1996. p10.
72. Ibid. p382.
73. B. Stora, (ed.) *Algeria, 1830–2000: A Short History.* Ithaca, NY: Cornell University Press, 2004. p36
74. A.G. Hargreaves and M. J. Heffernan, *French and Algerian Identities from Colonial Times to the Present: A Century of Interaction.* Chicago: E. Mellen Press, 1993. pp68–72.
75. Willis, *Algeria.* p288.
76. Stora, *Algeria.* p37.
77. Ibid.
78. Hargreaves and Heffernan, *French and Algerian Identities.* p73.
79. Lorcin, *Algeria and France.* pp192–197.
80. A. Horne. *A Savage War of Peace, Algeria 1954–1962.* New York: New York Review Books, 2006. p521.
81. Reudy, *Modern Algeria.* pp206–230.
82. Details of this developing tend are well analysed in D. Heraldstveit, *Political Islam in Algeria.* Oslo: Norwegian Institute for International Affairs, 1997.
83. Reudy, *Modern Algeria.* p229.

Section 2   Islam in Minority: Citizenship and the ummah

1 www.odci.gov gives the figures for Muslims in minorities in Secular states or states with a different state religion to Islam against those in officially Muslim states.
2 I. Ahmad, 'Islamic Fundamentalism in South Asia' in *Fundamentalisms Observed,* Marty and Apple (eds.) pp464–468 cited in W. F. Larson, *Islamic Fundamentalism in Pakistan: Implications For Conversion to Christianity.* New York: Colombia University, 1996. p33.
3 Choudhury, in *Muslim World,* describes Sayyid Ahmad Khan as 'a Muslim leader of great vision and personality'. p90.
4 Witness his clinical and scathing attack on colonial suspicions in 'Review on Dr. Hunter's Indian Musalmans: Are They Bound in Conscience to Rebel Against the Queen?', in H. Malik (ed. with notes), *Political Profile*

of Sayyid Ahmad Khan. Islamabad: Institute of Islamic History, Culture
and Civilisation, Islamic University, 1982. chapter six.

5   His Lucknow speech of 1882 would be but one example of this. See
Malik, *Profile.* pp342–355.

6   Malik, *Profile.* pp359–373.

Chapter 3   Should Muslims Always Obey Those in Authority Over Them, Even When They Are Not Muslims?

1. Sayyid Abul A'la Maududi, *Let Us Be Muslims.* K. Murad (ed.) (First
Printed 1940), Leicester: Islamic Foundation, 1985. pp273–302.

2. Maududi, *Muslims.* p295.

3. The Proclamation of Religious Freedom made by Queen Victoria as
the government took over rule of the subcontinent after the 1857–58
rebellion specifically guaranteed religious freedom for all imperial
citizens. Even so, he still describes British rule and the Indian Penal
Code as an impediment to a faithful life. Maududi, *Muslims.* p299.

4. Mujeeb, *Indian Muslims.* p401.

5. L. Gardet, 'Dīn', *EI2,* Vol. 2,. pp293–296.

6. Ibid, p293.

7. Ibid.

8. Ibid. p295.

9. Watt, *Political Thought.* p29. However, Watt goes on to suggest that
'religions, strictly speaking, have no political concepts attached to
them. What is found is that a religion sometimes favours the political concepts attached to them'. With regard to Islam, this is harder
to argue. Cf 'Role of Muhammad' in the 'Nature of the Caliphate'
section.

10. Penrice, *Dictionary.* p50. cf Lane, *Lexicon,* Vol. 3. pp943–945.

11. It is accepted that this line of argument would be articulated differently depending upon whether one were discussing the UK, USA or
any European state. However, even given these Constitutional differences, it seems clear that, until the last decade religion was very much
viewed as a private affair in the UK. For an interesting analysis on the
cultural changes in this area see, N. Spencer, *Doing God: A Future for
Faith in the Public Square.* London: Theos, 2006. pp15–17.

12. Maududi, *Muslims.* p296.
13. G.A. Perwez, *Islam: A Challenge to Religion.* Lahore: Indara-Tulu-e-Islam, 1968. p357.
14. This may be in the process of changing see fn 11.
15. M. Asad, *The Principles of State and Government in Islam.* Gibraltar: Dar al-Andalus, 1961. p3.
16. Z. Bangash, (Comp. and Ed.), *In Pursuit of the Power of Islam. Major Writings of Kalam Siddiqui.* London: The Muslim Institute, 1996. p172.
17. Maududi, *Muslims.* p300.
18. In her discussion of al-Afghani's ideas, Nikki Keddie says that al-Afghani's main concern in coming to India was to try and remove the influence of Sayyid Ahmad Khan and his followers, whom he believed were far too close to the British. N.R. Keddie, *An Islamic Response to Imperialism: Political and Religious Writings of Sayyid Jamal ad-Din "al-Afghani.* Berkeley and Los Angeles: University of California Press, 1968. pp47–51.
19. Jamal ad-Din al-Afghani, 'Jinsiyah wa al-Din al-Islamiyah', *Al-Urwah al al-Wurthqa*, No. 2, 20 March 1884, in R. G. Landen, (trans. and ed.), *The Emergence of the Modern Middle East: Selected Readings.* New York: Van Nostrand Reihnold Company, 1970. p108.
20. Landen, *Modern Middle East.* pp109–110.
21. Whilst al-Afghani might be correct in his assertion that Indian Muslims were happier under Ottoman rule, simply because they were Muslim rulers: certainly the same sentiment is expressed in Algeria. However, al-Afghani's role as Pan-Islamic ambassador on behalf of the Caliphate might very well be informing his writing at this point.
22. Interestingly, in his chapter on 'Islam and the Demand for Pakistan', Ishtiaq Ahmed acknowledges al-Afghani's influence on later Muslims, but asserts that Sayyid Ahmad Khan succeeded in isolating him from having widespread effect in India. I. Ahmed, *Islamic State.* p71.
23. M. Iqbal, *Struggle for Independence: 1857–1947* (Karachi, 1958) app. IV, pp. 14–18 as quoted in J. Donohue, and J.L.Esposito, *Islam in Transition (Muslim Perspectives).* New York, London: OUP, 1982. p91.
24. Schulze summed up Ataturk's work thus: 'Every policy now became state apologetics – the principle that the state incorporated the absolute sovereignty in society ...' R. Schulze, *A Modern History of the Islamic World.* London: I.B. Tauris, 2000. p68.

25. Donohue and Esposito, *Islam in Transition.* p91.
26. M. Sedgwick. *Muhammad 'Abdhuh.* London: Oneworld, 2010. p28.
27. A. Hourani, *Arabic Thought in the Liberal Age. 1789–1939.* Cambridge: CUP, 1983. p137.
28. Ibid. p138.
29. As discussed in A. Ahmad, 'Sayyid Ahmad Khan, Jamal ad-din al Afghani and Muslim India', *Studia Islamica* Vol 3, No. 13 (1960) pp55–78.
30. Ibid. p57.
31. See James, *Raj.* p206.
32. Malik, *Profile.* pp273–274.
33. Ibid.
34. Ibid, p300.
35. Malik, *Profile,* 306–308. In this they were not alone, both the Ottoman Caliphs and the Meccan 'ulamā had declared the British Empire dar al-Islam in 1857, 1884 and 1914 (Meccan's alone). See Ozcan, *Pan-Islamism.* p17, p175.
36. Sanyal, *Devotional Islam.* p273. For an in-depth discussion of the meaning and implication of these terms in Medieval Islam see Crone, *Political Thought,* p242, p287, pp359–362, p369. In Hanafi sharī'a Schacht, *Islamic Law.* pp131–133 and for a general etymological discussion of the terms see Lewis, *Political Language.* pp72–73.
37. Malik, *Profile.* p300.
38. Sir Sayyid Ahmad Khan, Aligarh Institute Gazette of the 2 February 1889, as quoted in Baljon, *Khan.* p20.
39. McDonough, *Khan and Maududi.* p40.
40. S. A. Khan, *Tafsir al-Quran.* Agra: Mufidi 'amm Press, 1903–1906.
41. C. Ali, *The Proposed Political, Legal and Social Reforms under Muslim Rule.* Bombay: Education Society's Press, 1883. pII.
42. Ibid, iii. Ali would almost certainly have been one of the Muslims that Maududi was implicitly criticising in the opening lines of his chapter on 'Political Theory'. A. Maududi, *Islamic Law and Constitution.* Lahore: Taj Company, 1960. pp124–125.
43. Davies has shown that Roman leaders came from a very small group of patrician families, who effectively held on to power through a system of patronage and were voted their status by the Senate alone. It is also important to note that the extent to which Roman dictators could be described as 'under the law' could be open to

some debate. N. Davies, *Europe, A History*. London: Pimlico, 1997. pp167–171.

44. C. Ali, *Legal and Social Reforms*. pIV.

45. Ibid, pVII.

46. Ibid, pXXXV. This concept appears to have been widespread, historian such as Qureishi and Ozcan both document leaflets and speeches in which the Ottoman rulers were still, even at the end of their power, regarded as great powers by both the Muslim community and indeed by many of the European powers. See Qureishi, *Khalifat Movement*. pp188–9; Ozcan, *Pan-Islamism*. p211.

47. C. Ali, *Legal and Social Reforms,* pXXVI.

48. Ibid. pXXXVII.

49. See R.B. Serjeant, 'The Constitution of Medina', *Islamic Quarterly,* Vol. 8 (1964).

50. Ali, *Reforms*, pXXXVII.

51. M. Arkoun, *The Unthought in Contemporary Islamic Thought*. London, Beruit: Saqi Books, 2002. pp325–6. An interesting summary of Arkoun's perspective and life work is provided by Gabrielle Marranci (ed.) in *Muslim Societies and the Challenge of Secularization: An Interdisciplinary Approach*. Dortrecht: Springer, 2010. p187.

52. Arkoun's perspective is summed-up succinctly by Meena Sharify-Funk in *Encountering the Transnational: Women, Islam and the Politics of Interpretation*. Farnham: Ashgate Publishing, 2008. p32.

53. He was Vice-Chancellor at Jamia Millia Islamia from 1962–67 and President until his fatal heart attack in 1969. See I. M. Abu-Rabi, *The Blackwell Companion to Contemporary Islamic Thought*. Oxford: Blackwell Publishing, 2006. p483.

54. Ibid. p485.

55. S. Abid Husain, *The Destiny of Indian Muslims*. New York: Asia Publishing House, 1965.

56. Ibid. p212. Muslims have been in all Indian national governments since independence. Something that Sayyid Ahmad Khan would have encouraged.

57. Husain, *Destiny*. p213.

58. Ibid. p217.

59. For a discussion of India's protectionist stance and emergence from it see B.M. Jain, *Global Power: India's Foreign Policy 1947–2006*. Lexington MD: Rowman and Littlefield, 2008.

60. Husain, *Destiny*. p245.
61. Ibid. p249.
62. Ibid. p251.
63. Ibid. pp252–3.
64. S. Shahabuddin and T.P. Wright Jr, 'India, Muslim Minority Politics and Society' in Esposito, *Islam in Asia*. p155.
65. Husain, *Destiny*. p253.
66. A route that Muslims appear to be increasingly aware of according to Saleem Kidwai. See S. Kidwai, 'Muslim and Indian Democracy' in M.A. Andrabi (ed), *Islam in India Since Independence*. Srinagar: Iqbal Institute, University of Kashmir, 1988. pp39–44.
67. Husain, *Destiny*. p250.
68. Ibid. pp251–252.
69. Ibid. p253.
70. Ibid. p254.
71. Ibid. p255.
72. The Pakistani Punjabi chief Justice of the Board of Enquiry into the riots against the Ahmadiyya Sect.
73. M. Munir, *From Jinnah to Zia*. Lahore: Vangard Books,1979. pp145–146.
74. M. ul-Haq, *Islam in Secular India* Simla: Indian Institute of Advanced Study, 1972. p8.
75. Ibid. p15.
76. ul-Haq, *Secular India*. p21.
77. B. Bhutto, *Reconciliation: Islam, Democracy and the West*. New York: HarperCollins, 2008. pp275–318.
78. See Watt, *Muhammad*. pp33–38.
79. Bhutto, *Reconciliation*. p319.
80. See Chapter Two's discussion of the use of sunnah when seeking precedent.
81. The transient nature of Muslim treaties with non-Muslims is explained in Sohil Hasmi's, *Islamic Political Ethics: Society, Pluralism and Conflict*. Princeton: Princeton University Press, 2002. pp158–160.
82. There is no direct reference to the struggle for Pakistan or anti-British or Hindu propaganda for example.
83. Khan's three volumes of tafsīr are quoted throughout Dar, *Khan*.
84. Indeed, as was discussed in Chapter Two, Schacht goes so far as to suggest that, for Muslims, shari'a had a greater theological significance than the Qur'an itself.

Chapter 4   From Ijtihad to Khilafah State: On What Level Should the Notion of the Muslim Community Function?

1. K.A. Faruki, *The Evolution of Islamic Constitutional Theory and Practice.* Karachi: National Publishing House, 1971. pp203–237.

2. Muhammad Ali's leading role in the 'Ahmadiyya' Sect, eventually rejected by many orthodox Muslims for its claims to prophethood for Ghulam Ahmad and denial of the duty of 'Jihad', are acknowledged. However, he led the 'Lahore Group', which did not acknowledge Ghulam Ahmad's prophethood and continued to remain at the centre of Indian politics, even after the end of the 'Khalifat Movement'. See Mujeeb, *Muslims.* pp435–438, cf Schimmel, *Subcontinent.* pp211–213 and Sanyal, *Devotional Islam.* p279.

3. Maududi, *Islamic Law.* p148.

4. The name has many differing spellings due to transliteration. I have gone with that used by Oussama Arabi in his fascinating chapter on the contract law elements of the Majalla in *Studies in Modern Islamic Jurisprudence.* Leiden: Brill, 2001. pp39–62.

5. Those wishing to investigate the development of the Majalla further, and it's lasting impact on the modern Middle East could look at Bernard Lewis' brief description in *The Emergence of Modern Turkey.* New York, Oxford: OUP, 2002. pp122–3, which also contains some useful footnotes for further reading.

6. The website gives a detailed breakdown of the various ministries and functions within the 'Khilafah state' and accords the minorities such as Christians and Jews reduced citizenship as is consistent with 'dhimmi theology'. The outline of the state and the place of minorities is constant also with the *Universal Islamic Declaration of Human Rights.*

7. Maududi, *Islamic Law.* pp148–149.

8. Ibid. p149.

9. Ibid. p150.

10. It would be useful to investigate whether their increased power allowed them freedom of movement and removal of their 'slave' status.

11. Maududi, *Islamic Law.* p150.

12. Ibid. p151.

13. In the course of his historical survey, Sharma advances a similar idea, but binds the idea of Muslim political power tightly to one man

without the reasoning that Maududi advances. S.S. Sharma, *Caliphs and Sultans: Religious Ideology and Political Praxis*. New Delhi: Rupa and Co., 2004. p262. One might observe that the same principle is seen in operation in the *Universal Islamic Declaration of Human Rights*.

14. A useful explanation of ijtihad can be found on the 'mideastweb' internet site at http://www.mideast web.org/Middle-East-Encyclopedia/ ijtihad.htm. A fascinating discussion of Ijtihad and Maslaha by Tariq Ramadan can be found in M.A. Muqtedar Khan (ed.) *Islamic Democratic Discourse: Theory, Debates and Philosophical Perspectives*. Lanham, MD: Rowman and Littlefield, 2006.

15. G.A. Perwez, *Qurani aein Kay Bunyadi Khat-o-Khal*. Lahore: Indara-Tulu-e-Islam. pp4–5, cited in I. Ahmad, *Islamic State*.p130.

16. This is entirely consistent with his exegesis of Q4:59 cited in Maududi, *Qur'an*. p52.

17. A strong echo of the Shi'a Pious Imam theory.

18. Maududi, *Islamic Law*. p152.

19. Other opinions on the need to have Islamic Law as part of the state structure to allow Muslims to be Muslims are outlined by Sharma, *Caliphs and Sultans*. pp25–32.

20. I. Ahmed, *Islamic State*. p174.

21. For a fuller summary of the salient points of Perwez's ideal form of government, see I. Ahmad, *Islamic State*. pp130–131. A brief overview of Perwez's opinions can also be found in Larson, *Pakistan*. pp166–168.

22. Landen, *Emergence*. p107.

23. See A. Özcan, *Pan-Islamism*. pp56–58.

24. B. Tibi, *Islam Between Culture and Politics*. Basingstoke: Palgrave Macmillan, 2001. p140.

25. Ibid. p107.

26. For example, in the biography of Maududi on the *Jama'at e Islami* website (www.jamaat.org accessed 27/5/05), Maududi's Arabic ancestry was clearly flagged up, as was Sayyid Ahmad Khan's in the introduction of Malik's, *Profile*. pXVI.

27. Landen, *Emergence*. pp108–109. An interesting theory on the attraction of al-Afghani's message for Muslims in India (as well as other parts of the world) is given in A. Jalal, *Self and Sovereignty: Individual and Community in South Asian Islam since 1850*. London and New York: Routledge, 2000. pp188–189.

28. Taken from A. Iqbal, (ed.). *Selected Speeches and Statements of Maulana Mohamed Ali*. Lahore: Publishers United Ltd, 1963.

29. This Proclamation is referred to frequently by separatist Muslims as a justification for a number of political moves. This is seen clearly in the discussions on the *Shariat Act* and the implications of the Proclamation will therefore be discussed at that point.

30. See Oliver-Dee, *The Caliphate Question*. pp33–36.

31. Iqbal, *Speeches*. p36.

32. Ibid. p43.

33. Oliver-Dee, *The Caliphate Question*. Chapter five contains an extensive discussion of the core phrase that relates to Muhammad 'Ali's issue here: what is meant by 'spiritual authority'?

34. Iqbal, *Speeches*. pp43–44.

35. His ally and one of the chief theologians of the Khilafat Movement, Abu'l Kalam Azad, expanded on this idea but took it further. He proposed the idea that the Caliph should be the supreme ruler and that each country with a large Muslim population should have an Imam who would be responsible to him. For a fuller description of Azad's ideas, see A. Ahmad, *Islamic Modernism in India and Pakistan 1857–1964*. London, Bombay and Karachi: OUP, 1967. The issue is fraught with ambiguity and logical leaps. For those wishing to examine the argument further, file IOR/L/PS/10/853/4 contains minutes of Muhammad 'Ali's arguments on this matter to Prime Minister David Lloyd-George in 1920 and 1921.

36. Ibid. p45.

37. M. Munawwar, 'Allamah Muhammad Iqbal' in W. Uz-Zaman and M. Saleem Akhtar, (eds.), *Islam in South Asia*. Islamabad: National Institute of Historical and Cultural Research, 1993. p381.

38. M. Mir, *Iqbal*. London: I.B. Tauris, 2005. pp122–128. See also R. Malik, *Iqbal: The Spiritual Father of Pakistan*. Chicago: University of Michigan Press, 2003 which contains fascinating letters from Iqbal to Jinnah on the political and social status of Muslims in India.

39. Donohoe and Esposito, *Transition*. p92.

40. Ibid. p93.

41. C.W. Troll, *Islam in the Indian Subcontinent – Muslims in Secular India* (Discussion Paper Series III – 2). Tokyo: Institute of Asian Cultures, Sophia University, 1986. p5; cf, A.T. Embree, *India's Search for National Identity*. New York: Alfred A. Knopf, 1972. pp124–125.

42. Troll, *Islam Secular India*. p93.
43. Shaida, 'Iqbal'. p101.
44. M. Ruthven. *Islam in the Modern World, 3rd ed.* London: Granta Books, 2006. pp301–305.
45. Andrew Rippin gives an excellent summary of the structure and style of the book in *Muslims: Their Religious Beliefs and Practices, 3rd ed.* London and New York: Routledge and Taylor Francis, 2005. p232.
46. M. 'Abduh, *The Theology of Unity*. Trans I. Musa'ad and K. Cragg. London: George Allen and Unwin, 1966. p123.
47. Ibid. p129. See also Sedgwick. *Abduh*.
48. As quoted in M.ul-Haq. *Muhammad Abduh: A Study of a Modern Thinker of Egypt,* Aligarh: Islamic Studies Publisher, 1970. p22.
49. Hourani, *Arabic Thought*. p156
50. A. Merad, *Le Réformisme Musulman en Algérie de 1925 à 1940*. Paris: Moulton and Co. 1967. pp444–447.
51. See C. Kurzman (ed.), *Modernist Islam, 1849–1940: A Sourcebook.* Oxford and New York: OUP, 2002. p93.
52. J.P. Entelis, *Islam, Democracy and the State in North Africa*. Bloomington, IN: Indiana University Press, 1997. p57. This was the motto of the Algerian 'Ulama which Badis set up in 1931.
53. Lapidus, *Islamic Societies*. p331.
54. H. Malik, *Moslem Nationalism in India and Pakistan,* Washington D.C.: Public Affairs Press, 1967. pp123–139.
55. Khan, *Khalifat*.
56. Ibid. p1.
57. H. Chadwick, *The Early Church*. London: Penguin, 1993. pp160–165.
58 A claim later substantiated in Arnold, *Caliphate*. Chapter nine.
59. Khan, *Khalifat*. pp6–17.
60. This is interesting, for it is the very antithesis of Muhammad Ali's argument, when he later called for the British to leave Turkey alone during the Khilafat Crisis after the First World War.
61. Ibid. p17.
62. Mujeeb, *Indian Muslims*. p555.
63. Troll, *Islam Secular India*. p6.
64. See the 'Conclusion' in the earlier chapter 'Maududi and Khan: Theological contextualisation and 'Authority' in Islam'.

Section 3   Islam in Minority: Shariʻa and the State

1. D.S. Powers, 'Orientalism, Colonialism, and Legal History: The Attack on Muslim Family Endowments in Algeria and India.' *Comparative Studies in Society and History,* Vol. 31, No.3 (July 1989). pp535–571.

Chapter 5   The Introduction of shariʻa into British Imperial India: Issues and Questions

1. *Indian Express,* 28 November 1998.
2. 'Laws of Inequality', *The Hindu,* 8 October 2003.
3. B. Agarwal, 'Women's Inheritance: Next Steps', *The Indian Express,* 17 October 2005.
4. Schacht, *Introduction.* p93
5. See also, Oliver-Dee, *The Caliphate Question.* pp43–48.
6. K. De Schweinitz, *The Rise and Fall of British India: Imperialism as Inequality.* London: Routledge, 1983. p148.
7. See L.A. Benton, *Law and Colonial Cultures: Legal Regimes in World History.* Cambridge. CUP, 2002. pp138–140.
8. Schacht, *Introduction.* p96. This is important to note as it feeds into the broader Anglo-French perception that, although shariʻa as a whole was incompatible with European Law, Family and Inheritance Law appears to have been broadly accepted in a manner that the rest of the fiqh was not.
9. IOR L/P&J/7/943, F201.
10. 'Statement of Objects and Reasons' is dated 27 March 1935.
11. Ibid. F200.
12. This attitude is revealed again and again by the supporters of the Bill, and it is useful to note that the use of non-Muslim sources for fiqh had been specifically banned in the writings of Ibn Khaldun. See Khadduri, 'Sources'. pp3–4.
13. See Schacht, *Introduction.* p3–6. See also Kamali, *Shariʻah.* pp14–38.
14. It is interesting to note the presence of the same dynamic in the opening of the Universal Islamic Declaration of Human Rights, published in 1980. 'Human rights in Islam are firmly rooted in the belief that God, and God alone, is the Law Giver and the Source of all human rights. Due to their Divine origin, no ruler, government, assembly or authority can curtail or violate in any way the human rights conferred

by God, nor can they be surrendered.' UIDHR, Foreword, Paris, 1980.

15. This is a deeply complex issue which has claim and counter claim. Those wishing to engage with the issue might find it useful to read the following: S.T. Mahmoud, *The Muslim Law of India.* Berkley, CA: University of California Press, 1980; J.L. Esposito, *Women in Muslim Family Law.* Syracuse, NY: Syracuse University Press, 2001.

16. IOR L/P&J/7/943, F188.

17. The work of Mohammed Ilyas and the Tablighi Jamaat since its inauguration in 1928 has been the subject of much speculation but little factual analysis as the Tabligh are notoriously reticent. It is frequently discussed in relation to Islamic fundamentalism but rarely researched historically. R.K.P. Multani's *Islamic Fundamentalism in South Asia.* Chicago, IL: Sumit Enterprises, 2007 is an example of this which does contain some historical analysis. A more historical approach can be found in J. Ali 'Islamic Revivalism: The Case of Tablighi Jamaat' in *Journal of Muslim Minority Affairs,* Vol. 23, Issue 1, April 2003. pp173–181.

18. It is therefore ironic that the one of the advisors to the Governor of the Punjab was of the opinion that one of the effects of the Bill would be to produce an 'obvious motive for female infanticide.' F188.

19. IOR L/P&J/7/943, F199.

20. The first batch of responses in the file are dated 6 August 1936, which followed their circulation via the Legislative Assembly Department of the Government of India on 3 October 1935. F187–198.

21. This oft-repeated refrain from the British officials has important echoes for the present which shall be discussed in the Conclusions chapter. That being said, there was one British official who was extremely articulate and rigorous in his examination of the Bill and the exposition of its implications. It is therefore unreasonable to paint all officialdom in the same light. His contribution will be examined shortly.

22. Amongst the notable exceptions to the pervading note of caution that governs British comment is that of Judge Horwill (Madras) who states that 'While it is undoubtedly a good thing that all Muslims in India should have the same Personal Law, I do not see why they should look back to the seventh century and to the customs of other countries for their law.' F187. Whilst one might take issue with his

initial premise, the sentiment at the heart of the statement is worthy of discussion.

23. See, for example, the comments from both the Governor of Madras and the Central Provinces.
24. See, for example. F195.
25. Ibid. F192.
26. Ibid. F189.
27. Ibid. F187.
28. See IOR L/P&J/7/943, F187–189 and again in further comments later in the process at F93–105. Particularly prominent in this frequent re-iteration of mass support are the local *Anjuman Ittihad-e-Islam* associations, whose support is unequivocal and vociferous from all parts of the Subcontinent who frequently couch their arguments in relation to religious purity.
29. Ibid. F188.
30. Ibid. F187. The governor was referring to the Bengal Civil Courts Act 1887, which allowed for the use of alternative systems of law to settle disputes in the area of inheritance and other family law matters. The text can be seen at http://bdlaws.gov.bd/pdf_part.php?id=59. The Act is explained and interpreted in Henry Moncrieff-Smith's article 'British India' in the *Journal of Comparative Legislation and International Law,* Third Series, Vol. 9, No. 3 (1927) pp151–160.
31. Although the motivations of Jinnah in supporting the Bill are touched upon within the wider context of the whole group of Muslim representatives within the Assembly, his own personal motives are not engaged with. Those wishing to understand more about Jinnah's personal motives would be well advised to read A.Akbar, *Jinnah, Pakistan and Islamic Identity: The Search for Saladin.* Basingstoke: Routledge, 1997; J. Singh, *Jinnah: India, Partition, Independence.* New York: OUP, 2010; S. Wolpert, *Jinnah of Pakistan.* Oxford, New York: OUP, 2005; Jalal, *The Sole Spokesman.* p104.
32. Ibid.
33. An excellent and articulate example of this dynamic is the advice given by a Mr. Koreshi, a retired Collector from Bombay District, who argues the merits of the Bill on the basis of theology and Muslim identity, without referring to the legal benefits of it. IOR L/P&J/7/943, F186.
34. Ibid. F178.

35. Justice A.D. Arshad goes on to suggest that the one of the reasons behind the Bill is the increased rate of apostasy amongst Muslim Women who attempted divorce as a way out of the mismanagement of the waqfs due to them. Ibid. F169.
36. The debate minutes are at Folios 155–166 and are dated 19 May 1937.
37. F155.
38. F158.
39. It is interesting to note that there is an implicit assumption in this perspective that an Islam that is not politically pre-eminent is therefore downtrodden.
40. The text of the declaration can be found at http://en.wikisource. org/wiki/Queen_Victoria's_ Proclamation . Mitra Sharafi's article 'The Semi Autonomous Judge in Colonial India' discusses Queen Victoria's proclamation in relation to the broader examination of personal law in the colonial period. *Indian Economic & Social History Review,* Vol. 46, No. 1 (2009) pp57–81. It is also quoted in Miles Taylor's article on Queen Victoria's early connections with India: 'Queen Victoria and India, 1837–61', *Victorian Studies,* Vol. 46, No. 2, Papers from the Inaugural Conference of the North American Victorian Studies Association (Winter 2004), pp. 264–274.
41. F159.
42. Such pragmatic political considerations were certainly the hallmark of British foreign policy in relation to identity issues throughout the imperial period. See Oliver-Dee, *The Caliphate Question.* pp52–56.
43. IOR L/P&J/7/943, F165.
44. The debate is extensive and it covers Folios 89–154 in the file. This is, in part, due to the quotation of the amendments themselves as each one is discussed. The discussion and associated meetings occurred on 1–9 September 1937 and again on 16 September when the Bill was finally passed.
45. Repeated reference is made to this meeting, but it is first mentioned at F150.
46. Ibid. F152.
47. See Chapter Two.
48. Ibid. F128. Yamin Khan (Agra) and George Joseph (Madura) amongst others. Yamin Khan expresses the view that shari'a as a term does not adequately cover the phrase 'Muslim Personal Law'. On the evidence

of Chapter One this observation is not without foundation. The central concern of the use of this particular term broadens out the possible scope of the remit covered by the Bill as shari'a covers far more than simply Personal Law.

49. Ibid. F127.
50. James, *Raj.* p285.
51. IOR L/P&J/7/943, F124.
52. Ibid. F132.
53. Ibid. F122.
54. See Chapter One where the development of shari'a in its early stages was examined.
55. IOR L/P&J/7/943, F122–3.
56. Ibid. F3–109.
57. Anderson, 'Colonial Encounter'. p83.
58. M. Iqbal, *The Reconstruction of Religious Thought in Islam.* New Delhi: Kitab Bhavan, 2000 (First Published 1930). pp149–150. The ideas of Iqbal himself as well as Khan are discussed in S. Khatoon, *The Development of Islamic Rationalism on the Subcontinent with Special Reference to Waliullah, Sayyid Ahmad Khan and Muhammad Iqbal.* Thesis for the University of Karachi, 1980.

Chapter 6   Case Study: French Imperial Interaction with shari'a

1. Victor, *Between God.* p242.
2. See A. Christelow, *Muslim Law Courts and the French Colonial State in Algeria.* Princeton, NJ Princeton University Press, 1985. pp112–114.
3. C-R. Ageron and R. Brett, *Modern Algeria: A History From 1830 to the Present* (First Published in French, 1964) London: Hurst and Co., 1991. pp20–22.
4. Christelow, *Muslim Law Courts.* p41.
5. P. Silverstein, *Algeria in France: Transpolitics, Race and Nation.* Bloomington, IN: Indiana University Press, 2004. p51.
6. Luciani was himself a jurist and author of the book *Taité des successions musulmanes.* Paris: Leroux, 1890.
7. O. Arabi, *Studies in Modern Islamic Law and Jurisprudence.* The Hague, New York and London: Klumer Law International, 2001. p125.

8. David Santillia published his *Code Tunisien des Obligations et des Contracts* in 1906 and, Morand authored his *Revue Algerian et Tunisienne de Legislation et de Jurisprudence* in 1907, although the *Code Morand* itself was not published until 1916.

9. It is a question that could also be asked of the British, but for which there is no recorded rationale.

10. Arabi, *Modern Islamic Law.* p126.

11. Ibid.

12. See Oliver-Dee, *The Caliphate Question.* pp35–37.

13. The aims of British imperial policy in the late eighteenth century are discussed in R. Hyam, 'The Primacy of Geopolitics: The Dynamics of British Imperial Policy, 1763–1963'. *The Journal of Imperial and Commonwealth History,* Volume 27, Issue 2 (1999). pp27–52.

14. Arabi, *Modern Islamic Law.* p125.

15. Ibid. p133.

16. Ibid. p134, quoting A. Haydar, *Durur al-Hukkam Sharh Majallat al-Ahkram.* Haifa: Abbasid Press, 1925. Vol. 1. p40 and 42. Leaving aside the implications for Morand for a moment though, this is a fascinating legal dynamic that has further implications for the discussion in the previous chapter in relation to the perceived 'requirement' to bring in shari'a as against customary law in India.

17. Ibid. p135.

18. Ibid. p121 quoting J-R Henry and F. Balique, *La Doctrine Coloniale du Droit Musulman Algerian: Bibliography Systematique et Introductions Critique.* Paris: Centre National de la Recherché Scientifique, 1979. p48. One of Morond's chief opponents was his colleague at the Law Faculty in Algeria, Emile Larcher. Arabi, *Modern Islamic Law.* p122.

19. See Ageron, *Algeria.* pp257–288. See also K. Adamson, *Algeria: A Study in Competing Ideologies.* London: Continuum, 1998. pp60–78. Although Adamson takes a primarily economic and sociological perspective in relation to Islam in Algeria, she makes several useful observations upon the dynamics of post-independence Islam particularly.

20. Arabi, *Modern Islamic Law.* p134.

21. F. Opwis, 'Maslaha in Contemporary Islamic Legal Theory', *Islamic Law and Society.* Vol. 12. No. 2 (2005) pp182–223. It also appears as chapter four in A. Amanat and F. Griffel, *Shari'a: Islamic Law in the Contemporary Context.* Berkley, CA: Stanford University Press, 2007.

22. See M. Khadduri, 'The Maslaha (Public Interest) and Illa (Cause) in Islamic Law', *New York University Journal of International Law & Politics* (1979–1980) pp213–227; T. Ramadan, 'Ijtihad and Maslaha: The Foundations of Governance' in M.A. Muqtedar Khan (ed.), *Islamic Democratic Discourse: Theories, Debates and Philosophical Discourses*. Lanham (MA): Rowman and Littlefield, 2006; J. Olidort, *Maslaha: A Mechanism for reform in Islamic Legal Theory*, Boston, MA: Brandis University Press, 2007.

23. M. Morand, *Études de Droit Musalman Algerien*. Algiers: Adolph Jordan, 1910. p141.

Chapter 7   The New World: Citizenship, Identity and the New Europe

1. The full text of both the speech and his Radio 4 interview can be found at www.archbishopofcanterbury.org/1575.

2. Ibid.

3. The Archbishop's remarks were summarised and explained on his website www.archbishopof canterbury.org/1581?q=sharia. The use of the term 'secularism' is contentious in terms of its negative or positive conotations. Yahya Birt, Dilwar Hussain and Ataullah Siddiqui (eds) book *British Secularism and Religion* makes a useful contribution in this field.

4. See Footnote 1.

5. An in-depth discussion of the Archbishop's lecture was published in the *International Journal of Public Theology*, Volume 2, Number 4, 2008, by Jonathan Chaplin (Director of the Kirby Laing Institute for Christian Ethics in Cambridge) entitled 'Legal Monism and Religious Pluralism: Rowan Williams on Religion, Loyalty and Law'. An edited version of this article appeared in *Fulcrum Magazine* and can be found at http://www.fulcrum-anglican.org.uk/page.cfm?ID=278.

6. Razia Butt, 'Gordon Brown Backs Archbishop of Canterbury in Sharia law Row', *The Guardian*, 11 February 2008.

7. Baroness Sayeeda Warsi 'Sharia Would Not Help Integration But Disunity' *The Sun*, 9 February 2008.

8. Joanna Sugden and Ruth Gledhill, 'The Archbishop of Canterbury "Should Resign" Over Sharia Row', *The Times*, 8 February 2008.

9. No Author Attributed, 'Williams Attcked Over Sharia Law Comments', *The Daily Telegraph*, 8 February 2008.

10. Ibid.
11. Lord Chief Justice Phillips, Equality Before the Law, East London Muslim Centre, 3 July 2008.
12. As reported by Melanie Phillips, 'A Caledonian Caliphate', *The Spectator*, 25 June 2008.
13. Frances Gibb, 'Case Dismissed: Lord Chief Justice Lays Down Law on Sharia', *The Times*, 5 July 2008.
14. www.spectator.co.uk/melaniephillips/page_16, 14 July 2008.
15. Madeleine Bunting. 'Lord Phillips : Talking Sense on Sharia', *The Guardian*, 4 July 2008.
16. See, for example FoxNews.com on 15 September 2010 article entitled 'Britain Adopts Islamic Law, Gives Sharia Courts Full Power to Rule on Civil Cases' and *The Telegraph* newspaper the following day. The 'Equalities Bill' was introduced in June 2011 with the specific aim of curbing the activities of the shari'a courts, particularly in connection with women.
17. Richard Edwards, 'Sharia Courts Operating in Britain', *The Daily Telegraph*, 14 September 2008.
18. For example: Editorial, *The Observer*, 18 July 2005; Nail Ferguson,*The Sunday Telegraph*, 17 July 2005; Anushka Asthana, *The Observer*, 10 July 2005.
19. One example would be Andrew Brown, 'How English can a Muslim Be?' *The Independent*, 28 October, 1993.
20. DCLG survey *'Mapping Faith'* , 28 October 2009.
21. M. Anwar. 'Muslims in Western States: The British Experience and the Way Forward'. *Journal of Muslim Minority Affairs*. Vol. 28, No. 1 (2008) pp125–137.
22. Ibid. pp134–135.
23. Professor Suleiman is the Director of the *Prince Alwaleed Bin Talal Centre of Islamic Studies*, Cambridge.
24. Y. Suleiman, (ed.), *Contextualising Islam in Britain.* Cambridge: CUP, 2009. p73.
25. See Chapter One.
26. The Preventing Violent Extremism strategy document, first published in April 2007 is available to download as PDF from http://www.communities.gov.uk/documents/communities/pdf/320752.pdf.
27. The document above does not contain any mention of other communities becoming involved in the Muslim integration issue.

28. See *The Telegraph's* coverage of the proposals at http://www.telegraph. co.uk/news/politics/7904718/David-Cameron-National-Citizen-Service-will-tackle-tragic-waste-of-young-people.html.

29. The speech specifically attacked the failure of state-sponsored multiculturalism and provoked a strong response both in the UK and abroad. The text of the speech can be found at http://www.number 10.gov.uk/news/speeches-and-transcripts/2011/02/pms-speech-at-munich-security-conference-60293.

30. P. Mandler, 'What is "National Identity'? Definitions and Applications in Modern British Historiography', *Modern Intellectual History*, Vol. 3, No. 2 (2006) pp271–291.

31. Ibid, p272.

32. Ibid, p272.

33. See for example A.E. McGrath, *The Intellectual Origins of the Reformation*. London: Blackwell Publishing, 2003 and L. James, *Raj*. London: Abacus, 1997.

34. McGrath, *Reformation*.p189.

35. L. Colley, *Britons, Forging the Nation 1707–1837*. London, New Haven, CT: Yale University Press, 1994.

36. An overview of the new strategy can be found at http://www.homeoffice.gov.uk/counter-terrorism/review-of-prevent-strategy/.

37. P. Jenkins, *God's Continent: Christianity, Islam and Europe's Religious Crisis*. New York: OUP, 2007; M. Gurfinkiel, 'Islam in France: The French Way of Life is In Danger', *Middle East Quarterly*, Vol. IV, No. 1 (1997). Both works produce impressive statistical data upon which they base their analysis. The broader principle of demography in relation to religious impact in the secular state is analysed in Eric Kaufmann's 'Breeding For God' article in *Prospect* magazine in which the lecturer in politics at Birbeck college, Universtity of London, advances his 'Second Demgraphic Transition' theory. *Prospect,* Issue 128. November 2006. pp26–30.

38. A. Barras. 'Contemporary *Laïcité*: Setting the Terms of a New Social Contract? The Slow Exclusion of Women Wearing Headscarves'. *Totalitarian Movements and Political Religions,* Vol.11, No. 2 (2010). pp229–248.

39. Jenkins, *God's Continent.* p197. A detailed account of the events are covered in Vicente Llorent Bedmar and Veronica Cobano-Delgado Palma's article 'The Muslim Veil Controversy in French and Spanish Schools.' *Islam and Christian–Muslim Relations* Vol. 21. No. 1 (2010) pp61–73.

40. See http://www.jacktimes.com/politics/laws/wearing-muslim-head-scarves-banned-by-the-french-government.html. The day before the veil ban came into effect, the ruling French party, the UMP, held a debate on the status of Islam in Europe generally and in France in particular. The debate was very controversial, but Nicolas Sarkozy argued that the airing of such sensitive discussion might help take the wind out of the sails of the right-wing parties that had done so well in recent elections. The event was reported on the *al-Jazeera* website.http://english.aljazeera.net/news/europe /2011/04/201145203442292956.html.

41. Jenkins, *God's Continent.* pp197–198.

42. J. Bowen, *Why the French Don't Like Headscarves.* Princeton: Princeton University Press, 2006. p2. The French law of 1905 is analysed in Eileen Barker's (ed.), *The Centrality of Religion in Social Life: Essays in Honour of James A. Beckford.* Aldershot: Ashcroft Publishing, 2008. pp43–45 and in W. Cairns and R. McKeon, *Introduction to French Law.* London: Cavendish Publishing, 1995. p117.

43. Ibid. p5.

44. Bowen, *Headscarfs.* p33. A fascinating article in *The Economist* also explores some of the French concerns with radicalisation, particularly in French prisons. 'Jailhouse Jihad', *The Economist,* 18 September 2008.

45. Ibid. pp4–5.

46. C. Labourde, 'Secular Philosophy and Muslim Headscarves in Schools', *The Journal of Political Philosophy.* Vol. 13, No. 3 (2005), pp 305–329. See also T.J. Gunn 'Religious Freedom and Laïcité: A Comparison of the United States and France' *Brigham Young University Law Review.* Issue 419 (2004).

47. Ibid. p307.

48. P. Weil, *la france et ses étrangers: l'aventure d'une politique de l'immigration.* Paris: Calmann-Lévy, 1991. p187.

49. Favell, *Integration.* p42.

50. O. Fouquet, J-C. Mallet, J Merlin, *etre francais, aujourd'hui et demain.* Paris: Union générale d'éditions, 1988.

51. Favell, *Integration.* p45.

52. See R. John Matthies' excellent article 'Kicking the Anthill: The Destabilization of the Extremist Base in France'. *Journal of Muslim Minority Affairs,* Vol. 28. No. 1 (2008) pp139–146.

53. Gino Raymond, Professor of French at Bristol University, has written an excellent article that traces the course of the integration-

assimilation debate on the French left and showing how Nicolas Sarkozy has managed to keep the left-wing parties off-balance over the period of the debate. G.G. Raymond, 'From Islam en France to Islam de France: contradictions of the French left's responses to Islam' *Patterns of Prejudice* Vol. 43. No. 5 (2009). pp481–496. See also M. Adrian, 'France, the veil and Religious Freedom'. *Religion, State & Society,* Vol. 37, No. 4 (2009) pp345–374.

54. 'Shari'a Calling' *The Economist*, 12 November 2009.

Conclusions

1. A. Favell, *Philosophies of Integration and the Idea of Citizenship in France and Britain (Migration, Minorities and Citizenship Series).* 2nd ed. Basingstoke: Palgrave, 2001.

2. Ibid. p1.

3. Ibid. pp1–2.

4. The files examined in the *The Caliphate Question* also evidence British manoeuvrings of this nature suggesting that their passive acceptance of the *Shariat Act* could be characterised in this way.

BIBLIOGRAPHY

Books and Journal Articles

Abbas, Tahir. *Muslim Britain: Communities Under Pressure.* London, New York: Zed Books Ltd, 2005.

Abu-Rabi, Ibrahim M. *The Blackwell Companion to Contemporary Islamic Thought.* Oxford, Blackwell Publishing, 2006.

Abduh, Muhammad. *The Theology of Unity.* Trans I. Musa'ad and K. Cragg. London: George Allen and Unwin, 1966.

Abun-Nasr, Jamil M. *Muslim Communities of Grace: The Sufi Brotherhoods in Islamic Religious Life.* New York, Chicester, UK: Colombia University Press, 2007.

Adrian, Melanie. 'France, the Veil and Religious Freedom'. *Religion, State & Society,* Vol. 37. No. 4, (2009). pp345–374.

al-Afghani, Jamal. 'Jinsiyah wa al-Din al-Islamiyah', *Al-Urwah al al-Wurthqa,* No. 2, 20 March 1884, in R. G. Landen, (trans. and ed.), *The Emergence of the Modern Middle East: Selected Readings.* New York: Van Nostrand Reihnold Company, 1970.

Ageron, Charles R. *Modern Algeria: A History from 1830 to the Present.* London: Hurst and Co., 1991. (French Original, 1964.)

Ageron, Charles R. and R. Brett, *Modern Algeria: A History From 1830 to the Present.* (First Published in French, 1964.) London: Hurst and Co., 1991.

Ahmed, Akbar S. *Jinnah, Pakistan and Islamic Identity: The Search for Saladin.* Basingstoke: Routledge, 1997.

Ahmed, A. 'Sayyid Ahmad Khan, Jamal al-din al Afghani and Muslim India', *Studia Islamica* Vol 3, No. 13 (1960). pp55–78.

Ahmed, A. *Islamic Modernism in India and Pakistan 1857–1964.* London, Bombay and Karachi: OUP, 1967.

Ahmed, Ibrahim. *The Concept of an Islamic State, An Analysis of the Ideological Controversy in Pakistan.* London: Frances Pinter 1987.

Ahmed, Rafiuddin. (ed.), *Understanding the Bengal Muslims.* New Delhi: OUP, 2001.

Ali, Chaudri M. *The Emergence of Pakistan.* New York: Columbia University Press, 1967.

Ali, Chiragh. *The Proposed Political, Legal and Social Reforms under Muslim Rule.* Bombay: Education Society's Press, 1883.

Ali, J. 'Islamic Revivalism: The Case of Tablighi Jamaat', *Journal of Muslim Minority Affairs,* Vol. 23. Issue 1 (April 2003). pp173–181.

Ali, Yusuf. (trans). *The Holy Quran.* Birmingham: IPCI, Islamic Vision, 1999.

Amanat, A. and F. Griffel, *Shari'a: Islamic Law in the Contemporary Context.* Berkley (CA) Stanford University Press, 2007.

Ameli, Saied R. *Globalization, Americanization and British Muslim Identity.* London: Islamic College for Advanced Studies Press, 2002.

Anderson, Michael R. 'Islamic Law and the Colonial Encounter in British India' in C. Mallat and F. Connors (eds.) *Islamic Family Law.* Leiden: Brill, 1990.

Andrabi, Mohammed A. (ed.), *Islam in India Since Independence.* Srinagar: Iqbal Institute, University of Kashmir, 1988.

Ansari, Khizar H. *The Emergence of Socialist Thought among North Indian Muslims (1917–1947).* Lahore: Book Traders, 1990.

——. *Muslims in Britain,* London: Minority Rights Group, 2002.

Arabi, Oussama. *Studies in Modern Islamic Law and Jurisprudence.* The Hague, New York and London: Klumer Law International, 2001.

Arkoun, Mohammed. *The Unthought in Contemporary Islamic Thought.* London, Beruit: Saqi Books, 2002.

Arnold, Thomas W. *The Caliphate,* with a Final Chapter by S. Haim. London: Routledge and Keegan Paul, 1965.

Asad, Muhammad. *The Message of the Qur'an: Translated and Explained.* Gibraltar: Dar al-Andalus, 1980.

Baljon, Johannes M.S. *Reforms and Religious Ideas of Sayyid Ahmed Khan.* Leiden: E.J. Brill, 1949.

——. *Religion and Thought of Shah Wali Allah Dilhawi 1703–1762.* Leiden: E.J. Brill, 1986.

Bangash, Zafar. (Comp. and Ed.), *In Pursuit of the Power of Islam. Major Writings of Kalam Saddiqui.* London: The Muslim Institute, 1996.

Barker, Eilleen. (ed.), *The Centrality of Religion in Social Life: Essays in Honour of James A. Beckford.* Aldershot: Ashcroft Publishing, 2008.

Barras, Amélie. 'Contemporary Laïcité: Setting the Terms of a New Social Contract? The Slow Exclusion of Women Wearing Headscarves'. *Totalitarian Movements and Political Religions,* Vol.11, No. 2 (2010). pp229–248.

Bedmar, Vincente L. and V. Cobano-Delgado Palma, 'The Muslim Veil Controversy in French and Spanish Schools.' *Islam and Christian– Muslim Relations* Vol. 21. No. 1 (2010). pp61–73.

Bell, Richard. *The Qur'an*, Translated Volume I. London: T and T Clark, 1937.

Bems, Eva. *Human Rights: Universality and Diversity.* Leiden: Martinus Lindhoff Publishers, 2001.

Bennoune, Mahfoud. *The Making of Contemporary Algeria, 1830–1987.* Cambridge: CUP, 1988.

Benton, Lauren A. *Law and Colonial Cultures: Legal Regimes in World History.* Cambridge: CUP, 2002.

Berrigan, Somaiyah (ed.), *An Enlightening Commentary into the Light of the Holy Qur'an by a Group of Muslim Scholars.* Isfahan: Imam Ali Islamic Research Center, 2000.

Betts, Raymond F. *Assimilation and Association in French Colonial Theory, 1890–1914.* New York: Columbia University Press, 2005 (Originally Published 1961).

Bhutto, Benazir. *Reconciliation: Islam, Democracy and the West.* New York: HarperCollins, 2008.

Birt, Yahya. D. Hussain and A. Siddiqui (eds.) *British Secualrism and Religion: Islam, Society and the State.* Markfield: Kube Publishing, 2011.

Black, Anthony. *The History of Islamic Political Thought.* Edinburgh: Edinburgh University Press, 2001.

Bowen, John R. 'Does French Islam Have Borders? Dilemmas of Domestication in a Global Religious Field', *American Anthropologist,* Vol. 106, No. 1 (2004) pp43–55.

———. *Why the French Don't Like Headscarves.* Princeton: Princeton University Press, 2006.

Brett, Michael. 'Legislating for Inequality in Algeria: The Sénatus-Consulté of 14th July 1865.', *Bulletin of the School of Oriental and African Studies,* Vol. 51. No. 3 (1988). pp451–465.

Burgat, François. *Face to Face with Political Islam.* London: I.B.Tauris, 2003.

Burke, Edmund, E. Abrahamian and I. Lapidus, (eds.) *Islam, Politics and Social Movements.* London: I.B.Tauris, 1988.

Burke, Edmund. 'Pan-Islam and Moroccan Resistance to French Colonial Penetration, 1900–1912'. *Journal of African History.* Vol. XIII, No. I (1972). pp97–118.

Cairns, Walter. and R. McKeon, *Introduction to French Law.* London: Cavendish Publishing, 1995.

Calder, Norman. 'Shari'a' *Encyclopedia of Islam, 2nd ed.,* Vol. 8. Leiden: Brill, 1964.

Chadwick, Henry. *The Early Church.* London: Penguin, 1993.

Chaudhuri, Nirad C. *The Autobiography of an Unknown Indian.* New York: Macmillan,1951.

Chaplin, Jonathan. 'Legal Monism and Religious Pluralism: Rowan Williams on Religion, Loyalty and Law', *International Journal of Public Theology*, Vol. 2, No. 4 (2008).

Choudhury, Golam W. *Islam and the Modern Muslim World*. London: Scorpion Publishing Ltd, 1993.

Christelow, Allan. *Muslim Law Courts and the French Colonial State in Algeria*. Princeton, NJ: Princeton University Press, 1985.

Clarke, Andrew F. 'Imperialism, Independence, and Islam in Senegal and Mali'. *Africa Today*, Vol. 46, No. 3 (Summer 1999). pp149–167.

Colley, Linda. *Britons, Forging the Nation 1707–1837*. London, New Haven, CT: Yale University Press, 1994.

Cragg, Kenneth. *The Pen and the Faith. Eight Modern Muslim Writers and the Qur'an*. London: G. Allen and Unwin, 1985.

Crone, Patricia. *Medieval Islamic Political Thought*. Edinburgh: Edinburgh University Press, 2004.

Danziger, Raphael. *Abd al-Qadir and the Algerian Resistance to the French and Internal Consolidation*. New York: Holmes and Meier, 1977.

Davis, Uri. *Citizenship and the State*. Reading, MA: Ithaca Press, 1997.

Department of Communities and Local Government (UK) '*Mapping Faith*'. 28 October 2009.

De Schweinitz, Karl. *The Rise and Fall of British India: Imperialism as Inequality*. London: Routledge, 1983.

Dueck, Jennifer. 'The Middle East and North Africa in the Imperial and Post-Colonial Historiography of France'. *The Historical Journal* (2007), Issue 50. pp935–949.

Durie, Mark. *The Third Choice: Islam, Dhimmitude and Freedom*. n.p: Deror Books, 2010.

Dutton, Yasin. *The Origins of Islamic Law: The Qur'an, The Muwatta, and the Madinan 'amal*. London: Curzon, 1999.

Eisenstadt, Shmuel N. and L. Roniger, 'Patron–Client relations as a Way of Structuring Social Exchange'. *Comparative Studies in Society and History*, Vol. 22, Issue 1 (1980). pp418–441.

Embree, Ainslie T. *India's Search for National Identity*. New York: Alfred A. Knopf, 1972.

Entelis, John P. *Islam, Democracy and the State in North Africa*. Bloomington, IN: Indiana University Press, 1997.

Emerit, Marcel. 'Algeria', *Encyclopedia of Islam, 2nd ed.*, Vol. 1. Leiden: Brill, 1964.

Enyat, Hamid. *Modern Islamic Political Thought*. Basingstoke: Macmillan Education, 1982.

Esposito, John. (ed.), *Islam in Transition (Muslim Perspectives)*. New York, London: OUP, 1982.

———. (ed.) *Islam in Asia: Religion, Politics and Society*. Oxford: OUP, 1987.

————. *Women in Muslim Family Law.* Syracuse, NY: Syracuse University Press, 2001.

El Fadl, Khaled A. 'Islamic Law and Muslim Minorities: The Juristic Discourse on Muslim Minorities from the Second/Eighth to the Eleventh/Seventeenth Centuries' *Islamic Law and Society,* Vol. 1, No. 2 (1994).

————. 'Islam and the Theology of Power'. *Middle East Report,* No. 221. 2001.

Fateh, Tarek. *Chasing a Mirage: The Tragic Illusion of an Islamic State.* Toronto: Wiley, 2008.

Favell, Adrian. *Philosophies of Integration and the Idea of Citizenship in France and Britain (Migration, Minorities and Citizenship Series),* 2nd ed. Basingstoke: Palgrave, 2001.

Faruki, Kemal. *The Evolution of Islamic Constitutional Theory and Practice.* Karachi: National Publishing House, 1971.

Fouquet, Olivier, J-C. Mallet and J. Merlin, *etre francais, aujourd'hui et demain* Paris: Union générale d'éditions, 1988.

Gardet, Louis. 'Din', *Encyclopedia of Islam 2nd ed.,* Vol. 2, Leiden: Brill, 1964. pp293–296.

Geaves, Ron. *The Sufis of Britain: An Exploration of Muslim Identity.* Cardiff: Cardiff Academic Press, 2000.

Gibb, Hamilton A. R. *Modern Trends in Islam.* Chicago: University Press, 1945.

————. *The Formative Period of Islamic Thought,* Edinburgh: Edinburgh University Press, 1973.

Gonzalez, Nathan. *The Sunni-Shi'a Conflict: Understanding Sectarian Violence in the Middle East.* Anaheim, CA : Nortia Books, 2009.

Grover B L. and R.R. Sethi, (eds.), *Studies in Modern Indian History: 1707 to the Present Day.* New Delhi: S. Chand, 1963.

Gunn, Jeremy. 'Religious Freedom and Laïcité: A Comparison of the United States and France'. *Brigham Young University Law* Review. Issue 419 (2004).

Gurfinkiel, Michel. 'Islam in France: The French Way of Life is In Danger', *Middle East Quarterly,* Vol. IV, No. 1 (1997).

Hallaq, Wael B. *Shari'a: Theory, Practice and Transformations,* Cambridge: CUP, 2009.

Ibn Hanbal, A. *Al-Musnad.* Vol 2. A. Shakir and H. Ahmad al-Zayn (eds.). Cairo: Dar al-Hadith, 1995.

Hargreaves, Alec G. and M. J. Heffernan, *French and Algerian Identities from Colonial Times to the Present: A Century of Interaction.* Chicago: E. Mellen Press, 1993.

ul-Haq, Mushir. *Muslim Politics in Modern India,1857–1947.* Meerut, India: Meenakshi Prakashan, 1970.

——. *Islam in Secular India.* Simla: Indian Institute of Advanced Study, 1972.

Harrison, Christopher. *France and Islam in West Africa, 1860–1960.* Cambridge: Cambridge University Press, 2006.

Hasan, Mushirul. (ed) *Communal and Pan-Islamic Trends in Colonial India.* New Delhi: Manohar, 1981.

——. *Islam and Indian Nationalism : Reflections on Abdul Kalam Azad.* New Delhi: Manohar, 1992.

——. *Legacy of a Divided Nation.* London: Hurst & Co., 1996.

Hasmi, Sohil. *Islamic Political Ethics: Society, Pluralism and Conflict.* Princeton: Princeton University Press, 2002.

Haydar, Ali. *Durur al-Hukkam Sharh Majallat al-Ahkram, Vol. 1.* Haifa: Abbasid Press, 1925.

Henry, Jean-Robert and F. Balique, *La Doctrine Coloniale du Droit Musulman Algerian: Bibliography Systematique et Introductions Critique.* Paris: Centre National de la Recherché Scientifique, 1979.

Heraldstveit, Daniel. *Political Islam in Algeria.* Oslo: Norwegian Institute for International Affairs, 1997.

Hiro, Dilip. *Islamic Fundamentalism.* London: Paladin,1988.

Hiskett, Mervyn. *The Course of Islam in Africa.* Edinburgh: Ediburgh University Press, 1994.

Horne, Alistair. *A Savage War of Peace, Algeria 1954–1962.* New York: New York Review Books, 2006.

Hourani, Albert. *Arabic Thought in the Liberal Age. 1789–1939.* Cambridge: CUP, 1983.

Husain, Abid. *The Destiny of Indian Muslims.* London: Asia Publishing House, 1965.

ul-Haq, Mahmud. *Muhammad Abduh: A Study of a Modern Thinker of Egypt,* Aligarh: Islamic Studies Publisher, 1970.

Hyam, Ronald. 'The Primacy of Geopolitics: The dynamics of British Imperial Policy, 1763–1963', *The Journal of Imperial and Commonwealth History,* Volume 27, Issue 2 (1999). pp27–52.

Ikram, S M. *Modern Muslim India and the Birth of Pakistan.* Delhi: Renaissance, 1950.

Iqbal, A. (ed). *Selected Speeches and Statements of Maulana Mohamed Ali.* Lahore: Publishers United Ltd, 1963.

Iqbal, Mohammed. *Struggle for Independence: 1857–1947.* Karachi, 1958.

Iqbal, Mohammed. *The Reconstruction of Religious Thought in Islam.* New Delhi: Kitab Bhavan, 2000.

Jain, B M. *Global Power: India's Foreign Policy 1947–2006.* Lexington, MD: Rowman and Littlefield, 2008.

Jalal, A. *The Sole Spokesman: Jinnah, The Muslim League and the Demand for Pakistan.* Cambridge: CUP, 1982.

James, Lawrence. *Raj: The Making and Unmaking of British India.* London: Abacus, 1998.

Janin, H. and A. Kahlmeyer, *Islamic law: The Sharia from Muhammad's Time to the Present.* Jefferson, NC: McFarland and Co. Publishers, 2007.

Jenkins, Philip. *God's Continent: Christianity, Islam and Europe's Religious Crisis.* New York: OUP, 2007.

Judd, Denis. *Empire: The British Imperial Experience from 1765 to the Present.* London: Fontana Press, 1997.

Kamali, Muhammad H. *Shari'ah Law: An Introduction.* Oxford: Oneworld, 2008.

Karpat, Kemal H. *The Politization of Islam. Reconstructing Identity, State, Faith and Community in the Late Ottoman Period.* Oxford: OUP, 2001.

Keddie, Nikkie R. *An Islamic Response to Imperialism: Political and Religious Writings of Sayyid Jamal ad-Din al-Afghani.* Berkeley and Los Angeles: University of California Press, 1968.

Kedourie, Ellie. *The Chatham House Version and other Middle Eastern Studies.* London: Weidenfeld and Nicholson, 1970.

Khadduri, Majid. 'The Maslaha (Public Interest) and Illa (Cause) in Islamic Law', *New York University Journal of International Law & Politics* (1979–1980). pp213–227.

——. *The Islamic Law of Nations: Shaybani's Siyar.* Baltimore, MD: John Hopkins Press, 1996.

Khan, Sayyid A. *Tafsir al-Quran,* 7 Volumes. Agra and Aligarh: Agra: Mufidi 'amm Press, 1903–1906.

——. *The Truth about the Khaliphat.* K. Ahmed (Comp). New Delhi: Khosla Bros, 1920.

Khatoon, Saeeda. *The Development of Islamic Rationalism on the Subcontinent with Special Reference to Waliullah, Sayyid Ahmad Khan and Muhammad Iqbal.* Karachi: Thesis for the University of Karachi, 1980.

Kinkel, Caroline. *Osman's Dream: The Story of the Ottoman Empire 1300–1923.* London: John Murray, 2005.

Kurzman, Charles. (ed.), *Modernist Islam, 18490–1940: A Sourcebook.* Oxford and New York: OUP, 2002.

Labourde, Cecile. 'Secular Philosophy and Muslim Headscarves in Schools', *The Journal of Political Philosophy.* Vol. 13. No. 3 (2005). pp305–329.

Lambton, Anne. *State and Government in Medieval Islam.* Oxford: OUP, 1981.

Lane, Edward. *Arabic-English Lexicon, Book I, Vol. 5.* Beruit: Libraire du Liban, 1968. First Published London: 1881.

Lapidus, Ira. *A History of Islamic Societies.* Cambridge: CUP, 2002.

Lewis, Bernard. *The Emergence of Modern Turkey.,* 3rd ed. New York, London: OUP, 2002.

——. *The Political Language of Islam.* Chicago and London: University of Chicago Press, 1988.

Lewis, Martin D. 'One Hundred Million Frenchmen: The "Assimilation" Theory in French Colonial Politics'. *Comparative Studies in Society and History,* Vol. 4, No. 2 (1962). pp129–153.

Lewis, Philip. *Islamic Britain: Religion, Politics, and Identity among British Muslims.* London: I.B.Tauris, 2003.

——. *Young British and Muslim.* London: Continuum, 2007.

Litvak, Meir. *Middle Eastern Societies and the West: Accommodation or Clash of Civilization?* Tel Aviv: Tel Aviv University, 2006.

Lorcin, Patricia M. E. *Algeria and France, 1800–2000: Identity, Memory, Nostalgia.* Syracuse, NY: Syracuse University Press, 2006.

——. and P. Sanders, 'France and Islam: Introduction', *French Historical Studies,* Vol. 30, No. 3 (Summer 2007). pp343–349.

MacDonald, Donald B. *The Development of Muslim Theology, Jurisprudence and Constitutional Theory.* Exeter: Wheaton and Co. Ltd, 1902.

Mahmoud, Tahir. *The Muslim Law of India.* Berkley, CA: University of California Press, 1980.

Majid, Abdul. *Hindustan or Pakistan: Partition or Unity.* Lahore: Ilami Markaz, n.d.

Malik, Hafeez. *Moslem Nationalism in India and Pakistan,* Washington D.C.: Public Affairs Press, 1967.

——. (ed. with notes) *Political Profile of Sir Sayyid Ahmad Khan.* Islamabad: Institute of Islamic History, Culture and Civilisation, Islamic University, 1982.

Malik Ibn Anas. *al-Muwatta.* M. Rahimuddin (trans). New Delhi: Kitab Bhavan, 2000.

Malik, Rashida. *Iqbal: The Spiritual Father of Pakistan.* Chicago: University of Michigan Press, 2003.

Mandler, Peter. 'What is "National Identity"? Definitions and Applications in Modern British Historiography', *Modern Intellectual History,* Vol. 3, No. 2 (2006). pp271–291.

Matthie, R John. 'Kicking the Anthill: The Destabilization of the Extremist Base in France'. *Journal of Muslim Minority Affairs,* Vol. 28. No. 1 (2008). pp139–146.

Maududi, A'la. *Islamic Law and Constitution.* Lahore: Taj Company, 1960.

——. *Towards Understanding the Quran,* (trans. and ed. Z Ansari). Leicester: The Islamic Foundation, 1989.

Marranci, Gabrielle. (ed.), *Muslim Societies and the Challenge of Secularization: An Interdisciplinary Approach.* Dortrecht: Springer, 2010.

Martin, Bradford G. *Muslim Brotherhoods in Nineteenth Century Africa.* Cambridge: CUP, 2003.

Mayer, Ann E. *Islam and Human Rights: Traditions and Politics.* Boulder, CO: Westview Press, 1999.

McDonough, Sheila. *Muslim Ethics and Modernity: A Comparative Study of the Ethical Thought of Sayyid Ahmed Khan and Maulana Maududi.* Montreal: Wilfred Laurier University Press, 1984.

McGrath, Alister E. *The Intellectual Origins of the Reformation.* London: Blackwell Publishing, 2003.

Merad, Ali. *Le Réformisme Musulman en Algérie de 1925 à 1940.* Paris: Moulton and Co. 1967.

Metcalf, Barbara, D. *Islamic Revival in British India: Deoband, 1860–1900.* Princeton: Princeton University Press, 1982.

Moaddel, Monsoor and K. Talattof (eds.) *Modernist and Fundamentalist Debates in Islam: A Reader.* New York and Basingstoke: Palgrave Macmillan, 2002.

Moore, Kathleen. *The Unfamiliar Abode: Islamic Law in the United States and Britain.* New York: Oxford University Press USA, 2010.

Moncrieff-Smith, Henry. 'British India' *Journal of Comparative Legislation and International Law,* Third Series, Vol. 9, No. 3 (1927), pp151–160.

Morand, Marcel. *Études de Droit Musalman Algerien.* Algiers: Adolph Jordan, 1910.

Mujeeb, Muhammed. *The Indian Muslims.* London: George Allen and Unwin Ltd, 1967.

Multani, R.K.P. *Islamic Fundamentalism in South Asia.* Chicago: Sumit Enterprises, 2007.

Munir, Muhammad. *From Jinnah to Zia.* Lahore: Vangard Books,1979.

Muqtedar Khan, M A. (ed.) *Islamic Democratic Discourse: Theory, Debates and Philosophical Perspectives.* Lanham, MD: Rowman and Littlefield, 2006.

an-Na'im, Abdullahi A. *Islam and the Secular State: Negotiating the Future of Shari'a.* Cambridge, MA: Harvard University Press, 2008.

Nasr, Vali. *The Shia Revival: How Conflicts Within Islam Will Shape the Future.* London: W.W. Norton and Company, 2007.

Navdi, S. H.H. *Islamic Resurgent Movements in the Indo-Pak Subcontinent during the Eighteenth and Nineteenth centuries: A Critical Analysis.* Durban: Academia, the Centre for Islamic, Near and Far Eastern Studies, Planning Publication, 1987.

Niemeijer, Albert C. *The Khalifat Movement in India 1919–1924.* s-Gravenhage: Nederlandsche Boek – en Steendrukkerij and Smits, 1972.

Nouschi, André. 'North Africa in the Period of Colonialisation', Holt et al. (eds.) *The Cambridge History of Islam.* Cambridge, New York: CUP, 1983.

Olidort, Jacob. *Maslaha: A Mechanism for reform in Islamic Legal Theory.* Boston, MA: Brandis University Press, 2007.

Oliver-Dee, Sean. *The Caliphate Question: British Government and Islamic Governance.* Lanham, MD: Rowman and Littlefield, 2009.

Özcan, Azmi. *Pan-Islamism: Indian Muslims, the Ottoman Empire and Britain. (1877–1924).* Leiden, New York, Koln: Brill, 1997.

Opwis, Felicitas. 'Maslaha in Contemporary Islamic Legal Theory', *Islamic Law and Society*. Vol. 12. No. 2 (2005). pp182–223.

Palmer, Alan. *The Decline and Fall of the Ottoman Empire*. London: John Murray, 1992.

Pandey, Deepak. *The Role of the Muslim League in National Politics*. Delhi: Tiwari,1991.

Penrice, John. *A Dictionary and Glossary of the Koran*. Delhi: Low Price Publications, 1873.

Perwez, Ghulam A. *Islam: A Challenge to Religion*. Lahore: Indara-Tulu-e-Islam, 1968.

Peters, Rudolph and G.J.J. de Vries, 'Apostasy in Islam', *Die Welt des Islams*, New Series, Vol. 17, Issue 1/4 (1976–1977).

Powers, David S. 'Orientalism, Colonialism, and Legal History: The Attack on Muslim Family Endowments in Algeria and India.' *Comparative Studies in Society and History*, Vol. 31, No.3 (July 1989). pp535–571.

Prawdin, Michael. and G. Thailiand (eds.) *The Mongol Empire: Its Rise and Legacy*. New Brunswick, NJ: Transaction Publishers, 2006.

Priestley, Herbert I. *France Overseas: A Study in Modern Imperialism*. London: Routledge, 1967.

Qureshi, Naeem M. *Pan-Islam in British Indian Politics: A Study of the Khilafat Movement, 1918–1924*. Leiden: Brill, 1999.

Qutb, Sayyid. *In the Shade of the Qur'an*. A. Salahi and A. Shamis (trans. and eds.). Leicester: The Islamic Foundation, 2001.

Rapoport, Yossef. and S. Ahmed, *Ibn Taymiyya and His Times*. Oxford: OUP, 2010.

Rahmen, Javaid and S.C. Bureau (eds.), *Religion, Human Rights and International Law: A Critical Examination of Islamic State Practices*. Leiden: Martinus Nijhoff Publishers, 2007.

Ramadan, Tariq. 'Ijtihad and Maslaha: The foundations of Governance', M.A. Muqtedar Khan (ed.) *Islamic Democratic Discourse: Theories, Debates and Philosophical Discourses*. Lanham, MA: Rowman and Littlefield, 2006.

al-Rasheed, Madawi. 'The Shia of Saudi Arabia: A Minority in Search of Cultural Authenticity', *British Journal of Middle Eastern Studies*, Vol. 25, No. 1 (May 1998). pp121–138.

Raymond, Gino G. 'From Islam en France to Islam de France: Contradictions of the French Left's responses to Islam' *Patterns of Prejudice*. Vol. 43. No. 5, (2009). pp481–496.

Rizvi, Athar A. *Shah Wali-Allah and His Times: A Study of Eighteenth Century Islam, Politics and Society in India*. Canberra: Ma'rifat, 1980.

Rodinson, Maxine. *Mohammad*. A. Carter (trans. from the French). London: Penguin, 1961.

Rippin, Andrew. *Muslims: Their Religious Beliefs and Practices, 3rd ed.* London and New York: Routledge and Taylor Francis, 2005.

Ruthven, Malise. *Islam in the Modern World, 3rd ed.* London: Granta Books, 2006.

Saeed, Abdullah and H. Saeed, *Freedom in Religion, Apostasy in Islam.* Aldershot: Ashgate Publishing, 2004.

Sale, George. *The Koran Translated into English from the Original Arabic.* London: Frederick Warne and Co. Ltd, 1764.

Sanyal, Usha. *Devotional Islam and Politics in British India, Ahmad Riza Khan Barelwi and His Movement, 1870–1920.* Delhi: OUP, 1999.

Sarkar, Sumit. 'Indian Democracy: The Historical Inheritance' in A. Kohli (ed.), *The Success of India's Democracy.* Cambridge: CUP, 2001. pp23–46.

Sayeed, Khalid B. *Pakistan: The Formative Phase, 1857–1948.* London: OUP, 1968.

Schacht, Joseph. *An Introduction to Islamic Law.* Oxford: Clarendon Press, 1964.

Schimmel, Annemarie. *Islam in the Indian Sub-Continent.* Leiden-Koln: E. Brill, 1980.

Schulze, Richard. *A Modern History of the Islamic World.* London: I.B.Tauris, 2000.

Sedgwick, Mark. *Muhammad Abduh.* London: Oneworld, 2010.

Serjeant, Robert B. 'The Constitution of Medina'. *Islamic Quarterly,* Vol. 8 (1964).

Sharafi, Mitra. 'The Semi Autonomous Judge in Colonial India', *Indian Economic & Social History Review.* Vol. 46, No. 1 (2009) pp57–81.

Sharma, Kusum. *Ambedkar and the Indian Constitution.* New Delhi: Ashish Publishing House 1992.

Shatzmiller, Maya (ed.), *Nationalism and Minority Identities in Islamic Societies.* Quebec City: McGill University Press, 2005.

Sharify-Funk, Meena. *Encountering the Transnational: Women, Islam and the Politics of Interpretation.* Farnham: Ashgate Publishing, 2008.

Shinar, Pessah. 'A Controversial Exponent of the Algerian Salafiyya: The Kabyle Alim, Imam and Sharif Abu Ya'la Sa'id B. Muhammad al-Zawawi', D. Ayalon and M. Sharon (eds.), *Studies in Islamic History and Civilization: In Honour of Professor David Ayalon.* Jerusalem: Cana Ltd, 1986.

Silverman, Paul.'Martyrs and Patriots: Ethnic, National and Transnational Dimensions of Kabyle Politics', *The Journal of North African Studies,* Vol. 8, Issue 1 (Spring 2003). pp 87–111.

Silverstein, Paul A. *Algeria in France: Transpolitics, Race and Nation.* Bloomington, IN: Indiana University Press, 2004.

Singer, Barnett. and J. W. Langdon, *Cultured Force: The Makers and Defenders of the French Colonial Empire.* Madison, WI, London: University of Wisconsin Press, 2004.

Singh, Jaswant. *Jinnah: India, Partition, Independence.* New York: OUP, 2010.

Sharma, Shashi S. *Caliphs and Sultans: Religious Ideology and Political Praxis.* New Delhi: Rupa and Co., 2004.

Shotwell, James T. *Turkey at the Straits.* London: Mcmillan Company, 1940.

Smith, Tony. *The French Stake in Algeria 1945–62.* New York: Cornell University Press, 1976.

Spear, Perceival. *Oxford History of India.* Oxford: OUP, 1964.

Spencer, Nick. *Doing God: A Future for Faith in the Public Square.* London: Theos, 2006.

Stora, Benjamin. (ed.) *Algeria, 1830–2000: A Short History.* Ithaca, NY: Cornell University Press, 2004.

Suleiman, Yasir. (ed.) *Contextualising Islam in Britain.* Cambridge: CUP, 2009.

Taylor, Miles. 'Queen Victoria and India, 1837–61', *Victorian Studies,* Vol. 46, No. 2, Papers from the Inaugural Conference of the North American Victorian Studies Association (Winter, 2004). pp264–274.

Ibn Taymiyya, *Kitab al-Iman (Book of Faith).* Trans. S. H. Al-Ani, Shadia Ahmad Tel. Indiana: Iman Publishing House, 2009.

Thorp, Malcolm R. and A. J. Slavin (eds.) *Politics, Religion and Diplomacy in Early Modern Europe: Essays in Honour of De Lamar Jensen.* London: Sixteenth Century Journal Publishers, 1994.

Tibi, Bassam. *Islam Between Culture and Politics.* Basingstoke: Palgrave Macmillan, 2001.

Tillion, Germaine. *France and Algeria: Complimentary Enemies.* Charlottesville: Greenwood Press, 1976.

Tolan, John V. (ed.), *Medieval Christian Perceptions of Islam.* NewYork and London: 1996.

Triaud, Jean-Luke. 'Islam in Africa under French Colonial Rule' in N. Levitzon and R. L. Randall (eds.), *History of Islam in Africa.* Athens (OH): Ohio University Press, 2000.

Troll, Christian W. *Islam in the Indian Subcontinent – Muslims in Secular India.* (Discussion Paper Series III – 2). Tokyo: Institute of Asian Cultures, Sophia University, 1986.

van der Veer, Peter. *Religious Nationalism in India: Hindus and Muslims.* Berkeley, CA: University of California Press. 1994.

Verkaaik, Oskar. *Migrants and Militants: Fun and Urban Violence in Pakistan.* Princeton: Princeton University Press, 2004.

Viktor, Knut. *Between God and Sultan: A History of Islamic Law.* London: Hurst and Company, 2005.

Watt, William M. *Free Will and Predestination in Early Islam.* Chicago: Luzac, 1948.

Watt, William M. *The Formative Period of Islamic Thought.* Edinburgh: Edinburgh University Press, 1973.

Wehr, Hans. *Arab-English Dictionary, 4th ed.* J. Cowen (ed.), Urbana, IL: Spoken Language Services, 1994.

Weil, Patrick. *la france et ses étrangers: l'aventure d'une politique de l'immigration.* Paris: Calmann-Lévy, 1991.

Wolpert, Stanley. *Jinnah of Pakistan.* Oxford, New York: OUP, 2005.

Wood, Hugh M. 'The Treaty of Paris and Turkey's status in International Law', *American Journal of International Law.* Vol. XXXVII (1943).

Willis, Michael. *The Islamist Challenge in Algeria: A Political History.* New York: Ithaca Press, 1996.

Zaidi, A. Moin. *Evolution of Muslim Political Thought in India. Volume 1, From Syed to the Emergence of Jinnah.* New Delhi: Indian Institute of Applied Political Research, 1975.

Uz-Zaman, Waheed and M. Saleem Akhtar, (eds.) *Islam in South Asia.* Islamabad: National Institute of Historical and Cultural Research, 1993.

Zamoyski, Adam. *The Rites of Peace: The Fall of Napoleon and The Congress of Vienna.* London, New York: HarperCollins, 2008.

Internet and Newspaper Sources

'Shari'a Calling', *The Economist* 12 November 2009.

'Jailhouse Jihad', *The Economist* 18 September 2008.

Editorial. *The Observer,* 18 July 2005.

Asthana, Anushka. *The Observer,* 10 July 2005.

Brown, Andrew. 'How English can a Muslim Be?' *The Independent,* 28 October, 1993.

Bunting, Madeleine. 'Lord Phillips: Talking Sense on Sharia', *The Guardian,* 4 July 2008.

Butt, Razia. 'Gordon Brown Backs Archbishop of Canterbury in Sharia Law Row', *The Guardian,* 11 February 2008.

Edwards, Richard. 'Sharia Courts Operating in Britain', *The Daily Telegraph,* 14 September 2008.

Ferguson, Nail. *The Sunday Telegraph,* 17 July 2005.

Gibb, Frances. 'Case Dismissed: Lord Chief Justice Lays Down Law on Sharia', *The Times,* 5 July 2008.

No Author Attributed, 'Williams Attcked Over Sharia Law Comments', *The Daily Telegraph,* 8 February 2008.

Phillips, Melanie. 'A Caledonian Caliphate', *The Spectator,* 25 June 2008.

Sugden, Joanna and Ruth Gledhill, 'The Archbishop of Canterbury "Should Resign" Over Sharia Row', *The Times,* 8 February 2008.

Warsi, Sayeeda. 'Sharia Would Not Help Integration But Disunity', *The Sun,* 9 February 2008.

www.archbishopof canterbury.org/1581?q=sharia, 2 November 2010.

Ballard, Roger. *Popular Islam in Northern Pakistan and Its Reconstruction in Urban Britain* on CASAS site December 2004, http://www.art.man.ac.uk/CASAS/pdfpapers/ popularislam.pdf, 6 October 2008.

http://bdlaws.gov.bd/pdf_part.php?id=59, 21 July 2011.

FoxNews.com 'Britain Adopts Islamic Law, Gives Sharia Courts Full Power to Rule on Civil Cases'. 15 September 2011, 16 September 2011.

http://english.aljazeera.net/news/europe /2011/04/20114520344229256.html, 14 June 2011.

www.jamaat.org, 8 March 2011.

http://www.jacktimes.com/politics/laws/wearing-muslim-headscarves-banned-by-the-french-government.html, 15 Febuary 2012.

http://www.homeoffice.gov.uk/counter-terrorism/review-of-prevent-strategy/.
http://www.number 10.gov.uk/news/speeches- and-transcripts/2011/02/pms-speech-at-munich-security-conference-60293, 24 September 2011.

http://www.mideast web.org/Middle-East-Encyclopedia/ijtihad.htm, As above.

http://www.number 10.gov.uk/news/speeches-and-transcripts/2011/02/pms-speech-at-munich-security-conference-60293, As above.

http://www.telegraph.co.uk/news/politics/7904718/David-Cameron-National-Citizen-Service-will-tackle-tragic-waste-of-young-people.html, 18 May 2011.

http://www.telegraph.co.uk/news/politics/7904718/David-Cameron-National-Citizen-Service-will-tackle-tragic-waste-of-young-people.html, 7 April 2012.

http://www.communities.gov.uk/documents/communities/pdf/320752.pdf, 12 August 2010.

http://www.communities.gov.uk/documents/communities/pdf/320752.pdf, 2 September 2011.

http://en.wikisource.org/wiki/Queen_Victoria's_ Proclamation, 14 October 2011.

INDEX